In His Footsteps

In His Footsteps

The Early Followers of Jesus

MARILYN E. PHELAN
and JAY M. PHELAN

RESOURCE *Publications* • Eugene, Oregon

IN HIS FOOTSTEPS
The Early Followers of Jesus

Copyright © 2021 Marilyn E. Phelan and Jay M. Phelan. All rights reserved. Except for brief quotations in critical publications or reviews, no part of this book may be reproduced in any manner without prior written permission from the publisher. Write: Permissions, Wipf and Stock Publishers, 199 W. 8th Ave., Suite 3, Eugene, OR 97401.

Resource Publications
An Imprint of Wipf and Stock Publishers
199 W. 8th Ave., Suite 3
Eugene, OR 97401

www.wipfandstock.com

PAPERBACK ISBN: 978-1-6667-0186-9
HARDCOVER ISBN: 978-1-6667-0187-6
EBOOK ISBN: 978-1-6667-0188-3

05/17/21

To Harold, my thanks for your continuing help and support, and to Pat, Cara, Scott, Laura, Robert, Kimberly and our grandchildren-Ryan, Katherine, Claire, Grace, Michael, Rachel, Reece, and Sydney-I pray you will always keep the faith.
M.E. P.

To Cara, Ryan, Katherine, and Sydney
J. M.P.

"I Will Lift up My Eyes to the Hills—From Whence Comes My Help? My Help Comes from the Lord, Who Made Heaven and Earth"

Psalms 121:1–2, NKJV

Contents

Preface | ix
Abbreviations | xiii
Introduction | xv

1. The Plan of Redemption and the Message of Salvation Jesus' First Followers Brought to the World | 1
2. The Disciples of the Inner Circle: James, the Greater, and his Brother John, the Beloved; Andrew and his Brother Simon Peter, The Rock | 43
3. The Remaining Eight Disciples | 70
4. Paul (Saul of Tarsus) | 93
5. Other God-Fearing Followers of Jesus | 114
6. The Establishment of a Kingdom of Justice and Righteousness | 167

Bibliography | 187

Preface

THIS BOOK PROVIDES A history of the Christian faith through a study of the lives and ministries of the tremendous first believers who, in obeying Jesus' command to bring His message of salvation to the world, changed the world forever. The chapters detail how the early followers of Jesus could testify with indisputable proof of Jesus' divinity and His oneness with God in that most had met with, and knew personally, the risen Lord. As the book will provide for some a realization, and for others a reminder, of the unshakeable faith of the first believers, it can take the reader back to the first century to realize, or to remember again, how these devout Jewish and Gentile Christians willingly and fearlessly faced horrific persecution, and, for many, martyrs' deaths, to prove, without doubt, that Jesus came to the world as the Messiah in the fulfillment of God's plan of redemption. Despite the great hardships the first believers encountered from a most corrupt world and its governments, these tremendous early Christians nonetheless found peace in knowing that Jesus had overcome the world. A remembrance of their unshakeable faith can provide the reader with that peace as well.

In the first chapter, the book reviews and briefly analyzes some of the history of the Israelite nation and how God's plan of redemption began with that nation and then culminated in the coming of the Jewish Jesus, the Messiah. The first chapter additionally refers to the Mosaic Law, to biblical prophecies, and to other important events recorded in the Scriptures of which the followers of Jesus were most knowledgeable and of which they testified to prove to the Jewish people as well as to the Gentiles that God brought to fruition His plan of redemption through Jesus, the Christ. The last chapter presents the reader with biblical predictions regarding Israel and the wonderous miracle that, after over 2,500 years, Israel is again a nation—and one nation as prophesied by the prophet Ezekiel.

Preface

    We prepared these chapters from in-depth research into books of the Bible, from information we obtained from earlier years of teaching Bible classes, from impressions and conclusions provided by some renowned writers and historians, and for one author, from visits to Christian sites in Israel: in Patmos where John wrote the book of Revelation; in Egypt, Turkey, Greece, Cyprus, Crete, and Italy, which included visits to the Vatican, all countries where Paul, Barnabas, and their followers brought the message of salvation to the Gentiles, and to France where Lazarus and the Marys are credited with first bringing to that region the message of salvation. From previous writers of the early church and the first followers of Jesus, we were very fortunate to have obtained translations of some of the writings of the Greek Christian historian, Eusebius, who, in the third century, wrote a comprehensive history related to believers in the first three centuries of the early church. Eusebius' writings cover the period from the foundation of the church to 324 AD. He showed in his writings how the Christian religion is the fulfilment of the Old Testament. Eusebius witnessed some of the later trials and persecutions of the early Christians and reported that these "splendid martyrs of Christ" astounded eyewitnesses by their courage. For affirmation, he also referenced Clement of Rome who knew and wrote about lives of the early believers in about 100 AD. Clement was born in 35 AD and was a contemporary of John, the disciple. He also may have been Paul's fellow worker, whom Paul referred to in Philippians 4:3. We have cited to many of Eusebius' findings, some Eusebius sourced directly from Clement, to provide a history of the early church and the lives and deaths of the first believers. We also have referenced to valuable information we obtained from the historian, John Foxe, in his *Fox's Book of Martyrs*, which Foxe wrote in the 1500s. We acquired additional information from significant narratives about the twelve disciples in William Steuart McBirnie's book, *The Search for the Twelve Apostles*, which was written in the 1970s. McBirnie traveled to places where the twelve disciples lived and listened to local reports about the lives and deaths of the twelve disciples to inform more accurately about their lives and probable deaths and burials.

    Our principal source of information about the early followers of Jesus came directly from different translations of the Bible. The reader can find a distinct, but instructive and perhaps new, approach to a study of the Bible from our manner of chronicling details of the lives and ministries of the incredible first believers and the tremendously critical role they played in

Preface

bringing to the world Jesus' message of salvation. It is our hope that the reader will have as great a pleasure and blessing in reading this book as we had in writing it.

    Marilyn E. Phelan
    Jay M. (Pat) Phelan

Abbreviations

Bible

King James Version	KJV
New American Standard Bible	NASB
New International Version	NIV
New King James Version	KJV

Old Testament

Genesis	Gen
Exodus	Exod
Leviticus	Lev
Numbers	Num
Deuteronomy	Deut
Joshua	Josh
1—2 Kings	1-2 Kgs
Psalms	Ps
Isaiah	Isa
Jeremiah	Jer
Ezekiel	Ezek
Daniel	Dan
Micah	Mic
Zechariah	Zech
Malachi	Mal

New Testament

Matthew	Matt
Romans	Rom
1—2 Corinthians	1—2 Cor
Galations	Gal
Ephesians	Eph
Colossians	Col
1 and 2 Thessalonians	1-2 Thess
1 and 2 Timothy	1-2 Tim
Philemon	Phlm
Hebrews	Heb
James	Jas
1-2 Peter	1-2 Pet
Revelation	Rev

Abbreviations

Books

Bauckham, Richard. *The Christian World Around the New Testament*. Baker Academic, Grand Rapids, Michigan, 2017, hereinafter cited as: Bauckham, *The Christian World Around the New Testament*

Eusebius. *The History of the Church from Christ to Constantine*. Translated by G. A. Williamson, revised and edited by Andrew Louth. Penguin Books, 1965, hereinafter cited as: Eusebius, *The History of the Church*

Eusebius. *The Ecclesiastical History*. Translated by C.F. Cruse. Reprinted 1998 by Hendrickson Publishers, hereinafter cited as: Eusebius, T*he Ecclesiastical History*

Foxe, John. *Fox's Book of Martyrs*. Wilder Publications, 2009, hereinafter cited as: Foxe, *Fox's Book of Martyrs*

McBirnie, William Steuart. *The Search for the Twelve Apostles*, Revised Edition. Tyndale House, 2008, hereinafter cited as: McBirnie, *The Search of the Twelve Apostles*

Introduction

MANY OF JESUS' FIRST followers had been a part of Jesus' ministry on earth, and they and several others later met with the risen Lord. After numerous persons had received the wondrous and miraculous blessing of knowing personally the resurrected Jesus and countless more experienced the coming of the Holy Spirit, these first believers recognized that Jesus' coming, death, and resurrection fulfilled God's plan of redemption as set out in the Scriptures. They then willingly and fearlessly faced tremendous persecution and, for many, horrific deaths, in obedience to Jesus' command to bring His message of salvation to an otherwise lost world. A reference back to the "splendid martyrs of Christ,"[1] and the extent of their suffering in the name of Jesus, should confirm to the reader that Jesus is truly the Christ and Lord and Savior of the world.

The first followers of Jesus were the twelve disciples whom Jesus called at the beginning of His ministry to follow Him and to become, as the disciple Matthew recorded, "fishers of men."[2] Before Jesus' resurrection, these disciples had argued among themselves, had sought greatness and reward for themselves, and had completely deserted their Lord when He was crucified. Except for the disciple John, they had left Jesus to die alone through fear for themselves. One disciple, Peter, even denied knowing Jesus. In contrast, after Jesus' resurrection and His appearance to the disciples and to many others, and after the disciples, along with the others, had witnessed Jesus' ascension into heaven and had received a new source of power when the Holy Spirit descended on them at Pentecost, the disciples and the other new believers knew without a doubt that Jesus is the Messiah and one with God. They then boldly, without fear or

---

1. Eusebius, *The History of the Church*, 271.
2. Matt 4:19.

Introduction

concern, faced horrific torture and death in obeying Jesus' command to bring salvation "*. . . to the ends of the earth.*"[3]

One of the early followers of Jesus, Luke the physician, a Gentile who wrote one of the Gospels and the book of Acts, recorded the words of Peter, who was a Jewish disciple, a member of Jesus' inner circle, and a pillar in the first church: "God raised Him up on the third day, and granted that He should become visible, not to all the people, but to witnesses who were chosen beforehand by God, that is, to us, who ate and drank with Him after He arose from the dead. And He ordered us to preach to the people, and solemnly to testify that this is the One who has been appointed by God as Judge of the living and the dead. Of Him, all the prophets bear witness that through His name everyone who believes in Him receives forgiveness of sins."[4]

Examples of Jesus' followers being appointed by God to preach to the people and to testify to prophecies in the Scriptures that bore witness of Jesus being the Messiah include Philip the Evangelist, an early follower of Jesus, witnessing to a Gentile from Ethiopia by explaining a prophecy of Isaiah.[5] After listening to Philip's explanation of that prophecy, the Gentile then believed and was baptized. In another example, Paul and Silas, both early Jewish followers of Jesus, went to a Jewish synagogue in Berea, a city in Macedonia in northern Greece, and preached fulfilled prophecies. When the Berean Jews examined the Scriptures to see if what Paul said was true, many of them believed.[6]

The chapters in this book review the lives of many of the early followers of Jesus whose ministries, like those of Philip, Paul and Silas, testified to the truth that Jesus is the Lord and Savior of the world. These first believers, who sacrificed everything to follow Jesus and to obey His command to bring the message of salvation to an otherwise lost and condemned world, convinced millions to believe that message and then to cause a change from a totally corrupt society into one based on the equality of all. The book establishes that Jesus' message of salvation, which His early followers

---

3. Acts 1:8a, NKJV.

4. Acts 10:43, NASB. Words of the prophets, and a review of the lives of the witnesses Jesus chose to bring His message of salvation to the world, testify not only that Jesus is the Messiah and one with God; they also prove that the Scriptures are the inspired Word of God.

5. Isa 53. Discussion in Chapter 5.

6. Discussion at Acts 17:1–12 and in Chapters 4 and 5. Many Greek Gentiles believed as well.

Introduction

carried to the world, brought forth a new faith that did completely change the world. In this current world, where many now appear either to have rejected that message, or lend little credence or importance to it, it is the authors' hope and prayer that all will consider the great, unquestioned, faith of the first believers and that consideration will bring about a new or revived faith and, with it, the peace and hope that only trust in the Lord can provide.

About 700 years before Christ, the prophet Isaiah wrote the words of the Lord: "Woe to those who call evil good and good evil."[7] Later, just prior to his death in about 67 AD, Paul wrote to Timothy, one of his companions and another early faithful follower of Jesus, that the time would come when people would turn away from the truth and would gather around them teachers who would say what they wanted to hear.[8] These words have special meaning in this present world when so many are again calling evil good and good evil and will only listen to those who "say what they want to hear." The early followers of Jesus addressed this problem by letting the words of Jesus be their guide. The words of Jesus and the writings and histories of His early followers, as recorded in the New Testament, should be our guide. The Bible attests that justice and righteousness cannot come from corrupt governments but rather from a total and undisputed faith in the Lord. The first Christians, who knew without doubt that Jesus is the Messiah and the fulfillment of God's plan of redemption for the world, verified by their lives, ministries, and deaths that justice, righteousness, and peace only comes when we turn to a complete faith and trust in Jesus. A study of the faith of the amazing first believers should reaffirm the Christian faith and remind us all, as Joshua reminded the Israelite nation over 3,000 years ago, to serve the Lord always.

---

7. Isa 5:20a.
8. See 2 Tim 4:3a-4a.

1

The Plan of Redemption and the Message of Salvation Jesus' First Followers Brought to the World

I. Introduction
II. Review of Jewish History as a Prelude to the Coming of the Messiah
   A. Establishment of the Israelite Nation with the Twelve Israelite Tribes
      1. The Northern Kingdom, the Kingdom of Israel
      2. The Southern Kingdom, the Kingdom of Judah
   B. Fulfilment of Prophecies
      1. Prophecy of the Survival of a Remnant of the Southern Kingdom
      2. Prophecy of the Coming of John the Baptist
      3. Prophecy of Jesus's Coming and Important Details of His Ministry
         a. The Message of Salvation
         b. The Twelve Disciples and Seventy Others
         c. The Crucifixion
         d. Jesus's Burial and the Role of Joseph of Arimathea
         e. Jesus's Resurrection and Ascension and the Coming of the Holy Spirit
         f. The Great Commission
         g. The Reason for Twelve Disciples
      4. Fulfillment of Jewish Feasts
         a. Passover Feast
         b. Feast of Unleavened Bread

  c. Feast of Firstfruits
  d. Feast of Pentecost
III. The Early Church
 A. Jews of the Dispersion and Growth of the Church
 B. Stephen, a First Deacon and the First Martyr
 C. Spread of the Gospel to the World

I. Introduction

IN REVIEWING THE LIVES and ministries of the early followers of Jesus, this first chapter initially reviews scriptural prophecies and some history of the Jewish people to provide the reader with a better understanding of the faith of the early Christian patriarchs who completely changed the world with their unwavering faith in Jesus as the Savior of the world and their obedience to Jesus' command to bring His message of salvation to the world. These first Christians knew, without doubt, that Jesus is the Christ, the Messiah; most had met personally with the resurrected Jesus, and many had witnessed Jesus' ascension into heaven. The first believers received the blessing of the Holy Spirit ten days after Jesus' ascension, and with the help of the Holy Spirit, were able to face the tremendous persecution and horrible deaths that were inevitable consequences of their undying devotion and service to their Lord. This first chapter provides some background in, and knowledge of, the scriptural prophecies and important events in Jewish history that precluded, and culminated in, the coming of Jesus as the Messiah and in the later creation of the early church; thus, the first part of this chapter serves as a prelude to a study of the lives and ministries of the earliest followers of Jesus who were motivated by these prophecies and their Jewish history. The chapter briefly critiques the marvelous sacrifice of our Lord who came to seek and to save the lost and to whom the first believers owed their eternal allegiance.

  References to critical Scriptural prophecies that foretold God's plan of redemption and its consummation with the birth and death of the Lord Jesus and a brief review of important events in Jewish history provide the reader with direction in studying the remaining chapters. The earliest followers of Jesus referred to prophecies from the scriptures to prove to those who had not met personally with the resurrected Jesus that He indeed is the Messiah and is one with God. It is helpful for the reader also to consider these important prophecies and to examine other critical events in Jewish history, such as the establishment of the twelve Israelite tribes and the seven Hebrew feasts, which God commanded His people to celebrate in order to meet with Him in a special manner at appointed times. A knowledge of these relevant events in the history of the Israelite people, and the Jewish practices that were based on these events, affected the ministries of the early believers and will provide guidance to the reader in studying the unwavering faith of the first followers of Jesus. This first chapter should provide the reader with a better understanding of the motivation of these early patriarchs and the substance and depth of their faith. Additionally, a study of the prophecies confirms that the Bible is the inspired word of God and the roadmap to salvation.

Except for a few Gentile first believers, such as Luke and Titus, the early followers of Jesus were, like Jesus, devout Jews. As God-fearing Jews, they read and studied the Scriptures; they were familiar with the Law of Moses as well as the scriptural prophecies. In testifying of the risen Lord, they proved to the multitude to whom they witnessed that Jesus' coming was the fulfillment of the Law and the Prophets. In summarizing important events in Jewish history, this chapter first considers the division of the Hebrew or Israelite nation into twelve tribes[1] and explains the significance of that division in a study of the lives of the early followers, particularly the twelve disciples whose service to the Lord provided a reexamination of the role of the twelve tribes in a new spiritual context. It also refers to a division of the Israelite nation into two kingdoms, the Northern and the Southern Kingdoms, and to the survival of a remnant from the Southern Kingdom, the Kingdom of Judah, from whence came the Jewish nation. In reviewing Jewish practices and institutions that were of importance to Jesus and His followers, the chapter later provides a summary of the seven Hebrew feasts that Jesus and the early Jewish Christians celebrated in obedience to God's instructions to the Israelite nation. A knowledge of the seven feasts

---

1. Discussion of twelve tribes in Gen 49:1–28.

The twelve tribes were formed based on the twelve sons of Abraham's grandson, Jacob, who was later called Israel. They were Reuben, Simeon, Levi, Judah, Dan, Naphtali, Gad, Asher, Issachar, Zebulun, Joseph, and Benjamin. Gen 35:23–26 and Exod 1:1–4. Still, the twelve tribes actually refer to the sons of Jacob who had land portions in the land promised to Abraham. Jacob's son, Levi, had no portion because he and his descendants were the priestly line, whereas Jacob's son Joseph, had two portions, one for each of his sons, Ephraim and Manasseh. Thus, the twelve tribes include the names of ten of Jacob's sons, excluding Levi and Joseph, but two that are named for Joseph's sons—the tribes of Ephraim and Manasseh.

provides additional understanding of the divinity of Jesus to prove that, as many Christians contend, Jesus's coming, along with that of the Holy Spirit following Jesus' ascension into Heaven, fulfilled four of the feasts and that Jesus' second coming will satisfy the remaining three currently unfulfilled feasts. Additionally, the first chapter establishes that Jesus' message of salvation, which Jesus' early followers carried to the world, brought forth a new faith that completely changed the world.

This first chapter also introduces the early church and the first believers who were a part of its early ministry to the world.

II. Review of Jewish History as a Prelude to the Coming of the Messiah

A. Establishment of the Israelite Nation from the Twelve Israelite Tribes

Several thousand years ago, God called Abraham to establish a Hebrew nation to spread to the world the message of one God and to bring with that message God's plan of redemption for a grievously sinful world through the advent of the Messiah, the Lord Jesus. For this purpose, God promised Abraham a special land for him and his descendants. This land, the then land of Canaan, was later divided among twelve Israelite tribes that represented eleven of the twelve sons of Jacob, who was Abraham's grandson and who was later called Israel.[2]

The twelve tribes that became the Israelite nation consisted of two tribes designated for one of Jacob's sons, Joseph, but none for his son, Levi. The descendants of Levi were priests and because they were designated to serve God as His priests in the tabernacles first and then in the Israelite Temple, they were not given a portion of the promised land; rather their inheritance was the tithe which the other tribes paid to the Lord, and the Lord remitted to them for their service.

---

2. See Gen 35:10–12. Joseph and Mary, the mother of Jesus, were from the tribe of Judah. From the name Judah, the Israelites from the tribes of Judah, Benjamin, and Levi came to be called the Jewish people. Additionally, one of the three territorial divisions of the promised land was called Judea; the other two territories were called Galilee and Samaria. Part of Judea is in the now occupied West Bank, which is controlled partially by Israel and partially by the Palestinian Authority. East Jerusalem is located in the West Bank.

The Plan of Redemption and the Message of Salvation

As recorded in Numbers,[3] God said to Aaron, the brother of Moses who was from the tribe of Levi: "'You shall have no inheritance in their land, nor shall you have any portion among them; I am your portion and your inheritance among the children of Israel. Behold, I have given the children of Levi all the tithes in Israel as an inheritance, in return for the work which they perform, the work of the tabernacle of meeting. Hereafter the children of Israel shall not come near the tabernacle of meeting, lest they bear sin and die. But the Levites shall perform the work of the tabernacle of meeting, and they shall bear their iniquity; it shall be a statute forever, throughout your generations, that among the children of Israel they shall have no inheritance. For the tithes of the children of Israel, which they offer up as . . . offering to the Lord, I have given to the Levites as an inheritance . . .'"

After God had brought the tribes out from servitude in the land of Egypt, the tribes remained in the wilderness for forty years because of their sin in failing to honor God and to obey His commandments. Later, following the death of Moses, who had been the leader of the Israelite nation, God did permit Joshua, Moses' successor, to bring the tribes into the land promised to Abraham.[4]

In instructing Joshua on how the tribes should cross the Jordan river to enter the land promised to Abraham, God parted the waters of the Jordan to permit the Israelite tribes to cross on dry ground. Following the tribes crossing the Jordan, Joshua told each tribe to place a stone in the middle of the Jordan to serve as a reminder of what the Lord had done for them. "And it came to pass, when all the people were . . . passed over Jordan, that the Lord spake unto Joshua, saying, 'Take you twelve men out of the people, out of every tribe a man, and command ye them, saying, 'Take you hence out of the midst of Jordan, out of the place where the priests' feet stood firm, twelve stones, and ye shall carry them over with you, and leave them in the lodging place where ye shall lodge this night.' Then Joshua called the twelve men, whom he had appointed of the children of Israel, out of every

---

3. Num 18:20–24, NKJV.

4. Joshua was from the tribe of Ephraim, which has been referred to as the tribe of Joseph. Num 1:32–33. It was initially the most dominate of the tribes because it was located at the center of the land then called Canaan, which is now Israel. Additionally, the centers of the Israelite religion, Shechem and Shiloh, were located in the land provided this tribe. Shiloh was the location of the tabernacle that held the Ark of the Covenant, which King David later moved to Jerusalem where Solomon, his son, built the first temple. The tribe of Ephraim is now one of the ten lost tribes. Its land became Samaria, as differentiated from Judea or Galilee. Ancient Palestine was divided into Galilee, Samaria, and Judea. Samaria is now in the West Bank in the current nation of Israel.

tribe a man; And Joshua said unto them, 'Pass over before the ark of the Lord your God in the midst of Jordan, and take you up every man of you a stone upon his shoulder, according unto the number of the tribes of the children of Israel: That this be a sign among you, that when your children ask their fathers in time to come, saying, 'What mean ye by these stones, Then ye shall answer them, That the waters of the Jordan were cut off before the ark of the covenant of the Lord; when it passed over Jordan, the waters were cut off; and these stones shall become a memorial unto the children of Israel forever."[5]

When the Israelite tribes had crossed the Jordan on dry ground and the priests had brought the ark of the Lord from the Jordan, the waters of the Jordan returned. Joshua then instructed the Israelites that they would tell their children about the significance of the stones. "Then he spoke to the children of Israel, saying 'When your children ask their fathers in time to come, saying, 'What are these stones?' then you shall let your children know, saying, 'Israel crossed over this Jordan on dry land'; for the Lord your God dried up the waters of the Jordan before you until you crossed over, as the Lord your God did to the Red Sea, which He dried up before us until we had crossed over, that all the peoples of the earth may know the hand of the Lord, that it is mighty, that you may fear the Lord your God forever."[6]

God had instructed Joshua to place the twelve stones in the middle of the Jordan River as a remembrance of what God had done for them.[7] Joshua had thought then by "... all the people of the earth ..." knowing "... the hand of the Lord, that it is mighty ... ," they would serve the Lord their God forever.[8]

Unfortunately, the Israelite nation did not remember to serve the Lord forever. The children of Israel rebelled against God and did not

---

5. Josh 4:1–7, KJV. As recorded in Heb 9:4, the ark of the covenant contained a golden pot that contained manna, Aaron's rod that budded, and the tablets of the covenant—the Ten Commandments. See also Ex 16:32 (manna), Ex 40:20 (Ten Commandments), and Num 17:10 (Aaron's rod)

6. Josh 4:21–24, NKJV. In his farewell to the Israelite nation, Joshua instructed the tribes to "*choose for yourselves this day whom you will serve . . .*" and stated to them: "*But as for me and my house, we will serve the Lord.*" Josh 24:15, NKJV.

7. See Josh 3:14–17; 4.

8. Josh 4:24, KJV. In like manner, a study of the sacrificial life histories of the early followers of Jesus should provide Christians with a remembrance, not only of the tremendous and ultimate sacrifice of Jesus Christ, but also the extent of the sacrifices of the early believers in bringing to the world Jesus' message of salvation. That remembrance should also cause believers to serve their God forever.

follow His commandments. Most of the Israelite kings, as well as many of the people, worshiped pagan gods. Because of disagreements among themselves caused by their lack of faith, the twelve Israelite tribes later were divided into two nations.

1. The Northern Kingdom, the Kingdom of Israel

After the death of Solomon, King David's son, the ten northern tribes, led by members of the tribe of Ephraim, withdrew from the remaining two tribes–the tribes of Judah and Benjamin–and formed the Northern Kingdom called the Kingdom of Israel. The ten tribes of the Northern Kingdom were ruled by evil, corrupt kings, none of whom worshiped the Lord. As a result, members of these tribes lost fellowship with God, and having lost God's help and support, they were conquered by the Assyrians and carried into captivity in 722 BC. The ten tribes were ultimately lost in history.

2. The Southern Kingdom, the Kingdom of Judah

Some kings and members of the Southern Kingdom, also called the Kingdom of Judah, had followed the precepts and commandments of the Lord; thus, the Southern Kingdom continued to exist as a nation for a time. Unfortunately, though, many from the Southern Kingdom, including most of its kings, also refused to obey God's commandments. As a result, in 134 years following the destruction of the Northern Kingdom, members of the Southern Kingdom were also taken into captivity. The Babylonians captured the Southern Kingdom in 605 BC and destroyed Jerusalem and the Jewish temple in 586 BC. The tribes of Judah and Benjamin, as well as some from the tribe of Levi, were then brought into enslavement in Babylon.

During their captivity, a remnant from the tribes of Judah, Benjamin, and Levi, who were later referred to as the Jewish people, turned back to the Lord. God then used Cyrus, the Persian king, to conquer the Babylonians and to permit this remnant, approximately seventy years later, in 537 BC, to return to their homeland.

B. Fulfilment of Prophecies

The Old Testament prophets–Moses being the first and Malachi the last–predicted future events through divine revelation.[9] Malachi was followed by the New Testament prophet, John the Baptist, and then by Jesus, who prophesied as the very Word of God.[10] One of Jesus' early followers, the disciple Matthew, quoted Jesus' words in the Gospel of Matthew: "Do not think that I have come to destroy the Law or the Prophets. I did not come to destroy, but to fulfill."[11]

1. *Prophecy of the Survival of a Remnant from the Southern Kingdom*

It is important to note that the Israelites from the tribes of the Southern Kingdom were in captivity for about seventy years–from 605 BC until 537 BC. The approximate seventy years of their captivity corresponds almost precisely to Jeremiah's prophecy in 605 BC that the Israelites from the Southern Kingdom would be in captivity for seventy years. As recorded in Jeremiah,[12] "'And this whole land shall be a desolation, and an astonishment; and these nations shall serve the king of Babylon seventy years. And it shall come to pass when seventy years are accomplished, that I will punish the king of Babylon and that nation, saith the Lord, for their iniquity, and the land of the Chaldeans, and will make it perpetual desolations." Jeremiah

---

9. A prophet is one who has contact with God. A prophet speaks on God's behalf; the prophet's message from God is called a prophecy. Prophecies from the Scriptures were written to show the Israelites the consequences of sin and the tragic result of their choices to abandon the law of God. Still, the prophecies also set out God's plan of redemption to impart hope to a sinful world.

Believers should study the prophecies carefully and in depth. It is most important to consider, as did the early believers, that scriptural prophecies of several thousand years ago from prophets who were chosen and called by God, have been fulfilled just as they were foretold. Additionally, and most importantly, the scriptural prophecies establish that God is in control. That realization brings hope and peace.

10. Some of Jesus' prophecies were fulfilled shortly after His crucifixion, an example being Jesus' prediction of the destruction of the Jewish Temple in Jerusalem that actually occurred in 70 AD or forty years after Jesus predicted its destruction. While others of Jesus' prophecies remain to be fulfilled, they will all be fulfilled when He returns.

Refer to discussion in Chapter 6 regarding prophecies of Jesus, as well as some of His early followers, including those of the disciple John in Revelation who predicted events leading to, and occurring in, the end times.

11. Matt 5:17–18, NKJV.

12. Jer 25:11, KJV.

The Plan of Redemption and the Message of Salvation

amazingly also foresaw the return to Jerusalem of a remnant of the children of Israel after their approximate seventy years in captivity, writing: "For thus saith the Lord, That after seventy years be accomplished at Babylon I will visit you, and perform my good word toward you, in causing you to return to this place.'"[13]

Another amazing prediction was Isaiah's even earlier prophecy, in 670 BC, that Cyrus, the king of Persia, would be the person who would permit the Israelite captives to return to their homeland.[14] Cyrus became the king of Persia in 559 BC, over 100 years after Isaiah's prophecy wherein Isaiah specifically referred to Cyrus being the one who would help the Israelite remnant restore Jerusalem. In 539 BC, Cyrus conquered the Babylonian empire, and, in 537 BC, permitted the Israelites to return to Jerusalem to rebuild the Israelite Temple.[15] As recorded in Isaiah nearly 130 years earlier:[16] "Thus saith the Lord, . . . That confirmeth the word of his servant . . . that saith to Jerusalem, Thou shalt be inhabited' and to the cities of Judah, Ye shall be built, and I will raise up the decayed places thereof . . . That saith of Cyrus, He is my shepherd, and shall perform all my pleasure: even saying to Jerusalem, Thou shalt be built; and to the temple, Thy foundation shall be laid.'"

In returning to Jerusalem from captivity in Babylon, Ezra, who was a Israelite scribe and priest and the primary leader of the Israelites when they returned from exile in Babylon to rebuild the Temple in Jerusalem, recorded that:[17] "In the first year of Cyrus king of Persia, in order to fulfill the word of the Lord spoken by Jeremiah, the Lord moved the heart of Cyrus king of Persia to make a proclamation throughout his realm and also to put it in writing: 'This is what Cyrus king of Persia says: 'The Lord, the God of heaven, has given me all the kingdoms of the earth and He has appointed me to build a temple for Him at Jerusalem in Judah. Any of His people among you may go up to Jerusalem in Judah and build the temple of the Lord, the God of Israel, the God who is in Jerusalem, and may their God be with them.'"

---

13. Jer 29:10, KJV.

14. See Isa 44:24–28.

15. Isaiah prophesied, approximately 130 years before it occurred, that Cyrus would be used to guarantee return of a remnant of the conquered Southern Kingdom.

16. Isa 44:24, 26, 28, KJV.

17. Ezra 1:1–3, NIV.

The prophets Jeremiah and Isaiah made astonishing predictions about the Southern Kingdom, not only about its people being brought into captivity, but also of the tribes' return to Jerusalem. Jeremiah's prophecy in 605 BC, that the Babylonians would capture the tribes of the Southern Kingdom and bring them into enslavement in Babylon and that they would remain in captivity for seventy years but then return to Jerusalem,[18] was fulfilled approximately seventy years later, in 537 BC. Additionally, Isaiah's prediction in 670 BC, sixty-five years prior to Jeremiah's prophecy, that Cyrus, the king of Persia, would be the one who would permit the tribes to return to their homeland, was fulfilled about 130 years later, also in 537 BC.[19] The return of some of the children of Israel to Jerusalem is important because, after their return, and following great reprove from the prophets Ezra and Nehemiah, the Israelite remnant did rebuild the temple in Jerusalem. Additionally, Ezra reestablished the law of Moses and forbade the Israelites to marry heathen persons.[20] The Hebrew people did not again worship heathen gods, and from this remnant, many of whom became faithful worshipers of the one true God and steadfast followers of the Lord, came the later birth of Jesus, the Christ.

Another prophecy of equal importance as those of Jeremiah and Isaiah is the prophecy of the prophet, Ezekiel, regarding the Israelite nation. In about 570 BC, Ezekiel informed the children of Israel of the Lord's words: "And I will scatter thee among the heathen, and disperse thee in the countries . . . ."[21] This prophecy, further discussed in Chapter 6, was fulfilled when the Romans, beginning in 70 AD with the destruction of Jerusalem, dispersed the Jewish people throughout the world. Still, Ezekiel also recorded the Lord's words that Israel would one day again be a nation: "Still say unto them, Thus saith the Lord God; Behold, I will take the children of Israel from among the heathen, whither they be gone, and will gather them on every side, and bring them into their own land; . . . and they shall be no more two nations, neither shall they be divided into two kingdoms any

---

18. Discussion in Jer 19:10 and 25:11.
19. Isaiah's prophecy at Isa 44.
20. Discussion in the books of Ezra and Nehemiah.
   It is unfortunate though that many of the children of Israel did not repent of their sins. This may be the reason the Jewish nation did not exist as an independent nation for over 2,500 years, from the time the Southern Kingdom was carried into captivity in 605 BC until Israel became a state in 1948.
21. Ezek 22:15, KJV.

The Plan of Redemption and the Message of Salvation

more at all."[22] One can theorize that this prophecy was fulfilled when Israel became one nation in 1948. As noted previously, it had been two nations, the Kingdom of Israel and the Kingdom of Judah, and had not been any nation since 605 BC when the Kingdom of Judah was destroyed. Ezekiel amazingly predicted that God would bring the children of Israel back to their homeland and they would no longer be divided into two nations. Israel currently is one nation, not two as at the time of Ezekiel's prophecy.

2. Prophecy of the Coming of John the Baptist

Seven hundred years prior to the birth of John the Baptist, Isaiah prophesied about him, describing him as:[23] "The voice of him that crieth in the wilderness . . . and stating, 'Prepare ye the way of the Lord, make straight in the desert a highway for our God.'" Malachi, the last of the Old Testament prophets, also predicted the coming of a "messenger" who would herald the birth of Jesus, prophesying that God would send a prophet like Elijah who would prepare the way for the Messiah. As recorded in Malachi,[24] the Lord said: "Behold, I will send my messenger, and he shall prepare the way before me . . ." and ". . . I will send you Elijah the prophet before the coming of the great and dreadful day of the Lord,"[25] warning the Jewish people that they should change their sinful way of life.

At the Transfiguration, discussed in Chapter 2, Jesus told His disciples, James, John, and Peter, that Elijah came through John the Baptist. Luke recorded Jesus as saying to the Pharisees:[26] "The law and the prophets were until John" (referring to John the Baptist).

John the Baptist was the son of a priest named Zacharias and Elizabeth, the cousin of Mary, the mother of Jesus. Both Zacharias and Elizabeth were descendants of Aaron, and thus, would have had a priestly background and would have been from the tribe of Levi.

John the Baptist was born about six months before the birth of Jesus. He was a rough individual who lived in the wilderness located between Jerusalem and the Dead Sea. John the Baptist preached the Word of God there where he also prophesied the coming of Jesus. When the Jewish

22. Ezek 37:21–22, KJV.
23. Isa 40:3, KJV.
24. Mal 3:1, KJV.
25. Mal 4:5, KJV.
26. Luke 16:16, NKJV.

leaders in Jerusalem asked who he was, "John replied in the words of Isaiah the prophet, 'I am the voice of one calling in the wilderness. 'Make straight the way for the Lord.'"[27]

John the Baptist was a Nazirite and, as a Nazirite, took a vow of dedication to the Lord. Regarding the Nazirite vow, the Lord said to Moses:[28] "Speak unto the children of Israel, and say to them: 'When either a man or woman consecrates an offering to take the vow of a Nazirite, to separate himself to the Lord, he shall separate himself from wine and similar drink . . . . All the days of the vow of his separation no razor shall come upon his head; until the days are fulfilled for which he separated himself to the Lord, he shall be holy." Samson and John the Baptist were the prominent Nazarites.

James, John, and Andrew (possibly Peter) had been disciples of the prophet John the Baptist, who, when he was completing his work, asked of his followers: ". . . Who do you suppose I am? I am not the one you are looking for. But there is one coming after me whose sandals I am not worthy to untie."[29] After John the Baptist pointed James and John to Jesus, they left their discipleship with John the Baptist to follow Jesus.

John the Baptist was later imprisoned by Herod Antipas, the son of Herod the Great, because he had condemned some of Herod's actions. These included Herod having divorced his wife and marrying his brother's wife, Herodias, while his brother was still alive. When John the Baptist was imprisoned, Herodias persuaded her daughter, Salome, Herod's stepdaughter, to ask for John's head as a reward for the dance she had performed in the presence of Herod and his guests.[30] Herod then reluctantly granted her wish, had John beheaded, and gave his head to Salome as a gift.

John the Baptist stood up for what was right and rebuked the king. In so doing, a corrupt Herod nobility subjected him to a horrific death.

3. Prophecy of Jesus's Coming and Important Details of His Ministry

Isaiah foretold the coming of the suffering Messiah, who is Jesus the Christ, and of Jesus' ministry, sometime between 740 and 700 BC, a date over 700 years before Jesus' birth and crucifixion. As recorded in Isaiah:[31] "For unto

---

27. John 1:23, NIV.
28. Num 6:2–5a, NKJV.
29. Acts 13:25, NIV.
30. Discussion at Mark 6:17–29.
31. Isa 9:6–7, KJV.

us a child is born, unto us a son is given: and the government shall be upon his shoulders: and his name shall be called Wonderful, Counsellor, The Mighty God, The everlasting Father, The Prince of Peace. Of the increase of his government and peace there shall be no end." Isaiah further predicted Jesus' suffering for the sins of the world:[32] "He is despised and rejected of men; a man of sorrows, and acquainted with grief; and we hid as it were our faces from him; he was despised, and we esteemed him not. Surely he hath borne our griefs, and carried our sorrows: yet we did esteem him stricken, smitten of God, and afflicted. But he was wounded, he was bruised for our iniquities: the chastening of our peace was upon him; and with his stripes we are healed. All we like sheep have gone astray; we have turned everyone to his own way; and the Lord hath lain on him the iniquity of us all. He was oppressed and he was afflicted, yet he opened not his mouth; he is brought as a lamb to the slaughter, and as a sheep before her shearers is dumb, so he opened not his mouth. He was taken away from prison and from judgment; and who shall declare his generation? For he was cut off out of the land of the living, for the transgression of my people was he stricken. And he made his grave with the wicked, and with the rich in his death; because he had done no violence, neither was any deceit in his mouth. Yet it pleased the Lord to bruise Him, he hath put him to grief: when thou shalt make his soul an offering for sin, he shall see his seed, he shall prolong his days, and the pleasure of the Lord shall prosper in his hand. He shall see of the travail of his soul, and shall be satisfied; by his knowledge shall my righteous servant justify many; for he shall bear their iniquities. Therefore, will I divide him a portion with the great, and he shall divide the spoil with the strong; because he hath poured out his soul unto death, and he was numbered with the transgressors; and he bare the sin of many, and made intercession the transgressors."

Jesus was the suffering servant to whom Isaiah predicted would "justify many" and "bear their inequities." Jesus' birth, crucifixion and resurrection, which occurred over 700 years later, fulfilled Isaiah's prophecy that the suffering servant, Jesus, would bear "the sin of many."

a. The Message of Salvation

After they met with the resurrected Jesus, the early followers of Jesus finally came to realize that Jesus was indeed the Messiah sent from God to save an otherwise lost and dying world. Although, during their three-year ministry

---

32. Isa 53:3–12, KJV.

with Jesus prior to His crucifixion, the disciples recognized that Jesus was a special teacher sent from God, they were nonetheless confused about who He actually is. At one time during that ministry, Jesus' declared to His disciples: "Let not your heart be troubled; you believe in God, believe also in me. In my Father's house are many mansions; if it were not so, I would have told you. I go to prepare a place for you. And if I go and prepare a place for you, I will come again and receive you to Myself; that where I am, there you may be also. And where I go you know, and the way you know."[33] When Thomas, one of the disciples, then questioned Jesus about how the disciples were to know the way where He was going, Jesus responded:[34] "'I am the way, the truth, and the life. No one comes to the Father except through Me. If you had known Me, you would have known My Father also; and from now on you know Him and have seen Him.'" Jesus also cautioned His disciples:[35] "'A little while longer and the world will see Me no more, but you will see Me. Because I live, you will live also.'" Because He lives, the disciples were rewarded with eternal life, and all believers today, like them, will also live forever.

Jesus' message is brought to all sinners. He said to a tax collector named Zaccheus that ". . . 'the Son of Man has come to seek and to save that which was lost . . .'"[36] and to a ruler of the Jews, a Pharisee named Nicodemus:[37] "And as Moses lifted up the serpent in the wilderness, even so must the Son of Man be lifted up, that whoever believes in Him should not perish but have eternal life. For God so loved the world that He gave His only begotten Son, that whoever believes in Him should not perish, but have everlasting life." Jesus brought comfort to Nicodemus and to all believers when he told Nicodemus that "' . . . God did not send His Son into the world to condemn the world, but that the world through Him might be saved.'"[38]

Jesus further assured the multitudes that ". . . whoever loses his life for My sake will save it . . ."[39] and said to the Jews:[40] "Truly, truly, I say to you, he who hears My word, and believes Him who sent Me, has eternal life, and

---

33. John 14:1–4, NKJV.
34. John 14:6–7, NKJV.
35. John 14:19, NKJV.
36. Luke 19:10, NKJV.
37. John 3:14–16, NKJV.
38. John 3:17, NKJV.
39. Luke 9:24b, NKJV.
40. John 5:24, NASB.

does not come into judgment, but has passed out of death into life." Jesus has assured all believers that "... everyone who sees the Son and believes in Him may have everlasting life."[41] He told the multitudes who followed Him:[42] "... I am the light of the world; he who follows Me shall not walk in the darkness, but shall have the light of life" and assured them, as well as all believers today, that "... if anyone keeps My word he shall never see death."[43]

The disciple John affirmed that Jesus performed many signs in the presence of the disciples, and many that were not recorded. With respect to those that were memorialized, John stated:[44] "But these have been written that you may believe that Jesus is the Christ, the Son of God, and that believing you may have life in His name." When Jesus was arrested, just prior to His crucifixion, the Jewish high priest asked Him: "'Are you the Christ, the Son of the Blessed?' Jesus said, 'I am. And you will see the Son of Man sitting at the right hand of the Power, and coming with the clouds of heaven.'"[45]

b. The Twelve Disciples and Seventy Others

Jesus began His ministry after He called twelve disciples to join Him.[46] The names of these disciples were: James and his brother John, Peter and his brother Andrew, Philip, Bartholomew (also called Nathanael), Matthew, Thomas, another James called James the Less, Thaddaeus, Simon the Zealot, and Judas Iscariot. Jesus chose His twelve disciples from all walks of life. Five of the apostles were probably Jesus' cousins. James and John were the sons of Zebedee and Salome, who reportedly was the sister of Mary, the mother of Jesus. James, called James the Less, Thaddaeus, and Simon the

---

41. John 6:40b, NKJV.
42. John 8:12, NASB.
43. John 8:51b, NKJV.
44. John 20:31, NASB.
45. Mark 14:61b-62, NKJV.

46. Most refer to these first followers of Jesus as "disciples" while some called them "apostles." Jesus referred to the twelve both as disciples and as apostles. "Disciple" means "learner" or "follower." See "Disciple" in Oxford University Press dictionary. After Jesus' resurrection and when His followers then carried His message of salvation to the world, the early followers were called apostles. An "apostle" has been defined as "messenger" or "missionary." Refer to "Apostle" in the Oxford University Press dictionary. The Oxford University Press dictionary also refers to an "apostle" as one who is an ardent supporter of a belief, idea, or cause.

Zealot[47] were sons of Alphaeus (also called Cleophas) and Mary, another reported sister of Jesus' mother. James, John, Andrew and Peter were fishermen; one disciple—Matthew also called Levi—was a tax collector. There is no evidence of the occupations, prior to their becoming disciples, of Thomas, Philip, Nathanael (also called Bartholomew), and Judas Iscariot, nor of Matthias who succeeded Judas Iscariot. One of the disciples, Peter, was married; there is no evidence regarding the marital status of the other disciples. Possibly as many as seven of the disciples were fishermen; clearly James, John, Peter, and Andrew were fishermen. It is possible that Thaddaeus, Philip, and James the Less were as well. The predominance of the fishing profession in the lives of the disciples undoubtedly was the reason the fish became the first and prevailing symbolization of the Christian faith.

Matthew recorded Jesus calling his twelve disciples:[48] "And having summoned His twelve disciples, He gave them authority over unclean spirits, to cast them out, and to heal every kind of disease and every kind of sickness. Now the names of the twelve are these: The first, Simon, who is called Peter, and Andrew his brother; and James the son of Zebedee, and John his brother; Philip, and Bartholomew; Thomas and Matthew the tax-gatherer; James the son of Alphaeus; and Thaddaeus; Simon the Zealot and Judas Iscariot, the one who betrayed Him." As recorded in the Gospel of Mark:[49] "Then He appointed twelve that they might be with Him, and that He might send them out to preach and to have power to heal sicknesses and to cast out demons. And He appointed the twelve: Simon, to whom He gave the name Peter; James, the son of Zebedee and John the brother of James, to whom He gave the name Boanerges, that is "Sons of Thunder"; Andrew, Philip, Bartholomew, Matthew, Thomas, James the son of Alphaeus, Thaddaeus, Simon the Cananite; and Judas Iscariot, who betrayed Him." Luke referred to the twelve as follows:[50] ". . . He called His disciples

---

47. Simon the Zealot had been a member of a political activist group, but after he witnessed Jesus resurrection and ascension into heaven, he became a devout follower of the Lord. This activist group, called Zealots, later rose up against the Romans in a war that saw the destruction of Jerusalem, which began in 70 AD. Following its destruction, the surviving Zealots sought refuge on the mount of Masada. Then, after the Romans were able to scale Masada, the Zealots took their own lives rather than becoming Roman slaves.

48. Matt 10:1-4, NASB.

49. Mark 3:14-19, NKJV.

50. Luke 6:13-16, NKJV. Judas Iscariot betrayed Jesus and later destroyed himself as noted in Chapter 3. The remaining eleven disciples replaced him after Jesus' ascension by drawing lots; the lot fell to Matthias who is discussed in Chapter 3.

to Himself; and from them He chose twelve whom He also named apostles: Simon, whom He also named Peter, and Andrew his brother; James and John; Philip and Bartholomew; Matthew and Thomas; James the son of Alphaeus, and Simon called the Zealot; Judas the son of James, and Judas Iscariot, who also became a traitor."

When Peter asked Jesus what there would be for them from following Him, Jesus answered:[51] "... Assuredly, I say to you, that in the regeneration, when the Son of Man sits on the throne of His glory, you who have followed Me will also shall sit on twelve thrones, judging the twelve tribes of Israel." Some then have equated the twelve disciples with the twelve tribes of Israel and as a continuation of the Word of God from the Scriptures to the new religion of Christians who endorsed the message of Jesus.

Jesus also chose seventy other persons to spread His message. He instructed these persons how they should prepare for His coming to the cities and warned them that they often would not be treated well. As recorded in Luke,[52] "After these things the Lord appointed seventy others also, and sent them two and two before His face into every city and place where He Himself was about to go. Then He said to them, 'The harvest is great, but the laborers are few; therefore pray the Lord of the harvest to send out laborers into His harvest. Go your way; behold, I send you out as lambs among wolves. Carry neither money bag, knapsack nor sandals; and greet no one along the road. But whatever house you enter, first say 'Peace to this house.' And if a son of peace is there, your peace will rest on it; if not, it will return to you. And remain in the same house, eating and drinking such things as they give, for the laborer is worthy of his wages. Do not go from house to house. Whatever city you enter, and they receive you, eat such things as are set before you. And heal the sick there, and say to them, 'The kingdom of God has come near to you.' But whatever city you enter and they do not receive you, go out into its streets and say, 'The very dust of your city which clings to us, we wipe off against you. Nevertheless know this, that the kingdom of God has come near you.'"

c. The Crucifixion

Jesus was the suffering servant foretold by the prophet Isaiah, but through his death on the cross He brought salvation to a sinful world. In writings

51. Matt 19:28, NKJV.
52. Luke 10:1–11a, NKJV.

that became the New Testament, some of Jesus' first followers detailed the account of Jesus' crucifixion, which occurred sometime between 30 and 33 AD when Jesus was thirty three years of age.

Jesus was arrested in Jerusalem in a place called Gethsemane and was taken to Caiaphas, the Jewish high priest, where the Jewish scribes and elders were gathered. These chief priests and elders then ". . . plotted against Jesus to put Him to death. And when they had bound Him, they led Him away and delivered Him to Pontius Pilate the governor."[53] Pilate's wife instructed him:[54] "'Have nothing to do with that just Man, for I have suffered many things today in a dream because of Him.'" Nevertheless, the chief priests and elders persuaded the multitudes to put Jesus to death and then demanded that Pilate deliver Jesus to be crucified.

Pilate's soldiers took Jesus to the Praetorium, which was Pilate's residence and is believed to be the former palace of Herod the Great: "And they stripped Him, and put a scarlet robe on Him. And after having a crown of thorns, they put it on His head, and a reed in His right hand; and they kneeled down before Him and mocked Him, saying, 'Hail, King of the Jews!' And they spat on Him, and took the reed and began to beat Him on the head. And after they had mocked Him, they took His robe off and put His garments on Him, and led Him away to crucify Him."[55] "And when they had come to a place called Golgotha, that is to say, Place of a Skull, they gave Him sour wine mingled with gall to drink. But when he tasted it, He would not drink. Then they crucified Him, and divided His garments, casting lots, that it might be fulfilled which was spoken by the prophet: 'They divided My garments among them, and for My clothing they cast lots.' Sitting down, they kept watch over Him there. And they put up above His head the accusation written against Him: This is Jesus the King of the Jews."[56]

Jesus' crucifixion occurred on the day of the Passover feast, which is discussed below. At the Passover feast, on the day of Christ's crucifixion, the Jewish high priest, Caiaphas, began the procession to enter the Jerusalem Temple to slaughter a pure, spotless Passover lamb on the sixth hour (noon). John records that Pilate handed Jesus over to be crucified on the

---

53. Matt 27:1–2, NKJV. Pontius Pilate was the governor of Judea from approximately 26 to 37 AD.

54. Matt 27:19a, NKJV.

55. Matt 27:28–31, NASB. They also nailed Jesus' hands to the cross.

56. Matt 27:33–37, NKJV. The reference to words spoken by the prophet is at Psalm 22:18.

sixth hour:[57] "Now it was the day of preparation for the Passover; it was about the sixth hour. And he said to the Jews, 'Behold your King!' They therefore cried out, 'Away with Him, away with Him, crucify Him!' Pilate said to them, 'Shall I crucify your king?' The chief priests answered, 'We have no king but Caesar.' So he then delivered Him to them to be crucified."

Jesus was nailed to the cross on the sixth hour of the Passover feast, which was noon, and suffering so incredibly, He hung there, on the cross, for three hours. As recorded in Matthew:[58] "Now from the sixth hour until the ninth hour there was darkness over all the land." The ninth hour occurred when the high priest, as discussed below, would enter the Holy Place in the Jewish Temple to offer the blood of the Passover lamb to cover the sins of the nations. At that moment, on the ninth hour, Jesus cried out:[59] "It is finished! And bowing His head, He gave up His spirit." Matthew recorded the event as follows:[60] "And Jesus cried again with a loud voice, and yielded up His spirit. And behold, the veil of the temple was torn in two from top to the bottom; and the earth shook, and the rocks were split."

There were two veils in the Temple–one at the entrance to the Holy Place and the second at the entrance of the Holy of Holies. Both were torn in two when Jesus died. As recorded in Matthew:[61] "So when the centurion and those who were with him, who were guarding Jesus, saw the earthquake and the things that had happened, they feared greatly, saying, 'Truly this was the Son of God!'"

d. Jesus Burial and the Role of Joseph of Arimathea

Joseph of Arimathea,[62] a wealthy member of the Sanhedrin, was a believer but originally in secret for fear of the Jews. Later, however, he, rather than the twelve disciples, risked great danger in coming forward to claim the body of Jesus and in preparing Jesus' body for a proper burial. Joseph of Arimathea gave his own burial place as a burial site for Jesus. While most events in the life of Jesus are mentioned only in one or two of the four Gospels, Joseph of Arimathea is mentioned in all four Gospels. His role in

57. John 19:14–15, NASB.
58. Matt 27:45, NKJV.
59. John 19:30b, NKJV.
60. Matt 27:50–51, NASB.
61. Matt 27:54, NKJV.
62. Arimathea was an ancient city in Judea.

Jesus' burial was most significant because, but for his intervention, Jesus' body could have been destroyed, possibly burned, because Jesus was crucified to die as a criminal.

Jeremiah records the place where the bodies of criminals were thrown and where Jesus' body undoubtedly would have been cast:[63] "And they built the high places of Baal, which are in the valley of the son of Hinnom, to cause their sons and their daughters to pass through the fire unto Molech;[64] which I commanded them not, neither came it into my mind, that they should do this abomination, to cause Judah to sin." The valley of the son of Hinnom was associated with Gehenna or Sheol; it was a type of Hell. In contrast, the righteous were thought to rest at the side of the faithful and righteous Abraham, the father of the Israelite and Jewish nation. As recorded in Luke regarding the death of a poor but righteous man: "So it was that the beggar died, and was carried by the angels to Abraham's bosom."[65] Joseph of Arimathea risked death to claim Jesus' body from Pilate to provide a proper Jewish burial for the Lord.

After Pilate released Jesus' body to him, Joseph of Arimathea, along with Nicodemus, the Pharisee who came to speak to Jesus at night,[66] claimed the body of Jesus.[67] They wrapped Jesus' body in linen cloths with spices as the Jews do in preparation for burial to delay corruption of the body.[68] Their saving Jesus' body for a proper burial also fulfilled prophecies in Psalms and Isaiah. As it is written in Psalms:[69] "For Thou wilt not leave my soul in hell; neither wilt thou suffer thine Holy One to see corruption." Isaiah wrote:[70]

---

63. Jer 32:35, KJV.

64. A Canaanite god associated with child sacrifice.

65. Luke 16:22, NKJV. Abraham's bosom represented a place of comfort upon the death of a Hebrew person who during life had obeyed God's word. An old and beautiful spiritual picks up that serenity: "Rock my soul in the bosom of Abraham."

66. As recorded in John 3:1–3, NKJV: "There was a man of the Pharisees, named Nicodemus, a ruler of the Jews. This man came to Jesus by night and said to Him, 'Rabbi, we know that You are a teacher come from God; for no one can do these signs that You do unless God is with him.' Jesus answered and said to him, 'Most assuredly, I say to you, unless one is born again, he cannot see the kingdom of God.'"

67. Although Joseph of Arimathea and Nicodemus were at the trial of Jesus before the Sanhedrin, they did not consent to the unfairness of that trial nor to the decision of that court, a decision that was rendered after Jesus' extremely grossly unfair trial.

68. See Matt 27:57, Mark 15:43, Luke 23:50, and John 19:38.

69. Ps 16:10, KJV.

70. Isa 53:9, KJV.

The Plan of Redemption and the Message of Salvation

"And he made his grave with the wicked, and with the rich in his death; because he had done no violence, neither was any deceit in his mouth."

Some have speculated, but without any evidence, that Joseph of Arimathea was the uncle of Mary, the mother of Jesus.[71] If so, he would have been Jesus' great uncle. At the time of Jesus' crucifixion, Mary's husband, Joseph, undoubtedly was deceased. If Joseph of Arimathea was Jesus' great uncle, there is reason for Pilate to have permitted him, as Jesus' kinsman, to take Jesus' body. Still, it is also conceivable that Pilate would have respected the request of Joseph of Arimathea regardless of his relationship to Jesus because, as a wealthy member of the Sanhedrin, Joseph of Arimathea was regarded as a powerful person in the Jewish community.

As written in Matthew,[72] "As evening approached, there came a rich man from Arimathea, named Joseph, who had himself become a disciple of Jesus. Going to Pilate, he asked for Jesus' body, and Pilate ordered that it be given to him. Joseph took the body, wrapped it in a clean linen cloth, and placed it in his own new tomb that he had cut out of the rock. He rolled a big stone in front of the entrance to the tomb and went away." Mark records the event as follows: "Joseph of Arimathea, a prominent member of the Council, who was himself waiting for the kingdom of God, went boldly to Pilate and asked for Jesus' body. Pilate was surprised to hear that he was already dead. Summoning the centurion, he asked him if Jesus had already died. When he learned from the centurion that it was so, he gave the body to Joseph. So Joseph bought some linen cloth, took down the body, wrapped it in the linen, and placed it in a tomb cut out of rock. Then he rolled a stone against the entrance of the tomb."[73] Luke reported:[74] "Now there was a man named Joseph, a member of the Council, a good and upright man, who had not consented to their decision and action. He came from the Judean town of Arimathea and he himself was waiting for the kingdom of God. Going to Pilate, he asked for Jesus' body. Then he took it down, wrapped it in a linen cloth and placed it in a tomb cut in the rock, one in which no had yet been laid. It was Preparation Day, and the Sabbath was about to begin. The women who had come with Jesus from Galilee followed Joseph and saw the tomb and how His body was laid in it. Then they went home and prepared spices and perfumes. But they rested on the Sabbath in obedience

---

71. Discussion at http://www.earlybritishkingdom.com/bios/joseph/html.
72. Matt 27:57–60, NIV.
73. Mark 15:43–46, NIV.
74. Luke 23:50–56, NIV.

to the commandment." John recorded the burial as follows:[75] "After this, Joseph of Arimathea, being a disciple of Jesus, but secretly for fear of the Jews, asked Pilate that he might take away the body of Jesus; and Pilate gave him permission. So he came and took the body of Jesus. And Nicodemus, who at first came to Jesus at night, also came; bringing a mixture of myrrh and aloes, about a hundred pounds. Then they took the body of Jesus, and bound it in strips of linen with the spices, as the custom of the Jews is to bury. Now in the place where He was crucified there was a garden; and in the garden a new tomb in which no one had yet been laid. So there they laid Jesus, because of the Jews' Preparation Day, for the tomb was nearby."

Joseph of Arimathea became a devout apostle; some historians have reported that he carried the message of salvation, accompanied by Lazarus, Martha, and Mary Magdalene, to Gaul in what is now the Provence of France, and from there to Glastonbury, England.[76] Only the disciple and apostle, John, outlived Joseph of Arimathea. John and Joseph of Arimathea were two of the very few apostles who died a natural death.

e. Jesus' Resurrection and Ascension and the Coming of the Holy Spirit

Three days after His crucifixion, on the day of His resurrection, Jesus appeared to Mary Magdalene first and then to eleven of His disciples. Mark wrote that after Jesus had risen, "He first appeared to Mary Magdalene and that she then . . . went and reported to those who had been with Him while

---

75. John 19:38–42, NKJV.

76. They reported that Philip the Apostle sent Joseph of Arimathea to England shortly after he arrived in France and that Joseph of Arimathea allegedly established the first church in Glastonbury, England. Joseph of Arimathea also is credited with bringing to Glastonbury the Holy Grail, the cup Jesus used at the Last Supper and in which Joseph of Arimathea supposedly received some of Jesus' blood at the cross. Https://www.earlybritishkingdoms.com/bio/joseph.html.

(The probable involvement of Lazarus and Mary Magdalene in bringing the gospel message to France is discussed in Chapter 5.)

A possible myth about Joseph of Arimathea involved a staff that he allegedly carved from the tree from whence came the crown of thorns placed on Jesus' head at His crucifixion. As Joseph of Arimathea rested at Glastonbury, he supposedly set the staff on the ground while he was sleeping. When he awoke in the morning, he found the staff had taken root and had grown into a thorn tree. Whether or not this is a myth, it is true that a thorn tree grew in Glastonbury that blossomed twice a year, near the time of Easter and at Christmas. Discussion at Https://www.greenmantlenursery.com/glastonburythorn.html.

The Plan of Redemption and the Message of Salvation

they were mourning and weeping."[77] Luke recorded the event as follows:[78] "Now on the first day of the week, very early in the morning, they, and certain other women with them, came to the tomb bringing the spices which they had prepared. But they found the stone rolled away from the tomb. Then they went in and did not find the body of the Lord Jesus. And it happened as they were greatly perplexed about this, that behold, two men stood by them in shining garments. Then as they were afraid and bowed their faces to the earth, they said to them, 'Why do you seek the living One among the dead? He is not here, but is risen, Remember how He spoke to you when He was still in Galilee, saying, 'The Son of Man must be delivered into the hands of sinful men, and be crucified, and the third day rise again.' And they remembered His words. Then they returned from the tomb and told all these things to the eleven and to all the rest. It was Mary Magdalene, Joanna, Mary the mother of James, and the other women with them, who told these things to the apostles. And their words seemed to them [the disciples] as idle tales, and they did not believe them. But Peter arose and ran to the tomb; and stooping down, he saw the linen clothes lying by themselves; and he departed, marveling to himself at what had happened."

Later, though, Luke reported that after Jesus appeared to the women and then also to the disciples: "These all continued with one accord in prayer and supplication with the women and Mary the mother of Jesus, and with His brothers."[79] Luke also recorded that both the women and men, who then had become faithful and fearless apostles, were imprisoned and even put to death for their zeal in spreading the gospel.[80]

Thomas, a disciple also known as Didymus, was not with the other disciples when Jesus first appeared to them. The other disciples later said to Thomas,[81] "'We have seen the Lord!' But he said to them, 'Unless I shall see in His hands the imprint of the nails, and put my finger into the place of the nails, and put my hand into His side, I will not believe.'" A week later, Thomas was with the disciples when Jesus again appeared to them. After Jesus said to Thomas: "'Reach your finger here, and look at My hands; and reach your hand here, and put it into My side. Do not be unbelieving,

---

77. Mark 16:9–10, NASB. See also John 20:9–21.
78. Luke 24:1–12, NKJV.
79. Acts 1:14, NKJV.
80. See Acts 8:1–4.
81. John 20:25, NASB.

but believing."[82] ". . . Thomas answered and said to Him, 'My Lord and my God.'"[83] Jesus replied to Thomas:[84] "'Because you have seen Me, have you believed? Blessed are they who did not see, and yet believed.'"

The resurrected Jesus stayed with His disciples for forty days.[85] When Jesus appeared to them in Jerusalem, He instructed them:[86] ". . . These are the words which I spoke to you while I was still with you, that all things must be fulfilled which are written in the Law of Moses and the Prophets and the Psalms concerning Me." He then informed them of the coming of the Holy Spirit. As stated in Acts, "On one occasion, while He was eating with them, He gave them this command: 'Do not leave Jerusalem, but wait for the gift My Father promised, which you have heard Me speak about. For John baptized with water, but in a few days you will be baptized with the Holy Spirit.'"[87] In opening their minds to understand the Scriptures, Jesus further said to them:[88] "This is what is written: The Messiah will suffer and rise from the dead on the third day and repentance for the forgiveness of sins will be preached in His name to all nations, beginning at Jerusalem. You are witnesses of these things. I am going to send you what my Father has promised; but stay in the city until you have been clothed with power from on high." Jesus told his apostles ". . . you shall receive power when the Holy Spirit has come upon you; and you shall be My witnesses both in Jerusalem, and in all Judea and Samaria, and even to the remotest part of the earth."[89]

Luke recorded that ". . . after He had said these things, He was lifted up while they were looking on, and a cloud received Him out of their sight.

---

82. John 20:27, NKJV. One of the soldiers had pierced Jesus' side with a spear.

83. John 20:28, NKJV.

84. John 20:29, NASB.

85. See Acts 1:3.

86. Luke 24:44, NKJV.

87. Acts 1: 4–5, NIV. John recorded, John 14:16–17, NASB, that Jesus assured the Twelve: "And I will ask the Father, and He will give you another Helper, that He may be with you forever; that is the Spirit of truth, whom the world cannot receive, because it does not behold Him or know Him, but you know Him because He abides with you, and will be in you." John further recorded Jesus as promising that ". . . the Helper, the Holy Spirit, whom the Father will send in My name, he will teach you all things, and bring to your remembrance all that I said to you." John 14:26, NASB.

88. Luke 24:46–49, NIV.

89. Acts 1:8b, NASB. Paul later questioned believers: "Do you not know that you are the temple of God and that the Spirit of God dwells in you?" 1 Cor 3:16, NKJV.

The Plan of Redemption and the Message of Salvation

And as they were gazing intently into the sky while He was departing, behold, two men in white clothing stood beside them; and they also said, 'Men of Galilee, why do you stand looking into the sky? This Jesus, who has been taken up from you into heaven, will come in just the same way as you have watched Him go into heaven.'"[90]

Following Jesus' resurrection and ascension, the remaining eleven disciples decided they must find another to replace Judas Iscariot. The eleven decided to nominate two men: Joseph, called Barsabbas, and Matthias. They then prayed:[91] "'You, O, Lord, who know the hearts of all, show which of these two You have chosen to take part in this ministry and apostleship from which Judas by transgression fell, that he might go to his own place.' And they cast their lots, and the lot fell to Matthias. And he was numbered with the eleven apostles."

On the Feast of Pentecost that occurred fifty days after the Passover of Jesus' crucifixion, which would be fifty days from the day Jesus was crucified, the Holy Spirit descended upon the followers of Jesus who were all together in one place.[92] A sound from heaven then came as a rushing mighty wind and there appeared on these believers tongues like as of fire. The event is recorded in Acts:[93] "And when the day of Pentecost had come, they were all together in one place. And suddenly there came from heaven a noise like a violent, rushing wind, and it filled the whole house where they were sitting . . . And they were all filled with the Holy Spirit."

f. The Great Commission

Jesus commissioned His disciples, as well as His other followers, to bring His message of salvation to the world. Earlier in Galilee, he had said to His disciples,[94] "All authority has been given to Me in heaven and on earth. Go therefore and make disciples of all nations, baptizing them in the name of the Father and of the Son and of the Holy Spirit, and teaching them to observe all I have commanded you; and lo, I am with you always, even to end of the age."

---

90. Luke 1:9–11, NASB.
91. Acts 1:24b-26, NKJV.
92. Acts 2:2. The Feast of Pentecost is discussed below.
93. Acts 2:2–4, NASB.
94. Matt 28:18–20, NASB.

Jesus' disciples, as well as the other early followers of Jesus, obeyed Jesus' command to become "... witnesses both in Jerusalem, and in all Judea and Samaria, and to the remotest part of the earth."[95] Unafraid and with great boldness, knowing without any doubt that Jesus was one with God and the Savior of the world, they risked everything, including their lives, to spread the Gospel to the "remotest part of the earth." Because of the almost unbelievable courageousness and fearless actions of Jesus' first early followers, which occurred only after these patriachs actually saw and met with the risen Christ, the world now can also, without any doubt, know and attest to Jesus' divinity and oneness with God.

g. The Reason for Twelve Disciples

Jesus chose twelve disciples to join Him in His ministry and to receive private instruction from Him about God's plan of redemption in order to equip the Twelve to bring Jesus' message of salvation to the world. There is some indication that Jesus wanted the twelve disciples to be a continuation of the twelve tribes of Israel but in a new, more complete, spiritual context. The number twelve represents completeness, but of more significance, the number equates to the twelve tribes of Israel.

As noted previously, Matthew recorded in his Gospel the words of Jesus:[96] "Truly I say to you, that you who have followed Me, in the regeneration when the Son of Man will sit on His glorious throne, you also shall sit upon twelve thrones, judging the tribes of Israel." Luke also reported Jesus as informing the disciples that they would "... sit on thrones judging the twelve tribes of Israel."[97]

There is further evidence in the book of Revelation that Jesus chose the twelve disciples to represent the twelve tribes in a new, more spiritual Israel. John describes the new Jerusalem in Revelation[98] as follows: "It had a great and high wall with twelve gates, and at the gates twelve angels; and names were written on them, which are those of the twelve tribes of the sons of Israel. There were three gates on the east and three gates on the north and three gates on the south and three gates on the west. And the

---

95. Acts 1:8, NASB.
96. Matt 19:28, NASB.
97. Luke 22:30b, NKJV.
98. Rev 21:12–14, NASB.

wall of the city had twelve foundation stones, and on them were the twelve names of the twelve apostles of the Lamb."

It is conceivable that Jesus replaced the twelve tribes of Israel with twelve disciples not only to bring His message of salvation to the world but also to bring about the full renewal of Israel by leading Israel to redemption. Paul wrote to the Ephesians:[99] "So then, you are no longer strangers and aliens, but you are fellow citizens with the saints, and are of God's household, having been built upon the foundation of the apostles and prophets, Christ Jesus Himself being the corner stone, in whom the whole building, being fitted together is growing into a holy temple in the Lord; in whom you also are being built together into a dwelling God in the Spirit."

Paul told the believers in Rome:[100] "It is not as though God's word has failed. For not all who are descended from Israel are Israel. Nor because they are his descendants are they all Abraham's children. On the contrary, 'It is through Isaac that your offspring will be reckoned.' In other words, it is not the children by physical descent who are God's children, but it is the children of the promise who are regarded as Abraham's offspring."

4. Fulfillment of Jewish Feasts

One of the most amazing portrayals of God's plan of salvation was the fulfillment of four of the seven Jewish feasts through the coming of Jesus and the Holy Spirit.[101] The word for "feasts" is "appointed times." At appointed times, during the seven feasts that were spread over seven months of the Jewish calendar, the Jewish people would be drawn especially close to God. These feasts demonstrated God's plan of redemption. As most Christians contend, the prophetical significance of three of the feasts was fulfilled by

---

99. Eph 2:19–22, NASB.

100. Rom 9:6–8, NIV.

101. Discussion of the feasts, summarized here, at Ray Vander Laan, "That the World May Know," https://www.thattheworldmayknow.com/jewish-feasts and https://www.pray4zion.org, See also "The Jewish Holidays–A Simplified Overview of the Feast of the Lord," https://hebrew4christians.com/Holiday/Introduction/introduction.html.

The Seven Feasts, recorded in Leviticus 23, include four spring feasts–the Passover Feast, the Feast of Unleavened Bread, the Feast of Firstfruits, and the Feast of Pentecost– and three fall feasts—the Feast of the Trumpets, the Day of Atonement (or Yom Kippur), and the Feast of the Tabernacles. As many Christians contend, Jesus death, burial, and resurrection and the coming of the Holy Spirit on Pentecost fulfilled the spring feasts. They contend the fall feasts are unfulfilled.

Jesus' death and resurrection with the Feast of Pentecost being fulfilled when the Holy Spirit descended upon the believers on the day of the Pentecost that followed Jesus' crucifixion.[102]

    102. The three fall feasts, which are unfulfilled, are as follows.

    The Feast of the Trumpets occurs on the first day of the seventh month, in September or October. The high priest would blow the trumpet so that the faithful would stop harvesting to begin their worship. Christians contend this Feast will be fulfilled at the second coming when the trumpet will sound to announce the arrival of the King of Kings. Some contend the church will be taken out of the world and that the trumpet represents the rapture of the church. Paul recorded in 1 Thess 4:15-17, NIV: "According to the Lord's word, we tell you that we who are still alive, who are left until the coming of the Lord, will certainly not precede those who have fallen asleep. For the Lord himself will come down from heaven, with a loud command, with the voice of the archangel and with the trumpet call of God, and the dead in Christ will rise first. After that, we who are still alive and are left will be caught up together with them in the clouds, to meet the Lord in the air. And so we will be with the Lord forever."

    The Day of Atonement, or Yom Kippur, which occurs on the tenth of seventh month, is the highest of Jewish holy days. It is the most important feast for the Jewish people. Before the Temple was destroyed, the atonement ritual began, as God had commanded Moses to tell his brother Aaron, the first high priest, with a high priest, that priest first being Aaron, coming into the holy of holies. A bull was sacrificed for a sin offering. Then two goats were brought, one to be sacrificed because of the Israelites' sinfulness and rebellion. The blood of the first goat was to appease the God's wrath for the sins of the people for another year. The other goat was used as a scapegoat. The high priest would place his hand on the goat's head, confess over it the sinfulness of the Israelite people, and a designated man would take the goat out and would release it into the wilderness. The goat carried on itself all the sins of the people, which were forgiven for another year. It removed the sins of the people into the wilderness where they were forgotten. This feast was described first in Leviticus 16:3-34. As set out in Leviticus 16:7-10, NKJV, regarding the first celebration of this feast, God commanded Moses to tell Aaron to take two goats and "... present them before the Lord at the door of the tabernacle of meeting." Aaron was to "... cast lots for the two goats: one lot for the Lord and the other lot for the scapegoat." Aaron was to "... bring the goat on which the Lord's lot fell, and offer it as a sin offering. But the goat on which the lot fell to be the scapegoat ... had to "... be presented alive before the Lord, to make atonement upon it, and to let it go as the scapegoat into the wilderness." As recorded in Leviticus 16:20-22, NKJV: "And when he has made an end of atoning for the Holy Place, the tabernacle of meeting, and the altar, he shall bring the live goat. Aaron shall lay both his hands on the head of the live goat, confess over it all the iniquities of the children of Israel, and all their transgressions, concerning all their sins, putting them on the head of the goat, and shall send it away into the wilderness by the hand of a suitable man. The goat shall bear on itself all their iniquities to an uninhabited land, and he shall release the goat in the wilderness."

    The Feast of Tabernacles, also called the Feast of Booths, occurs on the fifteenth day of the seventh month. God wanted the Israelites to celebrate the fact that He provided shelter for them in the wilderness. Each year on the Feast of Tabernacles, devout Jews build "booths" or tents outside their homes and worship in them. Tabernacles represent the Lord's shelter and a remembrance of how God protected the Israelites during the

The Plan of Redemption and the Message of Salvation

a. Passover Feast

Jesus' message to His disciples that they carried to the world was culminated at the celebration of the Passover, on the first Good Friday, which preceded Jesus' resurrection on the following Sunday. Jesus was crucified during the Passover, which is also called the Feast of Salvation.[103]

As noted previously, on the day of Christ's crucifixion at the Passover feast, the high priest, Caiaphas, began the procession to enter the Temple to slaughter a pure, spotless Passover lamb on the sixth hour (noon).[104] As recorded in Matthew:[105] "Now from the sixth hour darkness fell upon all the land until the ninth hour." Further, as noted previously, the ninth hour occurred when the high priest would enter the Holy Place to offer the blood of the Passover lamb to cover the sins of the nations, and at that moment, on the ninth hour, Jesus cried out:[106] "It is finished! And bowing His head, He gave up His spirit."

As noted previously, there were two veils in the temple–one at the entrance to the Holy Place and the second at the entrance of the Holy of Holies. Both were torn in two when Jesus died. As stated in Matthew:[107]

Exodus. Zechariah referred to the Feast of Tabernacles, at Zech 14:16-17, NIV: "Then the survivors from all the nations that have attacked Jerusalem will go up year after year to worship the King, the Lord Almighty, and to celebrate the Feast of Tabernacles. If any of the peoples of the earth do not go up to Jerusalem to worship the King, the Lord Almighty, they will have no rain." The prophet Micah, in Mic 4:1-7, KJV, referred to the Feast of Tabernacles: "But in the last days it shall come to pass, that the mountain of the house of the Lord shall be established in the top of the mountains, and it shall be exalted above the hills, and the people shall flow into it. And many nations shall come and say, 'Come, and let us go up to the mountain of the Lord and to the house of the God of Jacob, that He will teach us of His ways and we shall walk in His path; for the law shall go forth of Zion, and the word of the Lord from Jerusalem.'"

Further discussion of the three fall feasts, and remaining unfulfilled feasts, in Chapter 6.

103. Lev 23:5. Passover begins after dusk on fourteenth day of Nisan, the Jewish first month, which is in March or April, and ends at dusk of the fifteenth day. The Exodus took place in the Spring; thus, Nisan is the first religious month on the Jewish calendar. It is the Ecclesiastical (or religious) Jewish New Year. Passover recalled God's miraculous deliverance of the Israelite people from Egypt. Passover provides the memory of the angel of the Lord's passing over each Israelite family to prevent the death of their firstborn.

104. John records Pilate handing Jesus over to be crucified on the sixth hour. See John 19:14-15.

105. Matt 27:45, NASB.

106. John 19:30b, NKJV.

107. Matt 27:51, NKJV.

"Then, behold, the veil of the temple was torn in two from top to the bottom; and the earth quaked, and the rocks were split . . ."

The Passover feast was fulfilled when Jesus was crucified; Jesus is the Passover lamb. As Paul wrote to the Corinthians:[108] "For indeed Christ, our Passover, was sacrificed for us." Access to the Holy of Holies was once limited to the high priest and for only once a year (on Yom Kippur); with Jesus' sacrifice on the cross, it became open and accessible to all.

As Matthew recorded, the earth shook at the moment when Jesus died. It also shook when Moses came down from Mount Sinai to give the law to the Israelites. As stated in Exodus:[109] "Now Mount Sinai was completely in smoke, because the Lord descended upon it in fire. Its smoke ascended like the smoke of a furnace, and the whole mountain quaked greatly. And when the blast of the trumpet sounded long and became louder and louder, Moses spoke and God answered him by voice."

The book of Psalms also refers to the earth shaking:[110] "The earth shook, the heavens also dropped at the presence of God: even Sinai itself was moved at the presence of God, the God of Israel." The earth will shake again at the end when the earth trembles. As recorded in Hebrews:[111] "And His voice shook the earth then, but now He has promised saying, "Yet once more I will shake not only the earth, but also the heaven." This final shaking of the earth is recorded in Revelation:[112] "And I looked when He broke the sixth seal, and there was a great earthquake; and the sun became black as sackcloth made of hair, and the whole moon became as blood; and the stars of the sky fell to the earth." John further recorded in Revelation:[113] "Then there came flashes of lightning, rumblings, peals of thunder and a severe earthquake. No earthquake like it has ever occurred since mankind has been on earth, so tremendous was the quake. The great city split into three parts, and the cities of the nations collapsed."

Matthew also recorded the final event:[114] "Immediately after the tribulation of those days, the sun will be darkened, and the moon will not give her light, and the stars will fall from the sky, and the powers of the heavens

---

108. I Cor 5:7b, NKJV.
109. Exod 19:18–19, NKJV.
110. Ps 68:8, KJV.
111. Heb 12:26–27, NASB.
112. Rev 6:12–13a, NASB.
113. Rev 16:18–19b, NIV.
114. Matt 24:29–31, NKJV.

will be shaken, and then the sign of the Son of Man will appear in the sky, and then all the tribes of the earth will mourn, and they will see the Son of Man coming on the clouds of the sky with power and great glory. And He will send His angels with a great sound of a trumpet, and they will gather together His elect from the four winds, from one end of heaven to the other." Additionally, John recorded in Revelation:[115] "Then the sky receded as a scroll when it is rolled up, and every mountain and island was moved out of its place."

The writer of Hebrews recorded:[116] "And His voice shook the earth then but now He has promised, saying, 'Yet once more I will shake not only the earth, but also the heaven.' And this expression, 'Yet once more,' denotes the removing of those things which can be shaken, as of created things, in order that those things which cannot be shaken remain. Therefore, since we receive a kingdom which cannot be shaken, let us show gratitude, by which we offer to God an acceptable service with reverence and awe, for our God is a consuming fire." As the writer of Hebrews reported, God's Kingdom and His supreme power can never be shaken.

b. Feast of Unleavened Bread

The Feast of Passover was associated with the Festival of Unleavened Bread; the Israelites could not celebrate the Passover with leavened bread. Because there was not enough time for dough to rise when the children of Israel fled from Egypt, the Lord memorialized the event with the commandment to eat only unleavened bread for seven days. This celebration lasted seven days; for seven days the Israelites would eat unleavened bread and on the seventh day, there would be a feast to the Lord. Leaven in the Bible is symbolic with sin and evil. The Jews considered leaven as a symbol of death and decay. Leaven or yeast produces fermentation, especially in bread dough, and is the result of natural processes of decay. In contrast, unleavened bread symbolizes a holy walk. Sacrifices to God involve offering of objects in their least altered state. In this way, they are considered initially made by God. To fulfill God's commandment, Jews prepare for Passover by removing all traces of leaven from their homes. On the night before Passover, they symbolically remove the last vestiges of bread crumbs from their homes. Jews

---

115. Rev 6:14, NKJV.
116. Heb 12:26–29, NASB.

vacuum the house, wipe down cupboards, and physically remove all bread stuffs from their homes.[117]

Jesus was born in Bethlehem; the name "Bethlehem" in Hebrew is "House of Bread." John recorded Jesus as affirming:[118] "I am the living bread which came down from heaven. If anyone eats of this bread, he will live forever . . ." Additionally, Jesus' burial fulfilled the Feast of Unleavened Bread. Jesus was pure; His body was without sin; His body did not decay nor suffer the natural process of decomposition; Jesus' body did not return to dust.

Unleavened bread is a picture of Jesus' holiness, purity, and sinlessness. Jesus' broken body is our unleavened "bread of life." Christians are made "unleavened" (pure) by the sacrifice of Christ, the Bread of Life. Jesus celebrated the Feast of Unleavened Bread with his disciples when he instituted the Lord's Supper. Most Christians believe Jesus used unleavened bread for His Last Supper, and many churches use unleavened bread to celebrate the Lord's Supper because unleavened bread becomes a symbol of the body of our Lord.

Paul admonished Christians to live in purity and separation from the corrupting influence of sin in their lives. Because Christians are made "unleavened" (pure) by the sacrifice of Christ, their lives should reflect holiness and devotion to God. Paul urged Jesus' followers:[119] "Get rid of the old yeast, so that you may be a new unleavened batch—as you really are. For Christ, our Passover lamb, has been sacrificed. Therefore let us keep the festival, not with the old bread leavened with malice and wickedness, but with the unleavened bread of sincerity and truth."

---

117. This summary of the Feast of Unleavened Bread, as well as some of the other feasts, is attributed partially to discussion by Mark Levitt, edited by John Parson, "The Jewish Holidays," https://www.hebrews4christians.com/holidays/Introduction/introduction.html.

See Duet 16:3, NKJV, wherein the Lord commands the Israelites to eat unleavened bread for seven days, calling it the "bread of affliction," that they would eat for seven days to ". . . remember the day in which you came out of the land of Egypt all the days of your life." As recorded in Ex 13:6-7, NKJV: "Seven days you shall eat unleavened bread, and on the seventh day there shall be a feast to the Lord. Unleavened bread shall be eaten seven days. And no leavened bread shall be seen among you, nor shall leaven be seen among you in all your quarters. And you shall tell your son in that day, saying, 'This is done because of what the Lord did for me when I came up from Egypt.' It shall be a sign to you on your hand and as a memorial between your eyes, that the Lord's law may be in your mouth; for with a strong hand the Lord has brought you out of Egypt. You shall therefore keep this ordinance in its season from year to year."

118. John 6:51a, NKJV.

119. I Cor 5:7-8, NIV.

c. Feast of Firstfruits

The Feast of Firstfruits follows the Feast of Unleavened Bread.[120] The Jews acknowledged God's goodness in providing them with early crops. The Israelites were to reap the harvest and bring a sheaf of the firstfruits of the harvest to the priest. This feast is celebrated the same day of Jesus' resurrection, which some Christians celebrate as Easter. Jesus arose on the Feast of Firstfruits and in His resurrection, fulfilled this feast. As Paul recorded:[121] "But now Christ is risen from the dead, and has become the first fruits of those who have fallen asleep."[122]

Christ Jesus is the unblemished, pure Passover lamb, the unleavened Bread of Life, and the firstfruits of those raised from the dead.

d. Feast of Pentecost

Jesus was crucified during the Passover and ascended into Heaven forty days after His resurrection. He met with His early followers during this forty-day period, the period prior to His resurrection. Fifty days after His crucifixion and resurrection and ten days after His ascension into Heaven– on Pentecost, which is the feast the Israelites celebrate fifty days after Passover, the Holy Spirit came to His followers.

Pentecost was one of seven major annual Hebrew feasts; it was also called the Festival of Weeks. The Feast of Pentecost was a festival of thanksgiving for harvested crops, and while the children of Israel expressed thanks for the blessing of the harvest and were to bring a new meat offering to the Lord, the Feast of Pentecost was also celebrated to remember the time when God gave the Torah, the Law, to Moses on Mount Sinai.

On the Feast of Pentecost, which occurred fifty days after Passover on the day Jesus was crucified, the Holy Spirit descended upon the followers of Jesus who were all together in one place.[123] A sound from heaven came as a rushing mighty wind, and there appeared on these believers tongues like as of fire. Zechariah had referred to the Holy Spirit as "the spirit of grace and

---

120. Lev 23:10–11.

121. I Cor 15:20, NKJV.

122. Christ was not the first to rise from the dead; He raised Lazarus and others; even the disciple Peter raised Dorcas (discussion in Chapter 5). However, Jesus was the first and only one to die and then be resurrected in new life—to then live forever and never to die again.

123. Acts 2:1–2.

supplications:"[124] "And I will pour upon the house of David, and upon the inhabitants of Jerusalem, the spirit of grace and of supplications: and they shall look upon Me whom they have pierced."

At Mount Sinai, God confirmed with fire from heaven the validity of the Law of Moses. Exodus reads:[125] "Now Mount Sinai was all in smoke because the Lord descended upon it in fire; and the smoke ascended like the smoke of a furnace, and the whole mountain quaked violently. When the sound of the trumpet grew louder and louder, Moses spoke and God answered him with thunder." Psalms records the event:[126] "The earth shook, the heavens also dropped at the presence of God: even Sinai itself was moved at the presence of God, the God of Israel."

At Pentecost after Jesus' resurrection, God confirmed the validity of the Holy Spirit's ministry by sending fire as He had done when he confirmed the law of Moses with fire. At Mount Sinai, fire came down in one place. At Pentecost, fire came down on all the believers, symbolizing that God's presence is now available to everyone who believes in Him. The Holy Spirit fulfilled the Feast of Pentecost fifty days after Jesus crucifixion, on the Day of Pentecost, when, with fire coming down on the first believers, the Holy Spirit wrote the law in the hearts of all the believers, and the church then became comprised of both Jew and Gentile.

III. The Early Church

A. Jews of the Dispersion and Growth of the Early Church

As noted previously, members of tribes from the Southern Kingdom were taken as exiles to Babylon in 605 BC, but the tribes were permitted to return to Jerusalem, or Judea, in 537 BC. These approximate seventy years were the normal lifespan; thus, many of the Israelites in Babylon had known nothing of their homeland. History records that the great majority of members of the tribes from the Southern Kingdom did not return from Babylon to Jerusalem with Ezra in 537 BC. Many remained in exile in Babylon because, later in their captivity, they were treated well. Additionally, most of them had never seen Jerusalem or Judea. Only those who had

---

124. Zech 12:10a, KJV.
125. Exod 19:18–19, NASB.
126 Ps 68:8, KJV.

The Plan of Redemption and the Message of Salvation

a great religious zeal made the long and dangerous journey back to Judea. Those who remained were later referred to as the Jews of the dispersion.[127]

The Jews of the dispersion, or diaspora, were important in the spread of Christianity because the early believers carried the Gospel to the synagogues built all over the then areas settled and occupied by the Jews of the diaspora. Strong settlements of these Jewish people grew outside the former nation of Israel in every land and in major cities. Jews of the dispersion benefitted and influenced the nations where they were scattered and lived. Then when Greece later united the civilizations of Asia, Europe and Africa and established one universal language, and when Rome made the whole world its empire, with Roman roads making all parts of the world accessible, the time was ready for the coming of Christ. Additionally, Rome's highway system and the universal Greek language permitted the message of salvation to spread throughout the nations after Jesus' resurrection. The dispersion of the Jews among the nations paved the way for the propagation of the Gospel of Christ in Jewish synagogues and from there to the Gentile world.[128]

B. Stephen, a First Deacon and the First Christian Martyr

The number of the first believers as well as those who carried Jesus' message to the world grew rapidly.[129] However, as the early churches continued to grow and greatly increased in size, some needs and problems developed. One great need in the church was a means to distribute food to the poor; a dissension arose in the early church regarding this need. The Hellenistic, or Greek speaking, Jews, who probably were converted at Pentecost where the apostles spoke in their native tongue, thought the Hebrew speaking Jews were slighting them in the food distribution.[130]

The Twelve had a mission to preach so they appointed others to fill needs in the church. One of these persons was Stephen, who, as one of

---

127. See John 7:35, Acts 8:1–4 and 11:19.

128. See discussion at J. Vernon McGee, "How God Prepared the World for the Coming of Christ," Thru the Bible Radio Network, Pasadena, California, 1984.

129. As recorded in Acts 1:15, after Jesus' ascension, membership in the first church grew to 120, and, as recorded in Acts 2:41, after Pentecost, the number (this would be men only) grew to almost 3,000. Luke records in Acts 4:4 that the number of men who became believers had grown to 5,000. Today Christianity is the largest religion in the world; it consists of approximately 2.6 billion people or 1/3 of the world's population.

130. The Hellenistic Jews who resided in Jerusalem were somewhat second-class citizens to the Hebrew Jews.

the first deacons in the church, was appointed to oversee the distribution of food. As written in Acts:[131] "Now in those days, when the number of the disciples was multiplying, there arose a complaint against the Hebrews by the Hellenists, because their widows were neglected in the daily distribution. Then the twelve summoned the multitude of the disciples and said, 'It is not desirable that we should leave the word of God and serve tables. Therefore, brethren, seek out from among you seven men of good reputation, full of the Holy Spirit and wisdom, whom we may appoint over this business; but we will give ourselves continually to prayer, and to the ministry of the word.' And the saying pleased the whole multitude. And they chose Stephen, a man full of faith and of the Holy Spirit, and Philip, Prochorus, Nicanor, Timon, Parmenas and Nicolas, a proselyte from Antioch, whom they set before the apostles; and when they had prayed, they laid hands on them."

The appointment of these first seven deacons was the forerunner of the office of deacon in modern churches. Stephen and Philip were the most notable of the first seven deacons and the only two Luke discussed in the book of Acts. The life of Philip is discussed in Chapter 5 and the life of Stephen is discussed below. Little is known about the other five deacons.[132]

---

131. Acts 6:1–7, NKJV.

132. However, there are some reports about the five. See "Seven Deacons," Catholic Encyclopedia, 1913 and John Foxe, *Fox's Book of Martyrs*, 12.

It has been reported that Prochorus was Stephen's nephew, a Hellinistic Jew who resided in Jerusalem and who was filled with the Holy Spirit. He reportedly was a companion to John and Peter. It also has been reported that he was one of the seventy who are mentioned in Luke 10. Prochorus is also reported to have become a bishop of a church in Turkey and, because of his aggressive preaching, reportedly was put to death in Antioch.

Nicanor was reported to have been a Cypriot Jew who may have also been one of the seventy. There is a report that he suffered with Stephen, that he later returned to Cyrus, and that he was martyred there in 76 AD.

Timon is reported to have become a bishop either in Greece or in Syria where it is alleged that his preaching angered a local governor who put him to death with fire. Timon reportedly faced a martyr's death either in Greece, at Philipi, or in Syria in 44 AD.

Some reports indicate that Parmenas later preached in Asia and Macedonia. He reportedly was put to death in Philipi, a settlement in Macedonia, in 98 AD, during the reign of Trajan, the Roman emperor who at that time persecuted many Christians.

Nicolas is reported to have come from Antioch as a convert to Judaism. He was the first record of a convert being given an office in the early church. He reportedly was the leader of the dissident sect that is mentioned in Revelation 2:6 and 2:15. However, some contend that the sect made a vain claim that he was their leader so that they were given some authority for their claims.

The Plan of Redemption and the Message of Salvation

The story of Stephen's life is set out in the book of Acts. This record in Acts also furnishes an early view of happenings in the early church. Stephen was very young when the disciples appointed him as one of the first seven deacons, and he led a very short life. He was probably in his twenties when he became a deacon and is reported to have died a martyr's death when he was twenty-nine. His very short life and ministry is lasting evidence of how great faith in Christ can have profound effect on others and also evidence of what very young persons can do in spreading the Gospel of salvation.

It is not known where Stephen was born, but the name Stephanos is Greek; thus, Stephen was thought to be a Hellenistic Jew. It is recorded in Scripture that Stephen was "... full of faith and power..." who "... did great wonders and signs among the people."[133] To be able to perform "wonders and signs," Stephen had to have functioned like an apostle. It is also recorded that "... opposition arose ... "[134] from the Jewish community because of how forcefully Stephen preached the Gospel. "But some men from what was called the Synagogue of the Freedmen, including both Cyrenians and Alexandrians, and some from Cilicia and Asia, rose up and argued with Stephen. And yet they were unable to cope with the wisdom and the Spirit with which he was speaking."[135]

In trying to destroy Stephen, some Jews made up lies about him, causing him to be arrested and brought before the Sanhedrin, which was the Jewish supreme legal court in Israel.[136] As recorded in the book of Acts:[137] "Then they secretly persuaded some men to say, 'We have heard Stephen speak blasphemous words against Moses and against God.' So they stirred up the people and the elders and the teachers of the law. They seized Stephen and brought him before the Sanhedrin. They produced false witnesses, who testified, 'This fellow never stops speaking against this holy place and against the law. For we have heard him say that this Jesus of Nazareth will destroy this place and change the customs Moses handed down to us.'" As members of the Sanhedrin were listening to Stephen, "looking stedfastly

---

133. Acts 6:8, NKJV.

134. Acts 6:9, NIV.

135. Acts. 6:9–10, NASB.

136. The Sanhedrin, which was formed by Moses on instructions from God, was the supreme court in Israel. As recorded in Num 11:16–17, NIV: "The Lord said to Moses: 'Bring me seventy of Israel's elders who are known to you as leaders and officials among the people ... They will share the burden of the people with you so that you will not have to carry it alone.'"

137. Acts 6:11–14, NIV.

on him,[138] Luke records that they "... saw his face as it had been the face of an angel."[139]

Stephen witnessed boldly and powerfully to members of the Sanhedrin. His speech to them is the longest recorded sermon in Acts. He quoted the Old Testament, beginning with the call to Abraham,[140] which is recorded in Genesis:[141] "The Lord had said to Abram, 'Go from your country, your people and your father's household to the land I will show you. I will make you into a great nation, and I will bless you. I will make your name great, and you will be a blessing. I will bless those who bless you and whoever curses you I will curse and all peoples on earth will be blessed through you.'" Stephen pointed out to the Council, the Sanhedrin, how the Israelite nation had nonetheless rebelled against God throughout its history. He stated to them, "Our ancestors had the tabernacle of the covenant law with them in the wilderness. It had been made as God directed Moses, according to the pattern he had seen. After receiving the tabernacle, our ancestors under Joshua brought it with them when they took the land from the nations God drove out before them. It remained in the land until the time of David ... But it was Solomon who built a house for Him. However, the Most High does not live in houses made by human hands. As the prophet says: 'Heaven is my throne, and the earth is my footstool ... You stiff-necked people! Your hearts and ears are still uncircumcised. You are just like your ancestors: You always resist the Holy Spirit! Was there ever a prophet your ancestors did not persecute? They even killed those who predicted the coming of the Righteous One. And now you have betrayed and murdered Him—you who have received the law that was given through angels but have not obeyed it."[142] Stephen not only set out the history of Israel's rejection of God, he also pointed to their crucifying Jesus and called it a further example of their rebellion against God.[143] The Sanhedrin members refused to hear anymore from Stephen, drove him from the city, and stoned him to death.[144]

---

138. Acts 6:15, KJV.
139. Acts 6:15, KJV.
140. Acts 7:2–8.
141. Gen 12:1–3, NIV.
142. Acts 7:44–53, NIV.
143. Acts 7.
144. Acts 7:54–56, NASB.

The Plan of Redemption and the Message of Salvation

As stated in Acts:[145] "When the members of the Sanhedrin heard this, they were furious and gnashed their teeth at him. But Stephen, full of the Holy Spirit, looked up to heaven and saw the glory of God, and Jesus standing at the right hand of God. 'Look,' he said, "I see heaven open and the Son of Man standing at the right hand of God.' At this they covered their ears and, yelling at the top of their voices, they all rushed at him, dragged him out of the city and began to stone him. Meanwhile, the witnesses laid their coats at the feet of a young man named Saul. While they were stoning him, Stephen prayed, 'Lord Jesus, receive my spirit!' Then he fell on his knees and cried out, 'Lord, do not hold this sin against them.' When he had said this, he fell asleep." Although Saul, later called Paul, did not participate in the stoning, he approved of it. As Luke recorded: "Now Saul was consenting to his death."[146]

Stephen served God for only a short period of time, but his testimony saved many and has lasted through the ages. Although Stephen's testimony did not save Saul,[147] who was called Paul after his conversion, Saul recalled it later. As recorded in Acts,[148] when Paul shared how he came to faith in Christ, he stated, "And when the blood of your martyr Stephen was shed, I stood there giving my approval and guarding the clothes of those who were killing him."

Stephen died a martyr's death in 34 AD; it is not known where he was buried but undoubtedly in Jerusalem. As stated in Acts:[149] "And devout men carried Stephen to his burial, and made great lamentation over him."

C. Spread of the Gospel to the World

After Stephen's death, persecution of followers of Jesus continued in Jerusalem. Many then fled Jerusalem but in doing so spread the Gospel to the rest of the world. As recorded in the book of Acts: "At that time a great persecution arose against the church which was at Jerusalem; and they were all scattered throughout the regions of Judea and Samaria, except the

---

145. Acts 7:54–60, NIV.
146. Acts 8:1a, NKJV.
147. Saul was not saved as a result of Stephen's death; he was saved through his encounter with Christ as recorded in Acts 9. See discussion in Chapter 4.
148. Acts 22:20, NIV.
149. Acts 8:2, NKJV.

apostles."[150] In spreading the Gospel, God gave the Holy Spirit to the Gentiles as well: "So then those who were scattered because of the persecution that arose in connection with Stephen made their way to Phoenicia and Cyprus and Antioch, speaking the word to none except Jews alone. But there were some of them, men of Cyprus and Cyrene, who came to Antioch and began speaking to the Greeks also, preaching the Lord Jesus. And the hand of the Lord was with them, and a large number who believed turned to the Lord."[151]

The name of Christian first appeared in the city of Antioch following the Antioch church flourishing and growing rapidly with a large number of the apostles being there.[152] Paul started his missionary journey from Antioch. The first Gentile church reportedly was started in Antioch.

Eusebius noted that after Stephen was stoned to death and after James, the brother of John, as discussed in Chapter 2, was beheaded, and James, the half-brother of Jesus, faced the martyr's death discussed in Chapter 5, the remaining apostles left Judea because of being in constant danger. They then carried the Gospel into every land where they also encountered tremendous persecution and, for most, violent deaths.[153] Eusebius reported that the apostles were in "constant danger" from murderous plots and were driven out of Judea, but ". . . to teach their message they traveled into every land in the power of Christ, who had said, to them: 'Go and make disciples of all the nations in my name.'"[154]

Jesus' early followers willingly, and even gladly, suffered great hardships and torture in bringing Jesus' message of salvation to the world. As Eusebius confirmed, they put everything second to their faith in the Lord and endured great agonies to count themselves as followers of Jesus. Eusebius declared that ". . . words cannot describe the outrageous agonies endured by the martyrs . . ."[155] Eusebius confirmed that he was in places where followers of Jesus as late as 300 AD were still being executed and that he witnessed many of the executions, describing them as beheadings and

---

150. Acts 8:1b, NKJV. Most of the apostles, the Twelve, did not leave Jerusalem until after James, the half-brother of Jesus and the first bishop of the first church in Jerusalem, had suffered a martyr's death. Discussion of the life of James, the half-brother of Jesus, in Chapter 5.

151. Acts 11:19–21, NASB.

152. Eusebius, *The History of the Church*, 40. See also *Eusebius' Ecclesiastical History*, 39.

153. Eusebius, *The History of the Church*, 68.

154. Eusebius, *The History of the Church*, 68.

155. Eusebius, *The History of the Church*, 265.

The Plan of Redemption and the Message of Salvation

punishments by fire. Eusebius gave the following account of the persecutions that continued and occurred even during Eusebius' lifetime:[156]

> So many were killed on a single day that the axe, blunted and worn out by the slaughter, was broken in pieces, while the exhausted executioners had to be periodically relieved. All the time I observed a most wonderful eagerness and a truly divine power and enthusiasm in those who had put their trust in the Christ of God. No sooner had the first batch been sentenced, than others from every side would jump on to the platform in front of the judge and proclaim themselves Christians. They paid no heed to torture in all its terrifying forms, but undaunted spoke boldly of their devotion to the God of the universe and with joy, laughter, and gaiety received the final sentence of death; they sang and sent up hymns of thanksgiving to the God of the universe till their very last breath. Wonderful as these were, far, far more wonderful were those who were conspicuous for their wealth, birth, and reputation, and for learning and philosophy, yet put everything second to true religion and faith in our Saviour and Lord Jesus Christ.

The lives and deaths of the first, early followers, beginning with the Twelve and including Paul, James (half-brother of Jesus), Philip the Evangelist, Luke, John Mark, Barnabas, Silas, Timothy, Titus, Erastus, Apollos, Aquila and Priscilla, and other women, including Mary Magdalene and Lydia, are detailed in the following chapters. The first followers of Jesus were Jews except for Luke and Titus. These first believers *knew*, without doubt, that Jesus was resurrected, that He is one with God, and that, through Him, they, and all who believe, will have eternal life. As Paul assured the believers at Corinth: ". . . God both raised up the Lord and will also raise us up by His power."[157]

As God used ordinary apostles to spread His Word through extraordinary deeds and works, God can use anyone today. Paul stated in Ephesians,[158] "And He Himself gave some to be apostles, some prophets, some evangelists, and some pastors and teachers, for the equipping of the saints for the work of ministry, for the edifying of the body of Christ, till we all come to the unity of the faith and of the knowledge of the Son of God, to a perfect man, to the measure of the stature of the fullness of Christ." Jesus promised His followers throughout the ages that those who may be scorned

---

156. Eusebius, *The History of the Church*, 265.
157. I Cor 6:14, NKJV.
158. Eph 4:11, NKJV.

by family members or who sacrifice something valuable or important for His sake will have a reward "a hundred fold" that will include "eternal life." Jesus assured His followers: "And everyone who has left houses or brothers or sisters or father or mother or wife or children or lands, for My name's sake, shall receive a hundred fold, and inherit eternal life."[159]

Matthew closed his gospel with Jesus' admonition, promise, and commission:[160] "Go therefore and make disciples of all the nations, baptizing them in the name of the Father and the Son and the Holy Spirit, and teaching them to observe all that I commanded you; and lo, I am with you always, even to the end of the age." The story of the lives of the many devout and courageous believers who, filled with the Holy Spirit, accepted that commission and brought salvation to the world in such a short period of time, is an amazing testament to the wonder and grace of God and to these phenomenal followers of Jesus. Their stories follow.

---

159. Matt 19:29, NKJV.
160. Matt 28:19–20, NASB.

2

The Disciples of the Inner Circle
James, the Greater, and his Brother John, the Beloved; Andrew and his Brother Simon Peter, The Rock

Jesus had many followers, but He chose only twelve to be His disciples and thus to acquire that special training and knowledge needed to become apostles and to assist early believers in beginning the first churches. Four of the Twelve were a part of Jesus' inner circle. These were James, called the Greater, and his brother, John, who was called the Beloved, and Andrew and his brother Simon Peter, who was called the Rock. These four were devout Jews when Jesus called them, and they followed the teachings of Jesus to their deaths. After they encountered the risen Christ, they willingly and joyously faced persecution and death to bring the message of salvation to an otherwise lost world.

James, the Greater,[1] and John, his brother, were the sons of Zebedee and Salome and were fishermen from Bethsaida,[2] a town in Galilee east of the Jordan River.[3] They apparently followed their father's vocation as

---

1. James was called the Greater to distinguish him from James, the son of Alphaeus who was called James the Lesser, and from James, the half-brother of Jesus who was called James the Just.

2. John 1:44. Bethsaida was about eighty-one miles from Jerusalem and, along with Capernaum, was the site of nearly 80 percent of Jesus' ministry.

3. Luke records that Jesus fed 5,000 near Bethsaida. As stated in Luke 9:10, 14, 16, NASB: "And when the apostles returned, they gave an account to Him of all that they had done. And taking them with Him, He withdrew by Himself to a city called Bethsaida.

Zebedee was also a fisherman in Galilee.[4] Salome, called Mary Salome, was the mother of James and John and was purportedly the sister of Mary, Jesus' mother.[5] Although it is not clear, James and John probably then were Jesus' cousins.[6] Andrew and Simon Peter, his brother, also were fishermen from Bethsaida;[7] they were the sons of a fisherman named John.[8] Of these four—James, John, Andrew, and Peter—who became Jesus' inner circle, John and Peter became the greater of the four. They, along with James, Jesus' half-brother, were pillars of the early church and, along with Paul, were the leaders in spreading the message of salvation.

John at first was only in a subordinate position to his older brother, James, who was always mentioned in the Gospels first before him. However, John later became a prominent disciple because, as the "... disciple whom Jesus loved,"[9] and additionally as one of the three pillars of the

---

But the multitudes were aware of this and followed Him . . . (For there were about five thousand men). And He said to His disciples, 'Have them recline to eat in groups of about fifty each.' . . . And he took the five loaves and the two fish, and looking up to heaven, He blessed them, and broke them, and kept giving them to the disciples to set before the multitude."

4. Galilee, the tribal region of two of the ten lost tribes, Naphthali and Dan, includes the city of Nazareth, where Jesus grew up, and several small towns centered around the sea of Galilee, among them Capernaum and Tiberias. It is approximately sixty-three miles from Nazareth to Jerusalem. Jesus performed many miracles on the Sea of Galilee. Additionally, Jesus delivered the Sermon on the Mount on the Mount of Beatitudes located on the Northwest shore of the Sea of Galilee.

5. See John 19:25, NIV, wherein it is recorded: "Near the cross of Jesus stood His mother, His mother's sister, Mary the wife of Clopas, and Mary Magdalene." Most assume "His mother's sister" refers to Salome, who then would have been the sister of Mary, the mother of Jesus.

6. Salome was at the cross when Jesus was crucified and is identified as the mother of James and John. As recorded in Matt 27:56, NKJV: "And many women who followed Jesus from Galilee, ministering to Him, were there looking on from afar, among whom were Mary Magdalene, Mary the mother of James and Joses, and the mother of Zebedee's sons." Mark 15:40, NKJV, records: "There were also women looking on from afar, among whom were Mary Magdalene, Mary the mother of James the Less and of Joses, and Salome, who also followed Him and ministered to Him when He was in Galilee, and many other women who came up with Him to Jerusalem."

7. John 1:44.

8. Their father was also referred to as Jona and Jonah.

9. In John 13:22, 19:26, 20:2, 21:7, and 21:20, John called himself the disciple whom Jesus loved.

early church, he wrote five books of the Bible—the Gospel of John, three epistles,[10] and Revelation.

Peter was also a predominant disciple; he became the most vocal of Jesus' disciples. Nonetheless Peter had many faults until he fully realized that Jesus was one with God after he met with the resurrected Jesus. When Jesus first saw Peter, He said to him:[11] ". . . You are Simon the son of Jonah. You shall be called Cephas' (which is translated, a Stone)."[12]

James, John, Andrew and possibly Peter had been disciples of the first New Testament prophet, John the Baptist.[13] James, John, and Andrew undoubtedly acquired their great faith through their association with John the Baptist who brought in a new doctrine with his pointing to Jesus as the promised Messiah. Luke recorded Jesus' words:[14] "The Law and the Prophets were proclaimed until John."[15] Jesus followed John the Baptist as a prophet, but Jesus prophesied as the very word of God.

James and John were with John the Baptist when they saw Jesus passing by and heard John the Baptist announce:[16] ". . . Behold! The Lamb of God who takes away the sin of the world!" The next day John the Baptist again saw Jesus:[17] ". . . And looking at Jesus as He walked, he said, 'Behold, the Lamb of God!'" John the Baptist testified: "I have beheld the Spirit descending as a dove out of heaven, and He remained upon Him. And I did not recognize Him, but He who sent me to baptize in water said to me, 'He upon whom you see the Spirit descending and remaining upon Him; this is the one who baptizes in the Holy spirit.' And I have seen and have borne

---

10. 1, 2, and 3 John.

11. John 1:42, NKJV.

12. Cephas is Aramaic for the Greek name Peter. Cephas, or Peter, means "a rock."

13. See discussion of John the Baptist in Chapter 1. John the Baptist was the son of Zacharias, who was a priest, and Elizabeth, who Luke reported was a daughter of Aaron, and thus, would have had a priestly background. As a daughter of Aaron, Elizabeth would have been from the tribe of Levi. Luke refers to Elizabeth as a relative of Mary, the mother of Jesus. Mary was a descendant of David and thus would have been from the tribe of Judah. She probably though was Elizabeth's cousin. See Luke 1:5–6, 36.

14. Luke 16:16, NIV.

15. As discussed in Chapter 1, a prophet is one who receives the Word of God. Some of Jesus' early followers prophesied, John being one in his book of Revelation, but there are no current prophets. Mark declared, 13:22, NKJV: "For false christs and false prophets will rise and show signs and wonders to deceive, if possible, even the elect. But take heed; see I have told you all things beforehand."

16. John 1:29b, NKJV.

17. John 1:35b, NKJV.

witness that this is the Son of God."[18] As noted in Chapter 1, when John the Baptist was completing his work, he asked of his followers:[19] "Who do you suppose I am?" He confirmed to them that one greater than he would be coming after him. John, the disciple, recorded in his Gospel that John the Baptist avowed to them:[20] "I am not the one you are looking for. But there is one coming after me whose sandals I am not worthy to untie."

Although John the Baptist led James, John, and Andrew to Jesus, as recorded in Mark, Jesus also personally called James and John:[21] "He saw James the son of Zebedee and John his brother, who were also in the boat mending the nets. And immediately He called them; and they left their father Zebedee in the boat with the hired servants, and went away to follow Him." After Jesus also called them personally, they left their discipleship with John the Baptist to follow Jesus.

Jesus also personally called Andrew and Peter. Andrew was with John, the brother of James, when he also saw Jesus passing by and heard John the Baptist call Jesus the Lamb of God.[22] Andrew told his brother, Simon Peter, about Jesus and brought him to Jesus. In the Gospel of John, which John the disciple wrote, John himself reported of Andrew bringing Simon Peter to Jesus: "One of the two who heard John [the Baptist] speak, and followed [Jesus], was Andrew, Simon Peter's brother. He found first his own brother Simon, and said to him 'We have found the Messiah' (which translated means Christ). He brought him to Jesus."[23] Mark also recorded Jesus calling Andrew and Peter to become His disciples:[24] "And as He was going along by the Sea of Galilee, He saw Simon and Andrew, the brother of Simon, casting a net in the sea, for they were fishermen. And Jesus said to them, 'Follow Me, and I will make you become fishers of men.' And they immediately left the nets and followed Him." Andrew then also ended his discipleship with John the Baptist to follow Jesus.[25]

James, John, Andrew, and Peter were all part of Jesus' inner circle although Andrew to a lesser extent. The four of them were with Jesus on the

---

18. John 1:32–34, NASB.
19. Acts 13:25.
20. Acts 13:25.
21. Mark 1:19–20, NASB. See also Matt 4:21–22.
22. John 1:37, 40.
23. John 1:40–42, NASB.
24. Mark 1:16–18, NASB. See also Matt 4:18–20.
25. John 1:41.

Mount of Olives when Jesus predicted the end times. As recorded in Mark, "And as He was sitting on the Mount of Olives opposite the temple, Peter and James and John and Andrew were questioning Him privately, 'Tell us, when will these things be, and what will be the sign that all these things are going to be fulfilled?'"[26]

Peter, James and John were the privileged few to witness Jesus raising from the dead the twelve year old daughter of a ruler in the synagogue in Capernaum, who was named Jairus.[27] As recorded in Mark,[28] "While He was still speaking, some came from the ruler of the synagogue's house who said, 'Your daughter is dead. Why trouble the Teacher any further?' As soon as Jesus heard the word that was spoken, He said to the ruler of the synagogue, 'Do not be afraid, only believe.' And He permitted no one to follow Him except Peter, James, and John the brother of James. Then He came to the house of the ruler of the synagogue, and saw a multitude and those who wept and wailed loudly. When He came in, He said to them, 'Why make this commotion and weep? The child is not dead but sleeping.' And they ridiculed Him. But when He had put them all aside, He took the father and the mother of the child, and those who were with Him, and entered where the child was lying. Then He took the child by the hand and said to her 'Talitha cumi,' which is translated, 'Little girl, I say to you, arise.' Immediately the girl arose and walked; for she was twelve years old. And they were overcome with great amazement."

Additionally, Peter, James and John were with Jesus at the Transfiguration and witnessed there Jesus' divine nature along with the appearance of Moses and Elijah. At the Transfiguration, Peter referred to the Feast of Tabernacles and suggested putting up three shelters, one for Jesus, one for Moses, and one for Elijah. As written in Mark,[29] "Now after six days, Jesus took Peter, James, and John, and led up on a high mountain apart by themselves; and He was transfigured before them. His clothes became shining, exceedingly white, like snow, such as no launderer on earth can whiten them. And Elijah appeared to them with Moses; and they were talking with Jesus. Then Peter answered and said to Jesus, 'Rabbi, it is good for us to be here: and let us make three tabernacles; one for You, one for Moses, and

---

26. Mark 13: 3-4, NASB. Jesus' answer to them and His prophecy about the second coming are discussed in Chapter 6.

27. See Mark 5:22.

28. Mark 5:35-42, NKJV.

29. Mark 9:2-12, NKJV.

one for Elijah'—-because he did not know what to say; for they were greatly afraid. And a cloud came and overshadowed them; and a voice came out of the cloud, saying 'This is my beloved Son. Hear Him.' Suddenly when they had looked around, they saw no one anymore, but only Jesus with themselves. Now as they came down from the mountain, He commanded them that they should tell no one the things they had seen, till the Son of Man had risen from the dead. So they kept this word to themselves, questioning what rising from the dead meant. And they asked Him, saying 'Why do the scribes say that Elijah must first come?' Then He answered and told them, 'Indeed Elijah is coming first and restores all things. And how is it written concerning the Son of Man, that He must suffer many things and be treated with contempt? But I say to you, that Elijah has also come, and they did to him whatever they wished, as it is written of him.'"[30] Jesus earlier referred to John the Baptist as Elijah. "For all the prophets and the law prophesied until John. And if you willing to receive it, he is Elijah who is to come."[31]

Peter was married though there is no record of his marriage other than a reference in the gospel of Mark about his mother-in-law:[32] "And immediately after they had come out of the synagogue, they came into the house of Simon and Andrew, with James and John. Now Simon's mother-in-law was lying sick with a fever; and immediately they spoke to Him about her. And He came to her and raised her up, taking her by the hand, and the fever left her, and she waited on them."

Peter originally did not understand that the followers of Christ had to be servants to the people. "Then He poured water into the basin and began to wash the disciples' feet, and to wipe them with the towel with which He was girded. And so He came to Simon Peter who said to Him, 'Lord, do You wash my feet?' Jesus answered and said to him, 'What I do you do not realize now, but you shall understand hereafter.' Peter said to Him, 'Never shall You wash my feet!' Jesus answered him, 'If I do not wash you, you have no part with Me.' Simon Peter said to Him, 'Lord, not my feet only but also my hands and my head.'"[33] Jesus responded to Peter and the rest of

---

30. Moses represented the law and Elijah, a prophet who was taken up into heaven, symbolizes the prophets. Elijah and Moses appeared to show that Jesus fulfilled the law and the prophets, but that Jesus was far superior to both of them.

31. Matt 11:13-14, NKJV. Jesus apparently was saying that Elijah had already come through John the Baptist.

32. Mark 1:29-31, NASB.

33. John 13:5-9, NASB.

The Disciples of the Inner Circle

the disciples,[34] "Do you know what I have done to you? You call me Teacher and Lord; and you are right, for so I am. If I then, the Lord and the Teacher, washed your feet, you also ought to wash one another's feet. For I gave you an example that you also should do as I did to you."

Peter once asked of Jesus what reward the disciples would have:[35] "'Behold, we have left everything and followed you; what then will there be for us?' Jesus responded, 'Truly I say to you, that you who have followed Me, in the regeneration when the Son of Man will sit on His glorious throne, you also shall sit upon twelve thrones, judging the twelve tribes of Israel.'"[36]

Peter was the disciple who, during Jesus' ministry, reacted with the most faith in Jesus. When, early in Jesus' ministry, some persons had turned back and no longer wanted to follow Him, Jesus asked His disciples "... Do you also want to go away?"[37] Peter's response was "Lord, to whom shall we go? You have words of eternal life. And we have believed and have come to know that You are the Holy One of God."[38] Jesus blessed Peter for his great faith and his early recognition that Jesus was the Christ and one with God. "When Jesus came into the region of Caesarea Philippi, He asked His disciples, saying 'Who do men say that I, the Son of Man, am?' So they said, 'Some say John the Baptist, some Elijah, and others, Jeremiah or one of the prophets.' He said to them, 'But who do you say that I am?' Simon Peter answered and said, 'You are the Christ, the son of the living God.' Jesus answered and said to him, 'Blessed are you, Simon Bar-Jonah, for flesh and blood has not revealed this to you, but My Father who is in heaven. And I also say to you that you are Peter, and on this rock I will build My church, and the gates of Hades shall not prevail against it. And I will give you the keys of the kingdom of heaven; and whatever you bind on earth will be bound in heaven and whatever you loose on earth will be loosed in heaven.'"[39]

Although Peter had the greatest faith, he also had a doubtful nature until he met the risen Jesus. His doubtful nature was evident when he was in a boat that was a considerable distance from land and that was buffeted

---

34. John 13:12–15, NASB.
35. Matt 19:27, NASB.
36. Matt 19:28, NASB.
37. John 6:67, NKJV.
38. John 6:68–69, NASB.
39. Matt 16:13–19, NKJV.

by waves. As set out in Matthew,[40] "Now in the fourth watch of night Jesus went to them, walking on the sea. And when the disciples saw Him walking on the sea, they were troubled, saying, 'It is a ghost!' And they cried out for fear. But immediately Jesus spoke to them, saying, 'Be of good cheer, it is I; do not be afraid.' And Peter answered Him and said, 'Lord, if it is you, command me to come to You on the water.' He said, 'Come.' And when Peter had come out of the boat, he walked on the water to go to Jesus. But when he saw that the wind was boisterous, he was afraid; and beginning to sink he cried out, saying 'Lord, save me!' And immediately Jesus stretched out His hand and caught him, and said to him. 'O you of little faith, why did you doubt?' And when they got into the boat, the wind ceased. Then those who were in the boat came and worshiped Him, saying, 'Truly You are the Son of God!'"

Peter's doubtful nature and his temporary loss of faith began with his swearing he would never desert Jesus. Despite Peter's great faith when he was a part of Jesus' ministry, he abandoned Jesus after His arrest as Jesus had predicted. As Matthew recorded:[41] "Then Jesus said to them, 'All of you will made to stumble because of Me this night, for it is written: 'I will strike the Shepherd, And the sheep of the flock will be scattered. But after I have been raised, I will go before you to Galilee.' Peter answered and said to Him, 'Even if all are made to stumble because of You, I will never be made to stumble.' Jesus said to him, 'Assuredly, I say to you that this night, before the rooster crows, you will deny Me three times.' Peter said to Him, 'Even if I have to die with You, I will not deny You.' And so said all the disciples."

After Judas Iscariot had left the Passover supper to betray Jesus, Jesus told the remaining eleven that He would be going. "When therefore he had gone out, Jesus said, 'Now is the Son of Man glorified, and God is glorified in Him. If God is glorified in Him, God will glorify Him in Himself, and will glorify Him immediately. Little children, I am with you a little while longer. You shall seek Me, and as I said to the Jews, I now say to you also, Where I am going, you cannot come. A new commandment I give you, that you love one another, even as I have loved you, that you also love one another. By this all men will know that you are My disciples, if you have love for one another.' Simon Peter said to Him, 'Lord, where are You going?' Jesus answered, 'Where I go, you cannot follow Me now; but you shall follow later.' Peter said to Him, 'Lord, why can I not follow you right now? I

---

40. Matt 14:25–32, NKJV.
41. Matt 26:31–35, NKJV.

will lay down my life for you.' Jesus answered, 'Will you lay down your life for me? Truly, truly I say to you, a cock shall not crow, until you deny me three times!'"[42]

Later, when Jesus was arrested, Peter did deny Jesus. Matthew recorded Peter's denial in his Gospel: "Now Peter sat outside in the courtyard. And a servant girl came to him, saying, 'You also were with Jesus of Galilee.' But he denied it before them all, saying. 'I do not know what you are saying.' And when he had gone out to the gateway, another girl saw him and said to those who were there, 'This fellow also was with Jesus of Nazareth.' But again he denied it with an oath, 'I do not know the man.' And a little later those who stood by came up and said to Peter, 'Surely you also are one of them, for your speech betrays you.' Then he began to curse and swear, saying 'I do not know the Man!' Immediately a rooster crowed. And Peter remembered the word of Jesus who had said to him, 'Before the rooster crows, you will deny Me three times.' So he went out and wept bitterly."[43]

John also recorded Peter's denials in his Gospel. Annas, the high priest, knew John; thus, when Jesus was arrested, John was permitted to go with Jesus into the high priest's courtyard. As recorded in John's Gospel:[44] "And Simon Peter was following Jesus, and so was another disciple.[45] Now that disciple was known to the high priest, and entered with Jesus into the court of the high priest, but Peter was standing at the door outside. So the other disciple, who was known to the high priest, went out and spoke to the doorkeeper, and brought Peter in. The slave-girl therefore who kept the door said to Peter, 'You are not also one of this man's disciples too, are you?' He said, 'I am not.'"

Jesus did not disown Peter despite Peter having denied Him. On the Sunday following Jesus' crucifixion when three women went to Jesus' tomb to anoint His body, an angel at the tomb made special mention of Peter. Still, Peter and the other remaining disciples did not believe until they later met with the resurrected Lord. Mark recorded the event as follows:[46] "And when the Sabbath was past, Mary Magdalene, Mary the mother of James, and Salome bought spices, that they might come and anoint Him. Very early in the morning, on the first day of the week, they came to the tomb

---

42. John 13:31–38, NASB.
43. Matt 26:69–75, NKJV.
44. John 18:15–17, NASB.
45. John was referring to himself.
46. Mark 16:1–14, NKJV.

when the sun had risen. And they were said among themselves, 'Who will roll away the stone from the door of the tomb for us?' But when they looked up, they saw that the stone had been rolled away—for it was very large. And entering the tomb, they saw a young man clothed in a long white robe sitting on the right side; and they were alarmed. But he said to them, 'Do not be alarmed. You seek for Jesus the Nazarene, who was crucified. He has risen! He is not here. See the place where they laid Him. But go, tell His disciples—*and Peter*—that He is going before you into Galilee; there you will see Him, as He said to you.' So they went out quickly and fled from the tomb, for they trembled and were amazed. And they said nothing to anyone, for they were afraid. Now when He rose early on the first day of the week, He appeared first to Mary Magdalene . . . She went and told those who had been with Him as they mourned and wept. After that, He appeared in another form to two of them as they walked and went into the country. And they went and told it to the rest, but they did not believe them either. Later He appeared to the eleven as they sat at the table; and He rebuked their unbelief and hardness of heart, because they did not believe those who had seen Him after He had risen."

James and John also had their faults before they knew the risen Christ and followed His command to bring salvation to the world. Apparently, James and John thought of themselves as being Jesus' favorites. They both sought importance in what they thought would be an earthly kingdom that Jesus would establish to free Israel from Roman control. As recorded in Mark:[47] "Then James and John, the sons of Zebedee, came to Him, saying, 'Teacher, we want you to do for us whatever we ask.' And He said to them, 'What do you want me to do for you?' They said to Him, 'Grant that we may sit one on Your right and the other on Your left, in Your glory.' But Jesus said to them, 'You do not know what you ask. Are you able to drink the cup that I drink, or be baptized with the baptism that I am baptized with?' They said to Him, 'We are able.' So Jesus said to them, 'You will indeed drink the cup that I drink, and with the baptism I am baptized with you will be baptized; but to sit on My right hand and on My left is not mine to give, but it is for those for whom it is prepared.' And when the ten heard it, they began to be greatly displeased with James and John. But Jesus called them to Himself and said to them, 'You know that those who are considered rulers over the Gentiles lord it over them; and their great ones exercise authority over them. Yet it shall not be so among you; but whoever desires to become great

---

47. Mark 10:35–45, NKJV.

among you shall be your servant. And whoever of you desires to be first shall be slave of all. For even the Son of Man did not come to be served, but to serve, and to give His life a ransom for many.'"

Until after Jesus' resurrection and prior to their being filled with the Holy Spirit at Pentecost, James and John were evidently outspoken and short-tempered as well as being selfish. Mark referred to Jesus calling them the sons of thunder:[48] ". . . James, the son of Zebedee, and John the brother of James (to them he gave the name Boanerges, which means 'Sons of Thunder') . . . ." Their impetuousness, but also aggressiveness in wanting to protect Jesus, was apparent when they became very disturbed that people in a Samaritan village did not welcome Jesus. As written in Luke,[49] "And when His disciples James and John saw this, they said, 'Lord, do you want us to command fire to come down from heaven and consume them.' But He turned and rebuked them, and said "You do not know what kind of spirit you are of; for the Son of Man did not come to destroy men's lives, but to save them.'"

Despite their shortcomings, James, and John remained in Jesus' inner circle. John, along with Peter, prepared the Passover prior to Jesus resurrection. Jesus instructed John and Peter to "Go and prepare the Passover for us, that we may eat."[50] John wrote:[51] "Now before the Feast of the Passover, when Jesus knew that His hour had come that He should depart from this world to the Father, having loved His own who were in the world, He loved them to the end." John further recorded that while he, John, ". . . was reclining next to Him . . ."[52] he asked who among them would betray Jesus.[53]

Peter, James, and John were the three special disciples who were with Jesus in the Garden of Gethsemane just prior to Jesus' crucifixion. As stated in Mark,[54] "And they came to a place called Gethsemane, and He said to His disciples, 'Sit here until I have prayed.' And He took with Him Peter and James and John, and began to be very distressed and troubled. And He said to them, 'My soul is deeply grieved to the point of death; remain here and keep watch.'" Peter though fell asleep and for the first time abandoned Jesus

48. Mark 3:17, NASB.
49. Luke 9:54–56, NASB.
50. Luke 22:8, NKJV.
51. John 13:1, NKJV.
52. John 13:23, NIV.
53. John 13:25.
54. Mark 14:32–34, NASB.

in Jesus' great time of need. "Then He came to the disciples and found them sleeping, and said to Peter. 'What! Could you not watch with Me one hour? Watch and pray, lest you enter into temptation. The spirit indeed is willing, but the flesh is weak.' Again, a second time, He went away and prayed, saying, 'O My Father, if this cup cannot pass away unless I drink it, Your will be done.' And He came and found them asleep again, for their eyes were heavy. So He left them, went away again, and prayed the third time, saying the same words. Then He came to His disciples and said to them, 'Are you still sleeping and resting? Behold, the hour is at hand, and the Son of Man is being betrayed into the hands of sinners. Rise, let us be going. See, My betrayer is at hand!'"[55]

Peter tried to prevent the soldiers who came with Judas Iscariot from arresting Jesus. "Simon Peter therefore having a sword, drew it, and struck the high priest's slave, and cut off his right ear; and the slave's name was Malchus. Jesus therefore said to Peter, 'Put the sword into the sheath; the cup which the Father has given Me, shall I not drink it?'"[56]

John was the only disciple who was at the cross when Jesus was crucified. Jesus entrusted his mother to John as John stayed with Him at the cross. "But there were standing by the cross of Jesus, His mother . . . When Jesus therefore saw his mother, and the disciple whom he loved standing nearby, He said to His mother, 'Woman, behold your son.' Then He said to the disciple, 'Behold, your mother.' From that hour the disciple took her into his own household."[57]

There is speculation as to why Jesus assigned John as the protector of His mother. Undoubtedly Joseph, Mary's husband, was no longer alive and at this time Jesus' siblings did not believe in Him. As recorded in John,[58] "For even His brothers did not believe in Him." Perhaps Jesus wanted John to take His mother away from Jerusalem because He knew Jerusalem would later be destroyed, and He did not want His mother to experience the horrendous events that would occur there. It is rumored that John took Mary with him to Ephesus shortly before the destruction of Jerusalem, which began in 70 AD.

Jesus appeared to the disciples after His resurrection, a third time by the Sea of Galilee where He helped the disciples catch a net full of fish.

---

55. Matt 26:40–46, NKJV.
56. John 18:10–11, NASB.
57. John 19:25–27, NASB.
58. John 7:5, NKJV.

The Disciples of the Inner Circle

As John recorded,[59] "After these things Jesus showed Himself again to the disciples at the Sea of Tiberias, and in this way He showed Himself: Simon Peter, Thomas called the twin, Nathanael of Cana in Galilee, the sons of Zebedee, and two others of His disciples were together. Simon Peter said to them, 'I am going fishing.' They said to him, 'We are going with you also.' They went out and immediately got into the boat, and that night they caught nothing. But when the morning had now come, Jesus stood on the shore; yet the disciples did not know that it was Jesus. Then Jesus said to them, 'Children, have you any food?' They answered Him, 'No.' And He said to them, 'Cast the net on the right side of the boat, and you will find some.' So they cast, and now they were not able to draw it in because of the multitude of fish. Therefore that disciple whom Jesus loved said to Peter, 'It is the Lord.' Now when Simon Peter heard that it was the Lord, he put on his outer garment on (for he had removed it) and plunged into the sea. But the other disciples came in the little boat (for they were not far from land, but about two hundred cubits), dragging the net with fish. Then, as soon as they had come to land, they saw a fire of coals there, and fish laid on it, and bread. Jesus said to them. 'Bring some of the fish which you have just caught.' Simon Peter went up and dragged the net to land, full of large fish, one hundred and fifty-three; and although there were so many, the net was not broken. Jesus said to them, 'Come and eat breakfast.' Yet none of them dared ask Him, 'Who are you?' knowing it was the Lord. Jesus then came and took the bread and gave them, and likewise the fish. This is now the third time Jesus showed Himself to His disciples, after He was raised from the dead."

Jesus then questioned Peter to see if he could still follow Him and carry the message of salvation to the world. Jesus also predicted that Peter would die a violent death. "So when they had finished breakfast, Jesus said to Simon Peter, 'Simon son of John, do you love me more than these?' He said to Him, 'Yes, Lord, you know that I love you.' He said to him, 'Tend my lambs.' He said to him again a second time, 'Simon son of John, do you love me?' He said to Him, 'Yes, Lord; You know that I love You.' He said to him, 'Shepherd my sheep.' He said to him the third time, 'Simon son of John, do you love me?' Peter was grieved because He said to him the third time, 'Do you love me?' And he said to Him, 'Lord, You know all things; You know that I love you.' Jesus said to him, 'Tend my sheep. Truly, truly, I say to you, when you were younger, you used to gird yourself, and walk wherever you

---

59. John 21:1–14, NKJV.

wished; but when you grow old, you will stretch out your hands, and someone else will gird you, and bring you where you do not wish to go.' Now this He said, signifying by what kind of death he would glorify God. And when He had spoken this, He said to him. 'Follow me!'"[60]

Peter and the other disciples, except for John, had abandoned Jesus to leave Jesus to die almost alone, but after Jesus' resurrection, they became Jesus' fearless and powerful ". . . witnesses both in Jerusalem, and in all Judea and Samaria, and even to the remotest part of the earth."[61] At Pentecost, Peter quoted the prophet Joel to tell the crowd: "And it shall be in the last days, says God, 'That I will pour out of my Spirit on all flesh; Your sons and your daughters shall prophesy, Your young men shall see visions, Your old men shall dream dreams. And on My menservants and on My maidservants I will pour out my Spirit in those days; And they shall prophesy . . . And it shall be, that whoever calls on the name of the Lord shall be saved.'"[62]

Following Pentecost when they were filled with the Holy Spirit, James, John, Andrew, and Peter became indispensable leaders in the early church. Both James and Andrew allegedly were chosen to preach in Greece and in Scythia, a region in central Eurasia.[63] James is rumored to have made a pilgrimage to Spain.[64] Additionally, Andrew is reported to have been the apostle to the Greek world; he was founder of the church in Georgia.[65] However, because both James and Andrew were martyred early in the new Christian movement, they were less prominent than Peter and John in the operation of the early church. Peter and John became two of the most prominent leaders of the first believers and two of the three pillars of the early church.[66] As noted previously, John wrote five of the books in the New Testament, and Peter wrote two epistles.[67]

60. John 21:15–19, NASB.
61. Acts 1:8b, NASB.
62. Acts 2:17–18, 21,NKJV.
63. Eusebius, *The History of the Church*, 65, 344.
64. Discussion in McBirnie, *The Search for the Twelve Apostles*, 65–73.

Whether or not James traveled to Spain, James is the patron saint of Spain. James is further rumored to have returned to Judea after preaching in Spain.

65. Georgia is bounded by Russia, Turkey, and Armenia.
66. The third pillar of the early church was James, the half-brother of Jesus. Discussion of James, the half-brother of Jesus and first bishop of the church in Jerusalem, in Chapter 5.

67. Peter only wrote 1 and 2 Peter although some contend Mark's Gospel quotes Peter.

The Disciples of the Inner Circle

Although James, the brother who brought John to Jesus, was not the source of any biblical books,[68] he did give great testimony to the faith prior to his martyrdom.[69] James was the first disciple to suffer a martyr's death.[70] He was in Judea when he was martyred in 44 AD by Herod Agrippa for his aggressiveness in spreading the Word of God. After Herod Agrippa, the grandson of Herod the Great, was appointed governor of Judea, he wanted to establish himself with the Jewish people. He thought that ordering the persecution of the most prominent followers of Jesus would be popular with the people.[71]

Because James spoke boldly for Christ and perhaps also because he undoubtedly spoke against Herod for Herod's many depraved deeds and activities, Herod had James beheaded. As recorded in the book of Acts:[72] "Now about this time Herod the King laid hands on some who belonged to the church, in order to mistreat them. And he had James the brother of John put to death with a sword."[73]

John wrote a most powerful Gospel to prove that Jesus is the Son of God. The Gospel of John does not repeat most of the other gospels but rather shows how Jesus is the fulfillment of the prophecies. John points to Jesus being the replacement of the Israelite temple for believers to come to God. The Gospel of John is said to be one of the best books Christians can use for evangelism. Consider the overpowering words of John in the Gospel of John. John, who was a common uneducated fisherman, wrote a most clear and simple, but profound in meaning, gospel that undoubtedly was inspired by the Holy Spirit. John also wrote 1, 2, and 3 John and the book of Revelation. In Revelation John, speaking as a prophet, points to the end times to show that God remains in control. John's books alone can bring readers to believe in the saving grace of Jesus, the Christ.

68. This was possibly because he was put to death very early in the history of the church.

69. See *Eusebius, Ecclesiastical History*, 44.

70. James' death occurred ten years after the death of Stephen, who, as discussed in Chapter 1, was the first believer to be subjected to a violent death.

71. Discussion in Foxe, *Fox's Book of Martyrs*, 12.

72. Acts 12:1–2, NASB.

73. In his *Sixth Book of the Hypotyposes*, Clemens Alexandrinas reported that the man who brought James to trial was moved on seeing him and confessed that he also was a Christian. According to Clemens, both then were led away together and beheaded together. Both men reportedly were beheaded in 44 AD. Clemens was born in either Athens or Alexandria in 150 AD and was converted to Christianity. He became the leader of the Alexandrian Christian fellowship. See McBirnie, *The Search for the Twelve Apostles*, 62.

John Foxe records in *Fox's Book of Martyrs*, 12, that the death of James the Great occurred in 44 AD. See also Eusebius, *The History of the Church*, 44.

James' head is reported to be buried in the Chapel of James the Great in the Armenian Quarter of Jerusalem where Herod Agrippa had ordered him to be beheaded, but his body is buried in Spain in the City of Santiago de Compostela.[74]

Although Andrew was the first called disciple and was also in the inner circle, he played a lesser role than Peter, James, and John. Andrew did not witness Jesus' raising from the dead a synagogue official's' daughter as did James, John, and Peter; nor was Andrew present with Jesus at the Transfiguration as were James, John, and Peter. Moreover, Andrew also was not with Jesus in the Garden of Gethsemane just prior to Jesus' crucifixion as were James, John, and Peter.[75]

It was Andrew though who brought to Jesus a boy's five loaves of bread and two fish that Jesus used to feed a huge crowd, which had gathered to hear Him on a hill near the Sea of Galilee at Bethsaida. "One of His disciples, Andrew, Simon Peter's brother, said to Him, 'There is a lad here who has five small barley loaves and two fish, but what are these for so many people?' Jesus said, 'Have the people sit down.' Now there was much grass in the place. So the men sat down, in number about five thousand, Jesus therefore took the loaves, and having given thanks, He distributed to those who were seated; likewise also of the fish as much as they wanted. And when they were filled, He said to His disciples, 'Gather up the left over fragments that nothing may be lost.' And so they gathered them up, and filled twelve baskets with fragments of the five barley loaves, which were left over by those who had eaten. When therefore the people saw the sign which He had performed, they said, 'This is of truth the Prophet who is to come into the world.'"[76]

Andrew is the patron saint of Romania, Russia, Ukraine, and Scotland. He purportedly was crucified on an X-shaped cross in 62 AD, in Patras, Greece, although there is no precise record of the time, place, or manner of his death.[77]

---

74. Discussion in William Steuart McBirnie, *The Search for the Twelve Apostles*, 68, 77–78.

75. See Mark 5:35–42; 9:2–12, 32–34.

76. John 6:8–14, NASB.

77. See report of his death in Eusebius, *The History of the Church*, 344, and John Foxe, *Fox's Book of Martyrs*,13.
An X-shaped cross is now called a St. Andrew's cross. The flags of Scotland and Alabama both contain the St. Andrew's cross. Scotland's flag is called the Saltire or St. Andrew's Cross. The Scottish flag is a white shaped X-cross on a blue sky. The Alabama

The Disciples of the Inner Circle

After James' death, John continued to work for the Lord; he brought the message of salvation to many cities and governed churches in Asia.[78] Further, John, together with Peter, performed miracles in the name of Jesus. As recorded in Acts,[79] "Now Peter and John went up together to the temple at the hour of prayer, the ninth hour. And a certain man lame from his mother's womb was carried, whom they laid daily at the gate of the temple, which is called Beautiful, to ask alms of those who entered the temple; who, seeing Peter and John about to go into the temple, asked for alms. And fixing his eyes on him, with John, Peter said, 'Look at us!' So he gave them his attention, expecting to receive something from them. Then Peter said, 'Silver and gold I do not have, but what I do have I give you: In the name of Jesus Christ of Nazareth, rise up and walk!' And he took him by the right hand and lifted him up; and immediately his feet and ankle bones received strength. So he, leaping up, stood and walked and entered the temple with them—walking, leaping, and praising God. And all the people saw him walking and praising God. Then they knew that it was he who sat begging alms at the Beautiful Gate of the temple; and they were filled with wonder and amazement at what had happened to him."

Peter and John were arrested because they were proclaiming to the people that Jesus was resurrected. As Luke records:[80] "And they laid hands on them, and put them in jail until the next day, for it was already evening. But many of those who had heard the message believed; and the number of the men came to be to be about five thousand. And it came about on the next day, that their rulers and the elders and scribes were gathered together in Jerusalem . . . And when they had placed them in the center, they began to inquire, 'By what power, or in what name, have you done this?'" The persons who questioned John and Peter were amazed:[81] "Now when they saw the boldness of Peter and John, and perceived that they were unlearned and ignorant men, they marveled; and they took knowledge of them, that they had been with Jesus. And beholding the man which was healed standing with them, they could say nothing against it. But when they had commanded them to go aside out of the Council, they conferred among themselves, saying 'What shall we do to these men? For that indeed a notable miracle

---

flag is a crimson cross on a field of white.

78. See *Eusebius, Ecclesiastical History*, 86.
79. Acts 3:1–10, NKJV.
80. Acts 4:3–5, 7, NASB.
81. Acts 4:13–21, KJV.

hath been done by them is manifest to all them that dwell in Jerusalem, and we cannot deny it. But that it spread no further among the people, let us straitly threaten them, that they speak henceforth to no man in this name.' And they called them, and commanded them not to speak at all nor teach at all in the name of Jesus. But Peter and John answered and said to them, 'Whether it be right in the sight of God to hearken unto you more than unto God, judge ye. For we cannot but speak the things which we have seen and heard.' So when they had further threatened them, they let them go, finding nothing how they might punish them, because of the people; for all men glorified God for that which was done."

John and Peter later traveled to Samaria because ". . . the apostles who were in Jerusalem heard that Samaria had received the word of God . . ."[82] However, the Samaritans had not received the Holy Spirit. As Luke recorded: ". . . they had only been baptized in the name of the Lord Jesus;" thus, John and Peter ". . . laid hands on them, and they received the Holy Spirit."[83]

John and Peter, along with James, the half-brother of Jesus and first bishop of the church in Jerusalem, gave their blessing to Paul and Barnabas for them to become followers of Jesus and to carry the message of salvation to the Gentile world. Paul stated:[84] "For God, who was at work in Peter as an apostle to the circumcised, was also at work in me as an apostle to the Gentiles. James (the brother of Jesus), Cephas (Peter), and John, those esteemed as pillars, gave me and Barnabas the right hand of fellowship when they recognized the grace given to me. They agreed that we should go to the Gentiles, and they to the circumcised."

Peter visited Lydda, which was located twenty-two miles from Jerusalem, and made converts there. As recorded in the book of Acts:[85] "Now it came about as Peter was traveling through all those parts, he came down also to the saints who lived in Lydda. And there he found a certain man named Aeneas, who had been bedridden eight years, for he was paralyzed. And Peter said to him, 'Aeneas, Jesus Christ heals you; arise, and make your bed.' And immediately he arose. And all who lived in Lydda and Sharon saw him, and they turned to the Lord."

---

82. Acts 8:14a, NKJV.
83. Acts 8:16b,17b, NKJV.
84. Gal 2:8–9, NIV.
85. Acts 9:32–35, NASB.

The Disciples of the Inner Circle

After Lydda, Peter went to Joppa,[86] which is thirty miles from Jerusalem, and healed a follower of Jesus. "In Joppa, there was a disciple named Tabitha (in Greek her name is Dorcas); she was always doing good and helping the poor. About that time she became sick and died, and her body was washed and placed in an upstairs room. Lydda was near Joppa, so when the disciples heard that Peter was in Lydda, they sent two men to him and urged him, 'Please come at once!' Peter went with them, and when he arrived he was taken upstairs to the room. All the widows stood around him, crying and showing him the robes and other clothing that Dorcas made while she was still with them. Peter sent them all out of the room; then he got down on his knees and prayed. Turning toward the dead women, he said, 'Tabitha, get up.' She opened her eyes, and seeing Peter, she sat up. He took her by the hand and helped her to her feet. Then he called for the believers, especially the widows, and presented her to them alive. This became known all over Joppa, and many believed in the Lord."[87]

Peter also witnessed to the Gentiles despite criticism from the Jewish believers. He answered the call of a Gentile named Cornelius who lived in Caesarea, a city located on the coast of the Mediterranean Sea, about thirty miles from Joppa. It was the first city to have Gentile believers. "At Caesarea there was a man named Cornelius, a centurion in what was known as the Italian Regiment. He and all his family were devout and God-fearing; he gave generously to those in need and prayed to God regularly. One day at about three in the afternoon he had a vision. He distinctly saw an angel of God, who came to him and said 'Cornelius!' Cornelius stared at him in fear. 'What is it, Lord?' he asked. The angel answered, 'Your prayers and gifts to the poor have come up as a memorial offering before God. Now send men to Joppa to bring back a man named Simon who is called Peter. He is staying with Simon the tanner, whose house is by the sea.' When the angel who had spoke to him was gone, Cornelius called two of his servants and a devout soldier who was one of his attendants. He told them everything that had happened and sent them to Joppa."[88] Peter then went with them to Caesarea. "And as he talked with him, he entered, and found many people assembled. And he said to them: 'You yourselves know how unlawful it is for a man who is a Jew to associate with a foreigner or to visit him; and yet

---

86. Joppa is now known as Jaffa. Tel Aviv encompasses the ancient city. There is a church in Jaffa called the Church of St. Peter.

87. Acts 9:36–42, NIV.

88. Acts 10:1–8, NIV.

God has shown me that I should not call any man unholy or unclean. That is why I came without even raising any objection when I was sent for."[89]

Peter informed the Gentiles: "I most certainly understand now that God is not one to show partiality, but in every nation the man who fears Him and does what is right, is welcome to Him."[90] Later: "While Peter was still speaking these words, the Holy Spirit came on all who heard the message. The circumcised believers who had come with Peter were astonished that the gift of the Holy Spirit had been poured even on Gentiles. For they heard them speaking in tongues and praising God. Then Peter said, 'Surely no one can stand in the way of their being baptized with water. They have received the Holy Spirit just as we have.' So he ordered that they be baptized in the name of Jesus Christ."[91]

At first the circumcised criticized Peter, stating to him: "You went in to uncircumcised men and ate with them!"[92] Peter then explained to them why he had met with the Gentiles and had approved their baptism:[93] "Starting from the beginning, Peter told them the whole story. 'I was in the city of Joppa praying; and in a trance I saw a vision. I saw something like a large sheet being let down by its four corners, and it came right down to where I was. I looked into it and saw four-footed animals of the earth, wild beasts, reptiles, and birds. Then I heard a voice telling me, 'Get up, Peter. Kill and eat.' I replied, 'Surely not, Lord! Nothing impure or unclean has ever entered my mouth.' The voice spoke from heaven a second time, 'Do not call anything impure that God has made clean.' This happened three times, and then it was all pulled up to heaven again. Right then three men who had been sent to me from Caesarea stopped at the house where I was staying. The Spirit told me to have no hesitation about going with them. These six brothers also went with me, and we entered the man's house. He told us how he had seen an angel appear in his house, and say, 'Send to Joppa for Simon, who is called Peter. He will bring a message through which you and all your household will be saved.' As I began to speak, the Holy Spirit came on them as he had come on us at the beginning. Then I

---

89. Acts 10:27–29, NASB.

90. Acts 10:34–35, NASB.

91. Acts 10:44–48a, NIV. See discussion in Chapter 4 on the life of Paul of the problem relating to the Gentile believers being required to be circumcised as were the Jewish believers.

92. Acts 11:3b, NKJV.

93. Acts 11:4–18, NIV.

The Disciples of the Inner Circle

remembered what the Lord had said, 'John baptized with water, but you will be baptized with the Holy Spirit.' So if God gave them the same gift He gave to us who believed in the Lord Jesus Christ, who was I to think that I could stand in God's way?' When they heard this, they had no further objections and praised God, saying, 'So then, even to the Gentiles God has granted repentance that leads to life.'"

After Herod had James, the brother of John, put to death, he arrested Peter because he thought the Jews approved of these actions. As recorded in Acts:[94] "When he saw that this met with approval among the Jews, he proceeded to seize Peter also. This happened during the Festival of Unleavened Bread. After arresting him, he put him in prison, handing him over to be guarded by four squads of four soldiers each. Herod intended to bring him out for public trial after the Passover. So Peter was kept in prison, but the church was earnestly praying to God for him. The night before Herod was to bring him to trial, Peter was sleeping between two soldiers, bound with two chain, and sentries stood guard at the entrance. Suddenly an angel of the Lord appeared and a light shone in the cell. He struck Peter on the side and woke him up. 'Quick, get up!' he said, and the chains fell off Peter's wrists. Then the angel said to him, 'Putt your clothes and sandals.' And Peter did so. 'Wrap your cloak around you and follow me,' the angel told him. Peter followed him out of prison, but he had no idea that what the angel was doing was really happening; he thought he was seeing a vision. They passed the first and second guards and came to the iron gate leading to the city. It opened for them by itself, and they went through it. When they had walked the length of one street, suddenly, the angel left him. Then Peter came to himself and said, 'Now I know without a doubt that the Lord has sent forth His angel and rescued me from the Herod's clutches and from everything the Jewish people were hoping would happen.'"

After Peter was freed from prison, ". . . he departed and went to another place."[95] Some thought Peter went to Babylon and preached there. Peter later informed the Jews in Jerusalem that God had given the Gospel to the Gentiles. "And after there had been much debate, Peter stood up and said to them: 'Brethren, you know that in the early days God made a choice among you, that by my mouth the Gentiles should hear the word of the gospel and believe. And God, who knows the heart, bore witness to them, giving them the Holy Spirit, just as He also did to us; and He made no

---

94. Acts 12:3–11, NIV.
95. Acts 12:17b, NKJV.

distinction between us and them, cleansing their hearts by faith.'"[96] "Then all the multitude kept silent and listened to Barnabas and Paul declaring how many miracles and wonders God had worked through them among the Gentiles. And after they had become silent, James answered, saying, 'Men and brethren, listen to me; Simon has declared how God at the first visited the Gentiles to take out of them a people for His name. And with this the words of the prophets agree, just as it is written, 'After this I will return And will rebuild the tabernacle of David, which has fallen down; I will rebuild its ruins, And I will set it up; So that the rest of mankind may seek the Lord, Even all the Gentiles who are called by My name, Says the Lord, who does all these things. Known to God from eternity are all His works. Therefore I judge that we should not trouble those from among the Gentiles who are turning to God.'"[97]

It is reported that John Mark wrote his gospel, the Gospel of Mark, between 55 and 65 AD, based on Peter's remembrances.[98] Peter went to Antioch and arrived in Rome during the reign of Claudius. He took Mark with him as a companion and scribe. Mark became Peter's interpreter and scribe after he had accompanied Paul and Barnabas on their first missionary journey. Mark was not an eyewitness to Jesus' ministry, yet his gospel relates directly to Jesus life. Mark wrote Peter's sermons in his gospel. Peter referred to his close association with Mark as he sent greetings probably from the church in Babylon. "She who is in Babylon, chosen together with you, sends you greetings, and so does my son Mark."[99]

Peter also preached in Pontus, Galatia, Bithynia, Cappadocia, all in Asia Minor, and in Asia. Peter greeted the early Christians there:[100] "Peter, an apostle of Jesus Christ. To the pilgrims of the Dispersion in Pontus, Galatia, Cappadocia, Asia and Bithynia, elect according to the foreknowledge of God the Father, in sanctification of the Spirit, for obedience and sprinkling of the blood of Jesus Christ: Grace to you and peace be multiplied." Later

---

96. Acts 15:6–9, NASB.

97. Acts 15:12–19, NKJV.

98. Mark begins his Gospel with the preaching of John the Baptist, followed by Jesus calling Peter and Andrew. He reports of the disciples Peter, James, and John going to the home of Peter's mother-in-law to cure her of fever, all events of which Peter, but not Mark, would have had personal knowledge.

99. 1 Pet 5:13, NKJV. Some have decided Peter called Rome "Babylon" and thus was referring to the church in Rome.

100. 1 Pet 1:1–2, KJV.

The Disciples of the Inner Circle

Peter went to Rome where he was crucified, allegedly head downwards at his request.[101]

Peter is reported to have been crucified in 64 AD, during the reign of Nero. He reportedly was crucified upside down near Vatican Hill in Rome, which now is the site of St. Peter's basilica. There is no definite evidence of this fact, however, and many point to the fact that Paul did not mention Peter as being in Rome when he wrote his letter to the Romans. Still, the Epistle of Romans apparently was written in 57 AD, when Paul was in Corinth; thus, Peter may have arrived in Rome later. It is clear that Peter was one of the most devoted servants of the Lord who, without fear, suffered a violent death as a final testament of his undying knowledge that Jesus was one with God and the Savior of the world.

John, the disciple whom Jesus loved,[102] was especially instrumental in bringing the message of salvation to the world. John started the churches in Smyrna, Pergamum, Sardis, Philadelphia, Laodicea, and Thyatira, churches to which he refers in Revelation.[103] He later became the leader of the church in Ephesus that Paul had founded[104] although, because Paul does not mention John in his book to the Ephesians, John must not have lived in Ephesus with Mary, the mother of Jesus, until shortly before or after Paul's death.[105]

Domitian, who had served under Nero, was the Roman emperor from 96 to 98 AD; he exiled John to the Isle of Patmos[106] because of John's aggressive spreading of the Word of God. Most contend John wrote the book of Revelation while he was on the Isle of Patmos as an attack on Domitian[107] and the Roman empire.[108] In writing about his exile to Patmos, John

---

101. See Eusebius, *The History of the Church*, 65.

102. John referred to himself as the disciple whom Jesus loved at John 11:3; 13:23; 19:26, and 21:20.

103. Foxe, *Fox's Book of Martyrs*, 14.

104. Eusebius, *The History of the Church*, 83. See also *Eusebius, Ecclesiastical History*, 86.

105. Discussion in Foxe, *Fox's Book of Martyrs*, 81.
Paul wrote to the Ephesians from Rome in 60 AD and made no mention of John's presence there. Additionally, Paul was martyred in 64 or 66 AD. John then possibly left Jerusalem and went to Ephesus sometime after 64 or 66 AD. He would have been in Ephesus with Mary, the mother of Jesus, prior to the destruction of Jerusalem that occurred in 70 to 73 AD.

106. Patmos is a small Greek island by the Aegean Sea.

107. Domitian was the brother of Titus who is credited with destroying the Temple in Jerusalem beginning in 70 AD. Titus became the Roman emperor in 79 AD, nine years after the destruction of the Temple. Domitian followed Titus as emperor in 81 AD.

108. See, however, Eusebius, *The History of the Church*, 240–43. Eusebius decided

stated:[109] "I, John, your brother and fellow partaker in the tribulation and kingdom and perseverance which are in Jesus, was on the island called Patmos, because of the word of God and the testimony of Jesus. I was in the Spirit on the Lord's day, and I heard behind me a loud voice like the sound of a trumpet, saying: 'Write in a book what you see, and send it to the seven churches: to Ephesus and to Smyrna and to Pergamum and to Thyatira and to Sardis and to Philadelphia and to Laodicea.'"

John had been on the Isle of Patmos for about eighteen months when Domitian was murdered, in about 96 AD. Domitian reigned for fifteen years whereas John recorded that those who believe in Jesus will ". . . reign forever and ever.[110] Nerva, who succeeded Domitian as emperor, was the first of Rome's somewhat good emperors. He recalled John back to Ephesus in about 98 AD.[111]

John the apostle did not write Revelation, noting that the language and style in Revelation were not like the Gospel of John and John's Epistles. Eusebius concluded: "To sum up, anyone who examines their characteristics throughout will inevitably see that the Gospel and Epistle have one and the same colour. But there is no resemblance or similarity whatever between them and the Revelation; it has no connexion, no relationship with them; it has hardly a syllable in common with them." Eusebius agreed that a John wrote Revelation but stated that there was another John among the Christians of Asia as there are two tombs at Ephesus, each reputed to be for a person named John. Still, the difference in writing style in Revelation, as compared to the Gospel of John and the three epistles John wrote, can be attributed to the fact that John was very old at the time Revelation was written. John is alleged to have instructed someone else, perhaps a scribe, to write the words the Lord gave to him. This person would have had a different and unique writing style.

Eusebius stated that some of his predecessors rejected the book of Revelation, pronouncing it unintelligible and illogical and the title false. He affirmed that they also decided it was not John's work. Eusebius, however, did not reject the book of Revelation; he stated that many good Christians had a very high opinion of it and that his "mental powers" were ". . . inadequate to judge it properly." Eusebius took the view ". . . that the interpretation of the various sections is largely a mystery, something too wonderful for our comprehension." Eusebius concluded: "I do not understand it, but I suspect that some deeper meaning is concealed in the words; I do not measure and judge these things by my own reason, but put more reliance on faith, and so I have concluded that they are too high to be grasped by me. I do not condemn as valueless what I have not taken in at a glance, but rather am puzzled that I have not taken it in." Eusebius, *The History of the Church*, 241.

109. Rev 1:9–10, NASB.
110. Rev 22:5b, NKJV.
111. Foxe, *Fox's Book of Martyrs*, 14.

The Disciples of the Inner Circle

After his return to Ephesus, John directed the churches in Asia.[112] He would have been the only apostle alive at that time. It is clear from John's book of Revelation that he had a special relationship with the Asian churches.

John exhorted the early Christians not to be led astray. He stated in one of his epistles:[113] "Little children, let no one deceive you" and admonished them:[114] "Dear friends, do not believe every spirit, but test the spirits to see whether they are from God, because many false prophets have gone out into the world. This is how you can recognize the Spirit of God: Every spirit that acknowledges that Jesus Christ has come in the flesh is from God; but every spirit that does not acknowledge Jesus is not from God. This is the spirit of the antichrist, which you have heard is coming and now is already in the world."

John died in Ephesus sometime after 98 AD and before 120 AD. He allegedly was the only disciple who did not endure a tragic death; rather he lived to a very old age. He was buried in what is now the Basilica of St. John, located about two miles from Ephesus. However, when his tomb was opened during the reign of Constantine,[115] there was no body.[116] Moreover, no body was found for Mary, the mother of Jesus, who lived with John in

---

112. Eusebius, *The History of the Church*, 83.
113. 1 John 3:7a, NKJV.
114. I John 4:1–3, NIV.
115. Constantine, who lived from 280 to 337 AD, was the Roman emperor who adopted Christianity as the religion of the Roman empire. Some contend Constantine was the first Christian emperor in Rome; others do not think he was a Christian. They contend it was his mother, Helena, who was the Christian and that she convinced him Christianity should be the religion of the Roman empire. Still, regardless of whether Constantine became a believer, he did legalize Christianity in 313 AD in the Edict of Milan. After that, persecution of the Christians ended.

Constantine's mother, Helena, was a Greek and a Christian; she greatly influenced her son in his declaring Christianity to be the official religion. Helena located many of the Christian relics and had the Church of the Holy Sepulchre built on the site where she thought she had found the original cross on which Jesus was crucified. It is possibly the site where Jesus was buried and where He was resurrected three days later. The Church of the Holy Sepulchre is located in the Christian quarter of the old city of Jerusalem. Helena also had built churches on the Mount of Olives and in Bethlehem, where Jesus was born. She is sometimes referred to as Saint Helen and as Helena of Constantinople.

116. Discussion of John's later life in Foxe, *Fox's Book of Martyrs*, 81–93.
In the 1920s, when archaeological teams from Greece and Austria excavated the area where John was allegedly buried, they located John's tomb underneath the ruins, but when his tomb was opened, there was no body. Some contend John was carried to heaven, but there is nothing to confirm that.

Ephesus after Jesus, while He was dying on the cross, told John that Mary would be his mother.[117]

After John, the beloved disciple, saw the resurrected Jesus and knew without doubt that Jesus was one with God and is the Messiah, he wrote in his Gospel:[118] "In the beginning was the Word, and the Word was with God, and the Word was God. He was in the beginning with God. All things were made through Him, and without Him nothing was made that was made. In Him was life, and the life was the light of men. And the light shines in the darkness, and the darkness did not comprehend it. There came a man, sent from God, whose name was John. This man came for a witness, to bear witness of the Light, that all through him might believe. He was not that Light, but was sent to bear witness of that Light. That was the true Light which gives light to every man coming into the world. He was in the world, and the world was made through Him, and the world did not know Him. He came to His own, and His own did not receive Him. But as many as received Him, to them He gave the right to become children of God, to those who believe in His name; who were born, not of blood, nor of the will of the flesh, nor of the will of man, but of God. And the Word became flesh, and dwelt among us, and we beheld His glory, the glory as of the only begotten of the Father, full of grace and truth."

John centered the Gospel of John on these words:[119] "For God so loved the world that He gave His only begotten Son, that whoever believes in Him should not perish but have everlasting life." He closed his Gospel affirming that: "Many other signs therefore Jesus also performed in the presence of His disciples, which are not written in this book; but these have been written that you may believe that Jesus is the Christ, the Son of God, and that believing you may have life in His name."[120]

---

117. Many affirm strongly that Mary was bodily taken into Heaven at her death before her body could decay. Some churches in several countries celebrate what is called the Assumption of Mary. See discussion of Mary's life in Chapter 5. Her "assumption" is based on the manner in which the angel addressed her to announce she would be the mother of Jesus. As recorded in Luke 1:28b, NKJV, the angel appeared to Mary and "... said to her, 'Rejoice, highly favored one, the Lord is with you; blessed are you among women!'" Some also refer to Rev 12:1a, NKJV: "Now a great sign appeared in heaven: a woman clothed with the sun, with the moon under her feet, and on her head a garland of twelve stars. Then being with child . . ."

118. John 1:1–13, NKJV.

119. John 3:16, NKJV.

120. John 20:31, NASB.

The Disciples of the Inner Circle

John's final statement in his evangelistic Gospel was to report to believers that "... there are also many other things that Jesus did, which if they were written one by one, I suppose that even the whole world itself could not contain the books that would be written."[121]

---

121. John 21:25, NKJV. It is amazing how powerful are the words of an uneducated fisherman who could only have written the wonderful Gospel of John with inspiration from the Holy Spirit.

3

The Remaining Eight Disciples

I. Matthew, the Tax Collector
II. James, the Less, Son of Alphaeus
III. Philip, the Apostle
IV. Nathanael, also called Bartholomew
V. Thaddaeus, also called Judas or Jude
VI. Simon, the Zealot
VII. Thomas, the Doubter
VIII. Judas Iscariot, the Betrayer
IX. Matthias, the Chosen Successor

As noted in Chapter 1, James, John, Andrew, and Peter were part of an inner circle of the Twelve, although Andrew to a lesser extent; thus, their activities, particularly those of John and Peter, are more detailed in the four Gospels than those of the remaining eight disciples. Nevertheless, the other eight disciples, with the exception of Judas Iscariot, but including Matthias who succeeded Judas Iscariot, were most important leaders in the early church, and all played significant roles in bringing the message of salvation to the world. With the exception of Matthias, but he too to a lesser extent, these disciples also had the distinct and wondrous honor of being with Jesus throughout His ministry and later being a part of the miracle of seeing and meeting with the resurrected Jesus. Having witnessed the resurrection and having actually met with the risen Lord, they, as well as James, John,

Andrew, and Peter, knew without doubt, and could testify, that Jesus is Lord and Savior of the world.

I. Matthew, the Tax Collector

Matthew, the son of Alphaeus[1] was a tax collector whom Jesus called to become one of the Twelve. He was an especially significant disciple because he is the author of one of the four Gospels. Matthew referred in his gospel to the Twelve as follows:[2] "Now the names of the twelve apostles are these: the First, Simon, who is called Peter, and Andrew his brother; and James the son of Zebedee, and John his brother; Philip and Bartholomew; Thomas and Matthew the tax-gatherer; James the son of Alphaeus, and Thaddaeus; Simon the Zealot, and Judas Iscariot, the one who betrayed Him."

Matthew, who originally was called Levi,[3] was very different from those of the inner circle–Peter, Andrew, James and John. The latter four were very devout Jews; at least two of whom, and possibly all four, had been disciples of John the Baptist. In contrast, Matthew was a Jewish tax collector in the service of Rome, or possibly of Herod Antipas,[4] when Jesus called him to be a disciple. Most tax collectors at that time were dishonest outcasts who were hated by the Galileans.[5] As recorded in

---

1. The disciple, James the Less, was also the son of an Alphaeus; thus, some had reported that Matthew was the brother of the disciple referred to as James the Less. See discussion in McBirnie, *The Search for the Twelve Apostles,* 129. However, there is no evidence they were brothers. There probably were two different persons named Alphaeus, and the two were not brothers. Additionally, the mother of James the Less was a Mary, who apparently, like Salome the mother of James and John, was a sister of Mary, the mother of Jesus. This Mary would not have been the mother of the disciple, Matthew.

2. Matt 10:2-4, NASB.

3. Jesus reportedly changed Levi's name to Matthew, which means "gift of God."

4. Herod Antipas was son of Herod the Great and the ruler of Galilee from 4 BC to 39 AD. He is the Herod who beheaded John the Baptist. Herod Agrippa I, who is discussed in Chapter 2 with reference to the disciple James, ruled from 39 to 44 AD and is the Herod who put James, to death. Herod Agrippa I was the grandson of Herod the Great; his father was Aristobulus, another son of Herod the Great, but one whom Herod the Great had executed. Herod Agrippa II, the son of Agrippa I and the great-grandson of Herod the Great, was the last king of the Herodian dynasty.

5. Some might wonder why Jesus chose Matthew. Jesus obviously saw greatness in Matthew, and Matthew did become a most fearless and faithful follower of the Lord. As author of the Gospel of Matthew, he sought to prove to the Jewish people that Jesus is the Messiah.

Matthew was not the only tax collector who gave up his ill-gotten wealth to find

Mark:[6] "And as He passed by, He saw Levi the son of Alphaeus sitting in the tax office, and He said to him, 'Follow me!' And he rose and followed Him."

Matthew immediately gave up his lucrative job as a tax collector and followed Jesus, but pious Jews denounced Jesus' association with Matthew. After Jesus called Matthew to become one of his disciples, Matthew had a dinner for Jesus to introduce Jesus to his friends, most of whom were also hated tax collectors. Matthew recorded of the dinner:[7] "And it happened that as He was reclining at the table in the house, behold many tax-gatherers and sinners came and were dining with Jesus and His disciples. And when the Pharisees saw this, they said to His disciples, 'Why is your teacher eating with tax-gatherers and sinners?' But when He heard this, He said, 'It is not those who are healthy who need a physician, but those who are sick.'"[8] Luke records Jesus as saying, "I have not come to call the righteous, but sinners to repentance."[9]

Matthew was probably the most educated of the Twelve, and he was one of only two[10] of the disciples who wrote a gospel.[11] Matthew's gospel is the longest of the four Gospels and is called the most "Jewish" Gospel.[12]

---

salvation through belief in Jesus. As recorded in Luke 19:1–10, NIV: "Jesus entered Jericho and was passing through. A man was there by the name of Zacchaeus; he was a chief tax collector and wealthy. He wanted to see who Jesus was, but because he was short he could not see over the crowd. So he ran ahead and climbed a sycamore-fig tree to see Him, since Jesus was coming that way. When Jesus reached the spot, He looked up and said to him, 'Zacchaeus, come down immediately. I must stay at your house today.' So he came down at once and welcomed Him gladly. All the people saw this and began to mutter, 'He has gone to be the guest of a sinner.' But Zacchaeus stood up and said to the Lord, 'Look, Lord! Here and now I give half of my possessions to the poor, and if I have cheated anybody out of anything, I will pay back four times the amount.' Jesus said to him, 'Today salvation has come to this house, because this man, too, is a son of Abraham. For the Son of Man came to seek and to save the lost.'"

6. Mark 2:14, NASB. See also Matt 9:9.
7. Matt 9:10–12, NASB.
8. See also Mark 2:15–17.
9. Luke 5:32, NASB. See also Mark 2:17.
10. The other being John, the beloved disciple.
11. Still, some contend Peter was actually the author of the gospel of Mark—that Mark recorded the words of Peter.
12. Discussion in Eusebius, *The History of the Church*, 201. Eusebius states that the Gospel of Matthew was published for believers of Jewish origin.

Some historians attribute the Gospel of Matthew as being the first gospel to be written; others state that the Gospel of Mark was the first written and that it was then followed by the Gospel of Matthew.

It has been reported that Matthew wrote his gospel in Hebrew and that James, the Less, another disciple and the son of an Alphaeus,[13] translated the Gospel of Matthew into Greek.[14]

Matthew wrote his Gospel for the Jewish-Christian church to fulfill what was spoken by the prophets. He traced Jesus' genealogy back to David, the second king of Israel and to Abraham,[15] and referred to Jesus having been born in Bethlehem in Judea as foretold by the prophet Micah: "But you, Bethlehem, in the Land of Judah, Are not the least among the rulers of Judah; For out of you shall come forth a Ruler, who will shepherd My people Israel."[16]

Matthew is reported to have begun his preaching to the Jewish people[17] and to have remained in Israel for fifteen years after Jesus' ascension. He then purportedly preached in Persia, in Syria, and in Ethiopia, where the apostle Andrew joined him. Records indicate that Matthew was martyred in 60 AD,[18] and that his body is in Salerno, Italy.[19]

II. James, the Less, Son of Alphaeus

James, the son of Alphaeus, was called James the Less or James the Younger to distinguish him from James, the brother of John, who was called the Greater, and James the half-brother of Jesus, who was called James the Just and also James the Righteous.[20] As recorded in Luke:[21] "And when the day came, He called His disciples to Him; and chose twelve of them, whom He

---

13. As discussed above, James the Less was erroneously considered by some to have been Matthew's brother.

14. Discussion in Foxe, *Fox's Book of Martyrs*, 12.

15. Matt 1:1–17.

16. Matt 2:6, NKJV. The actual quote from Mic 5:2, KJV is: "But thou, Bethlehem, Ephrathah, though thou be little among the thousands of Judah, yet out of thee shall he come forth unto me that is to be ruler in Israel; whose goings forth have been from of old, from everlasting." Micah recorded at Mic 5:5, NIV: "And he will be our peace . . . ."

17. Eusebius, *The History of the Church*, 86.

18. Foxe, *Fox's Book of Martyrs*, 12.

19. McBirnie, *The Search for the Twelve Apostles*, 133–34. His body is reported to be in the Cathedral of San Matteo at Salerno, Italy.

20. James' father, Alphaeus, was also called Cleophas. Alphaeus was his Greek name; in Hebrew Alphaeus is pronounced Cleophas.

21. Luke 6:13–16, NASB.

also named as apostles . . . James, the son of Alphaeus, and Simon who was called the Zealot . . ."

As noted previously, some contend this James, the son of Alphaeus and called James the Less, was Matthew's brother because Matthew's father was also named Alphaeus, also called Cleophas; others contend that they were not related and that their fathers were two different persons both of whom were named Alphaeus or Cleophas.[22] Matthew does not refer to James the Less in his gospel, which indicates that the two possibly were not siblings or even related. Historians do record that Jude Thaddeus and Simon the Zealot, both of whom were also disciples of Christ, were brothers of James the Less and sons of Alphaeus, or Cleophas, and Mary, who may have been the sister of Jesus' mother.[23] Possibly then, James the Less, Jude Thaddeus, and Simon the Zealot, all disciples of Jesus, may have been Jesus' cousins.[24]

There is little information about the life of James the Less. He is only mentioned in connection with his mother, Mary. Mark refers in his Gospel to James' mother, Mary, being present when Jesus was crucified:[25] "And there were also some women looking on from a distance, among whom were Mary Magdalene, and Mary, the mother of James the Less and of Joses, and Salome."

James the Less reportedly was stoned for preaching Christ. One author reported his body was buried in Jerusalem but later taken to Constantinople for interment in the Church of the Holy Apostles.[26]

III. Philip the Apostle

Philip, a disciple who was a Jew with a Greek name, is only discussed in the Gospel of John. Philip possibly knew John, that being the reason John makes references to him in his Gospel. Philip may have been a fisherman

---

22. Nevertheless, McBirnie records in *The Search for the Twelve Apostles*, 138, that James the Less was a brother of Matthew.

23. John may be referring in his Gospel to James' mother, Mary, as being the sister of Jesus' mother, Mary. "*But there stood by the cross of Jesus His mother and His mother's sister, Mary the wife of Clopas, and Mary Magdalene.*" John 19:25, NKJV.

24. In *Eccesiastical History*, 134, Eusebius records Simon as being the son of Cleophas, whom Eusebius refers to as being the uncle of Jesus. This would mean that Simon the Zealot was Jesus' cousin, along with James the Less and Jude Thaddeus.

25. Mark 15:40, NASB.

26. McBirnie, *The Search for the Twelve Apostles*, 148.

The Remaining Eight Disciples

as were James, John, Andrew, and Peter, and may have also been a disciple of John the Baptist; however, there is no evidence to support any of these suppositions.

John records in his gospel that after Andrew had brought his brother, Peter, to Jesus, Jesus left for Galilee where he found and called Philip, who, like James, John, Andrew, and Peter, was from Bethsaida. Philip introduced one of the other disciples to Jesus—Nathaniel who was also called Bartholomew. As recorded in John:[27] "The next day He purposed to go forth into Galilee, and He found Philip. And Jesus said to him, 'Follow me.' Now Philip was from Bethsaida, of the city of Andrew and Peter. Philip found Nathanael and said to him, 'We have found Him of whom Moses in the Law and also the Prophets wrote, Jesus of Nazareth, the son of Joseph.' And Nathanael said to him, 'Can anything good come out of Nazareth?' Philip said to him, 'Come and see.'" Jesus later told Nathanael: ". . . 'Before Philip called you, when you were under the fig tree, I saw you.'"[28]

Philip was with Jesus when Jesus fed the 5,000. Jesus had asked Philip how to feed so many people; Philip then attempted to calculate the cost of feeding such a large group. John reported:[29] "Jesus therefore lifting up his eyes and seeing that a great multitude was coming to Him, said to Philip, 'Where are we to buy bread, that these may eat?' And He was saying to test him; for He Himself knew what He was intending to do. Philip answered Him, 'Two hundred denarii worth of bread is not sufficient for them, for everyone to receive a little.'" Andrew then found the boy with five loaves and two fishes.[30]

Philip had influence over the Greeks perhaps because he had a Greek name. John records that Philip did introduce some Greeks to Jesus. "Now there were certain Greeks among those who were going up to worship at the feast; these therefore came to Philip, who was from Bethsaida of Galilee, and began to ask him, saying 'Sir, we wish to see Jesus.' Philip came and told Andrew; Andrew and Philip came, and they told Jesus."[31]

At the last supper with Jesus, "Philip said to Him, 'Lord, show us the Father, and it is sufficient for us.'"[32] This request, which showed how

27. John 1:43–45, NASB.
28. John 1:48, NKJV.
29. John 6:5–7, NASB.
30. See John 6:8–11.
31. John 12:20–22, NASB.
32. John 14:8, NKJV.

little the disciples at that time understood about Jesus and His mission, did motivate Jesus to explain more fully what God is like. As recorded in John:[33] "Jesus said to him, 'Have I been with you so long, and yet you have not known Me, Philip? He who has seen Me has seen the Father; so how do you say, 'Show us the Father?' Do you not believe that I am in the Father, and the Father in Me? The words that I speak to you I do not speak on My own authority; but the Father who dwells in Me does the works. Believe Me that I am in the Father, and the Father in Me; or else believe Me for the sake of works themselves. Most assuredly, I say to you, he who believes in Me, the works that I do he will do also; and greater works than these he will do, because I go to My Father. And whatever *you ask in* My name, that I will do, that the Father may be glorified in the Son. If you ask anything in My name, I will do it. If you love Me, keep My commandments. And I pray the Father, and He will give you another Helper, that He may abide with you forever—the Spirit of truth, whom the world cannot receive, because it neither sees Him nor knows Him; but you know Him because He dwells with you, and will be in you. I will not leave you orphans, I will come to you. A little while longer and the world will see Me no more but you will see Me. Because I live, you will live also. At that day you will know that I am in My Father, and you in Me, and I in you. He who has My commandments and keeps them, it is he who loves Me. And he who loves Me will be loved by My Father and I will love him and manifest Myself to him.'"

After Jesus' resurrection, Philip, along with the remaining disciples, was at the Mount of Olives when the disciples chose Matthias to replace Judas Iscariot. "Then they returned to Jerusalem from the Mount called Olivet, which is near Jerusalem, a Sabbath day's journey away. And when they had entered, they went up to the upper room, where they were staying, that is, Peter and John and James and Andrew, Philip and Thomas, Bartholomew and Matthew, James the son of Alphaeus, and Simon the Zealot, and Judas the son of James. These all with one mind were continually devoting themselves to prayer, along with the women and Mary the mother of Jesus, and with His brothers."[34]

Philip is reported to have preached in Greece, Syria, and Phrygia, which was a part of Anatolia in what is now Asian Turkey; some also contend Philip visited France and England.[35] However, little was written about

---

33. John 14:9–21, NKJV.
34. Acts 1:12–14, NASB.
35. Discussion in McBirnie, *The Search for the Twelve Apostles*, 98. Philip is reported

The Remaining Eight Disciples

Philip after Jesus' death. Some, possibly in error, reported that Philip resided at Hierapolis in Turkey and that he reportedly suffered a martyr's death there.[36] Philip was reported to have been buried initially in Hierapolis,[37] with his body later taken from Hierapolis to Constantinople and then subsequently interred in a church in Rome.[38] However, this report may be incorrect in that the Philip who resided, died, and buried in Hierapolis was more likely Philip, the Evangelist, who is discussed in Chapter 5. The problem is that many, including Eusebius, assumed, incorrectly, that Philip the Apostle and Philip the Evangelist were the same person.[39]

IV. Nathanael, also called Bartholomew

Nathanael, the disciple who is called Bartholomew in all the gospels except the Gospel of John,[40] was born in Cana in Galilee. Philip called Nathanael to become a follower of Jesus. As recorded in John:[41] "Philip found Na-

---

to have traveled with Mary Magdalene, Mary, the wife of Cleopas, Mary Salome, and Lazarus to southern France to spread the Gospel there, but then he is alleged to have left with Joseph of Arimathea to travel to Glastonbury, England to proclaim the good news of salvation in England. Discussion of the visit of the Marys and Lazarus to France in Chapter 5.

36. See Eusebius, *The History of the Church*, 102-3, 171.

37. Eusebius, *The History of the Church*, 171. McBirnie reports in, *The Search for the Twelve Apostles*, 101,102-3, that Philip probably was martyred in Hierapolis, Turkey, by being pierced through the thighs and hung upside down. However, McBirnie, as well as Eusebius, assumed Philip the Apostle was also the Philip who was called the Evangelist. Philip the Evangelist lived in Hierapolis, Turkey. The Philip who was martyred in Hierapolis more probably was Philip the Evangelist.

McBirnie also refers to reports that Philip visited France. His possible visit to France with the Marys and Lazarus and his later journey to England with Joseph of Arimathea would point to Philip, the Apostle, as not having met a martyr's death. It is possible then that both he and the disciple John, lived to an old age.

38. McBirnie, *The Search for the Twelve Apostles*, 101.

39. The review in Chapter 5 of the life of Philip the Evangelist discredits the reports that Philip the Apostle was also Philip the Evangelist and thus lived in Hierapolis, Turkey. In Acts 6:2-6 Luke records Philip the Evangelist as having been chosen by the Twelve. The disciple and apostle, Philip, was one of the Twelve. Philip, the Evangelist, who in addition to Stephen, the first martyr for Christ, and five others, was one of the first "seven" deacons to be called, by the "Twelve," to serve other Christians. Discussion in Chapter 1. In Acts 21:8, Luke refers to having stayed, along with Paul, in the home of Philip the Evangelist. Luke relates to this Philip as being of the "seven," not one of the "twelve."

40. Nathanael is apparently an Eastern name for Bartholomew.

41. John 1:45-51, NASB.

thanael, and said to him, 'We have found Him, of whom Moses in the Law, and also the Prophets wrote, Jesus of Nazareth, the son of Joseph.' And Nathanael said to him, 'Can any good thing come out of Nazareth?' Philip said to him, 'Come and see.' Jesus saw Nathanael coming to Him, and said of him, 'Behold an Israelite indeed, in whom is no guile!' Nathanael said to Him, 'How do you know me?' Jesus answered and said to him, 'Before Philip called you, when you were under the fig tree, I saw you.' Nathanael answered Him, 'Rabbi, You are the Son of God; You are the King of Israel.' Jesus answered and said to him, 'Because I said to you that I saw you under the fig tree, do you believe? You shall see greater things than these.' And He said to him, 'Truly, truly, I say to you, you shall see the heavens opened, and the angels of God ascending and descending upon the Son of Man.'"

The actions of Nathanael as a follower of Jesus are only mentioned twice and only that he was with six of the other disciples when Jesus appeared to them after His ascension and was with the eleven when they chose a successor for Judas Iscariot. As recorded in John:[42] "After these things Jesus shewed Himself again to the disciples at the sea of Tiberias; . . . there were together Simon Peter, and Thomas called Didymus, and Nathanael of Cana in Galilee, and the sons of Zebedee, and two other of His disciples." Luke referred to Nathanael as Bartholomew when he reported of the meeting of the eleven to choose the disciple to replace Judas Iscariot. As recorded in Acts:[43] "And when they were come in, they went up into an upper room, where they were staying; that is Peter and John, and James and Andrew, Philip and Thomas, Bartholomew and Matthew, James the son of Alphaeus, and Simon the Zealot, and Judas the son of James."[44]

The three Gospels—Matthew, Mark, and Luke—refer to Nathanael as Bartholomew. Matthew records Jesus calling his twelve disciples as follows:[45] "And when He had called unto Him His twelve disciples, He gave them power against unclean spirits, to cast them out, and to heal all manner of sickness and all manner of disease. Now the names of the twelve are these: The first, Simon, who is called Peter . . . and Bartholomew . . ." Mark

---

42. John 21: 2, KJV.

43. Acts 1:13, KJV.

44. These remaining eleven disciples, after Judas Iscariot's departure, met at the Mount of Olives, which is close to Jerusalem, and chose Matthias to replace Judas Ischariot as the twelfth disciple.

45. Matt10:1–4, KJV.

states:⁴⁶ "Then He appointed twelve, that they might be with Him, and that He might send them out to preach, and to have power to heal sicknesses and to cast out demons. And He appointed the twelve; Simon (to whom He gave the name Peter) . . . Andrew, Philip, and Bartholomew . . . ." Luke referred to the Twelve as follows:⁴⁷ ". . . He called His disciples to Him; and chose twelve of them, whom He also named as apostles; Simon whom He also named Peter . . . and Bartholomew . . ."

The mission of Nathanael, or Bartholomew, reportedly lasted sixteen years.⁴⁸ He is known principally for going with Thaddeus, the disciple who was also called Jude or Judas, to bring Christianity to Armenia.⁴⁹ Thaddeus and Nathanael, also called Bartholomew, are both patron saints of the Armenia Apostolic Church. Additionally, Nathanael carried the Gospel to Ethiopia, Mesopotamia, Lycaonia, which is in Turkey, and Persia, which is now Eastern Iran, and traveled to India where Nathanael (Bartholomew) reportedly left Matthew's Gospel.⁵⁰ Eusebius recorded that Bartholomew, as one of the apostles, had preached in India and had left behind Matthew's account, which was found over a hundred years later ". . . in the hands of some there who had come to know Christ."⁵¹

Nathanael (Bartholomew) is reported to have been skinned alive and then crucified, head downward, in Armenia in 68 AD.⁵² Bartholomew's tomb and that of Thaddeus were in Armenia and treated as sacred shrines, but the relics of Bartholomew are preserved in the church of St. Bartholomew near Rome.⁵³

---

46. Mark 3:14–16, 18a, NKJV.

47. Luke 6:13–14, NASB.

48. McBirnie, *The Search for the Twelve Apostles*, 105.

49. Armenia is near the mountains of Ararat and is bordered by Turkey on the West, Georgia on the North, and Iran on the South. It is reported to have been the first state to adopt Christianity.

50. In *The Search for the Twelve Apostles*, 103, McBirnie quotes a story told in 1685 by Dorman Newman that a Hebrew Gospel of St. Matthew was found in India and that he had been assured it was left there by Bartholomew when he preached the Gospel in those parts.

51. Eusebius, *The History of the Church*, 157.

52. McBirnie, *The Search for the Twelve Apostles*, 105, 108.
Michelangelo portrayed the skinning of Bartholomew in his famous fresco, the "Last Judgment," which Michelangelo painted on the altar wall of the Vatican's Sistine Chapel.

53. McBirnie, *The Search for the Twelve Apostles*, 109–10.

V. Thaddaeus, also called Judas or Jude

The disciple, Thaddaeus, who was also called Judas and Jude,[54] is often referred to as Jude Thaddaeus. Matthew and Mark referred to him as Thaddaeus in their gospels;[55] Luke called him Judas.[56]

There is confusion as to the parents of Thaddaeus; he has been called both the "brother" and the "son" of James. If he were the "brother" of James, he would have been the brother of James the Less and the son of Cleophas and Mary, the possible sister of Mary, the mother of Jesus. He then would have been Jesus' cousin.[57] One historian speculated that Jude Thaddaeus was more likely the son of James the Great, the son of Zebedee.[58] Still other historians record Jude Thaddaeus and Simon the Zealot, both of whom were disciples of Christ, as being brothers of James the Less.[59] This also would mean that Jude Thaddaeus was the son of Cleophas and Mary, the possible sister of Mary, the mother of Jesus, and thus a possible cousin of Jesus.[60]

Jude Thaddaeus is the last disciple recorded to have questioned Jesus. He inquired about the following statements from Jesus:[61] "He who has My commandments and keeps them, it is he who loves Me. And he who loves

---

54. Judas is the Greek name for Judah, and Jude is Latin for Judah.

55. Matthew 10:3; Mark 3:18.

56. Luke 6:16.

57. In recent Bible translations—the New American Standard and the New International Version—Luke, at 6:16, referred to Thaddaeus as Judas the *son* of James. Still, some contend that "son" was referring to "brother" and that Jude was the "brother" of James the Less. Additionally, the King James Version records Jude as being the *brother* of James. If Jude Thaddaeus was the author of the Epistle of Jude as some also contend, then he will have acknowledged that he was the brother of James. Jude 1:1, NASB records" "*Jude, a bond-servant of Jesus Christ and brother of James . . .*" Still, some contend that Jude, another half-brother of Jesus, wrote the Epistle of Jude and, in referring to his being the brother of James, was referring to James the Just, who also was the half-brother of Jesus and the first bishop in the Jerusalem church.

58. See discussion in McBirnie, *The Search for the Twelve Apostles*, 151, where McBirnie theorizes that Judas Thaddaeus was the grandson of Zebedee and the nephew of the apostle John.

59. Eusebius, *Ecclesiastical History*, 134.

60. Eusebius referred to Simon the Zealot, who succeeded James the Just as bishop of the church in Jerusalem after James was martyred and who apparently was the brother of Jude Thaddaeus, as being the son of Cleophas, who was the *father* of James the Less. See Eusebius, *The History of the Church*, 95, 129; Eusebius, *Ecclesiastical History*, 81, 97. If this is correct, this would mean again that Jude Thaddaeus was the brother of James the Less, rather than the *son* of a James, and possibly was Jesus' cousin.

61. John 14:21, NKJV.

The Remaining Eight Disciples

Me will be loved by My Father, and I will love him, and manifest Myself to him." As recorded in the Gospel of John:[62] "Judas (not Iscariot) said to Him, 'Lord, how is it that You will manifest Yourself to us, and not to the world?'" "Jesus answered and said to him, 'If any man loves Me, he will keep My word; and My Father will love him, and We will come to him, and make Our home with him. He who does not love Me does not keep My words; and the word which you hear is not Mine, but the Father's who sent Me.'"[63]

Jude Thaddaeus was present after Jesus' ascension, at a gathering that the remaining eleven apostles brought to decide on a twelfth apostle to succeed Judas of Iscariot. As recorded in the book of Acts,[64] "And when they had entered, they went up into the upper room, where they were staying: Peter, James, John and Andrew; Philip and Thomas; Bartholomew and Matthew; James the son of Alphaeus and Simon the Zealot, and Judas the son of James."[65]

After Jesus death, the apostle Thomas sent Jude Thaddaeus to preach the gospel in Edessa, which was once a part of Mesopotamia.[66] He may have been one of the first apostles to leave Jerusalem to preach the Gospel.[67] Eusebius recorded that there is written evidence of Thaddaeus' preaching and performing evangelist work in the Record Office at Edessa, which Eusebius stated was at that time the royal capital of Osroene, the historical kingdom in Upper Mesopotamia in what is now Turkey. Eusebius wrote that King Abgar, whom Eusebius described as the brilliantly successful monarch of the peoples of Mesopotamia, was dying from a terrible physical disorder, and no human power could heal him. King Abgar had heard of Jesus and of His miracles and sent a request to give him relief from the disease. When King Abgar discovered that Thaddaeus was in Edessa and had heard that a man from foreign parts had arrived and was performing many wonders, King Abgar requested his presence.[68] Eusebius reported that Jude Thad-

---

62. John 14:22, NKJV.
63. John 14:23-24, NKJV.
64. Acts 1:13, NKJV.
65. A comment to this verse in the New American Standard version of the Bible states the reference to "Judas the *son* of James" could possibly mean *brother* of James.
66. Eusebius, *The History of the Church*, 30-31. Edessa was originally a Syrian city, but the area is now Urfa, Turkey. It is 400 miles from Jerusalem.
67. See discussion in McBirnie, *The Search for the Twelve Apostles*, 159.
68. Eusebius, *The History of the Church*, 32.

daeus restored King Abgar to health by the word of Christ, and that he amazed all the inhabitants of Edessa by his wonderful miracles.[69]

Jude Thaddaeus reportedly preached in Syria, Arabia, Mesopotamia and Persia.[70] One historian stated he also preached extensively with Bartholomew in Armenia; their shrines still exist there.[71] Thaddaeus has been called the first patriarch of the Armenian Church.[72] Some reports record that his body and that of Simon the Zealot, who may have been his brother and with whom he was also connected, were brought to Rome from Beirut, where some contend Thaddaeus was martyred; however, one historian asserted that Jude Thaddaeus was crucified at Edessa in AD 72.[73] Jude Thaddaeus' body is alleged to be in the same crypt with Simon the Zealot, in St. Peter's Basilica.[74]

---

69. Eusebius, *The History of the Church*, 36.
Eusebius reported that by Thaddaeus' actions, he exerted such an influence on the inhabitants of Edessa "... that he led them to reverence the power of Christ, and made disciples of the saving doctrine." Eusebius further stated: "From that day to this the whole city of Edessa has been devoted to the name of Christ, providing most convincing proof of our Saviour's goodness to them also." Eusebius, *The History of the Church*, 36.
See discussion in McBirnie, *The Search for the Twelve Apostles*, 159, wherein McBirnie states that if the Abgar legend is true, Jude would have been one of the first apostles to witness directly to a foreign king, a Gentile. He also determined there was no reason to doubt that Jude Thaddaeus, probably along with Bartholomew, and for a brief period with Thomas, had brought the salvation message to Edessa.

70. McBirnie, *The Search for the Twelve Apostles*, 153.

71. McBirnie, *The Search for the Twelve Apostles*, 105. McBirnie reported that Armenia was among the first to respond to the call of Christ and that both Thaddaeus and Bartholomew suffered martyrdom in Armenia, Thaddaeus in 50 AD and Bartholomew in 68 AD. See McBirnie, *The Search for the Twelve Apostles*, 153.

72. McBirnie, *The Search for the Twelve Apostles*, 155.

73. Foxe, *Fox's Book of Martyrs*, 13. McBirnie reported, in *The Search for the Twelve Apostles*, 157–58, that some contend Thaddaeus was martyred in Beirut, Syria, and some in Egypt. However, McBirnie claimed he investigated these claims carefully and found no evidence of either.

74. McBirnie, in *The Search for the Twelve Apostles*, 159, confirmed that Jude was buried with Simon the Zealot, stating that the "Persian tradition is that the two were slain at about the same time, or possibly together."

St. Jude's Children's Hospital in Memphis, Tennessee, was named for Jude Thaddaeus.

VI. Simon, the Zealot

The disciple, Simon the Zealot, also called the Canaanite,[75] was the son of Cleophas and Mary, the possible sister of Mary, the mother of Jesus;[76] thus, along with his brothers James the Less and probably Jude Thaddaeus, Simon may also have been Jesus' cousin.

One historian attributed to Simon the Zealot the question one of the disciples asked Jesus after Jesus appeared to the disciples following His resurrection:[77] "Lord is it at this time You are restoring the kingdom of Israel?" Jesus answered, "It is not for you to know times or epochs which the Father has fixed by His own authority; but you shall receive power when the Holy Spirit has come upon you; and you shall be My witnesses both in Jerusalem, and in all Judea and Samaria, and even to the remotest part of the earth."[78]

Simon had been part of a violent Jewish nationalist party, the Zealots. Historians report that the Zealots were responsible for a revolt in 68–70 AD that led to Titus, the future Roman emperor, completely destroying Jerusalem by 73 AD. It was the Zealots who took the last stand at Masada in 71 AD.[79] Simon must have left the Zealots after Jesus informed the disciples that they could not know when the Kingdom of Israel would be restored.[80]

---

75. See the reference in the King James Version of Matthew 10:4 and Mark 3:18.

76. Eusebius, *Ecclesiastical History*, 81.

77. Acts 1:6, NASB.
McBirnie refers to Simon being the person who asked Jesus the question about restoring the kingdom of Israel, in McBirnie, *The Search for the Twelve Apostles*, 168.

78. Acts:1:7–8, NASB.
McBirnie, in *The Search for the Twelve Apostles*, 168, theorized that Simon was first interested in Jesus as a Messiah who would restore the Kingdom of Israel and triumph over the Romans but that he gave up that concept after Jesus said they were not to know the time or season of the restoration of the Israelite kingdom.

79. Discussion in McBirnie, *The Search for the Twelve Apostles*, 167. Over 900 Jewish people committed suicide after a long siege by the Roman general Lucius Flavius Silva. These Jews chose to die rather than become Roman slaves. Masada currently is a symbol of heroism with Jews who often raise the cry "*Masada shall not fall again.*"
It is interesting that the Southern Kingdom was restored as the nation of Israel in 1948 after it had lost its status as a nation in 605 BC; thus, while Jesus did not inform the disciples of the time or season of the restoration, He did imply that its restoration would occur. Its restoration has now occurred. The nation of Israel was restored in 1948. Jerusalem has also been restored. The Jewish people recaptured Jerusalem in 1967 in what is called the Six Day War.

80. Discussion in McBirnie, *The Search for the Twelve Apostles*, 168.

Although there is little reference in the Bible to Simon the Zealot, other than to list him as one of the twelve apostles,[81] historians describe him as a fervent preacher who carried the message of salvation to Egypt, Cyrene, Africa, Spain, and Britain, and report that he wrought many miracles.[82] Simon also preached the Gospel with Jude Thaddaeus in Syria, Mesopotamia, and Persia (now Iran). Eusebius reported that after James the Just, the brother of Jesus, had suffered martyrdom, Simon was appointed the second bishop of the church in Jerusalem.[83]

Although Simon is alleged to have lived a long life, he also suffered martyrdom for his faith in Christ. Eusebius[84] reported that Simon suffered martyrdom at the age of 120, when Trajan was emperor, stating that after being tormented for many days, ". . . he died a martyr, with such firmness that all were amazed . . . that a man of a hundred and twenty years should bear such tortures. He was at last ordered to be crucified." Simon is reported by some to have suffered martyrdom in Persia; his body is in a tomb with Jude Thaddaeus in St. Peter's in Rome.[85]

VII. Thomas, the Doubter

The disciple, Thomas, was also known as Didymus, which means "twin," but there is no information as to a twin. Thomas was one of the twelve disciples who is portrayed in the Bible as being fearless and aggressive in his defense of Jesus but also as originally having doubts about Jesus' divinity. Thomas is referred to as "doubting Thomas;" however, after Jesus' resurrection, Thomas became a bold and faithful follower of the Lord. Thomas' uncertainty at times about Jesus' divinity provides assurance to other believers

---

81. See Matthew 10:4, Mark 4:18, Luke 6:15.

82. Discussion in McBirnie, *The Search for the Twelve Apostles*, 160, 174.

83. Eusebius, *Ecclesiastical History*, 134.
Still, in about 62 AD, after the death of the James, who was the half-brother of Jesus, the fellowship of Christians lost importance in Jerusalem. If Simon was the second bishop of Jerusalem, he would either have been put to death before or during the siege of Jerusalem that began in 70 AD or he would have left the church before that and then traveled to many other countries to spread the message of salvation.
Some contend the second bishop of the church in Jerusalem was another of Jesus' half-brothers, a half-brother named Simon. Matthew mentions the half-brother Simon in his Gospel, at Matt 13:55.

84. Eusebius, *Ecclesiastical History*, 98, and *The History of the Church*, 95.

85. McBirnie, *The Search for the Twelve Apostles*, 175.

The Remaining Eight Disciples

that they have Jesus' understanding and forgiveness when they at times also waiver in their faith.

John records that when Jesus told His disciples to go with Him to Lazarus' home in Judea after Jesus was told Lazarus had died, His disciples tried to dissuade Him from going there, but Thomas opposed the other disciples. "Now Jesus loved Martha, and her sister, and Lazarus. When therefore He heard that he was sick, He stayed then two days longer in the place where He was. Then after this He said to the disciples, 'Let us go to Judea again.' The disciples said to Him, 'Rabbi, the Jews were just now going to stone You, and are You going there again?'"[86] Jesus said to His disciples,[87] "Lazarus is dead and I am glad for your sakes that I was not there, so that you may believe; but let us go to him." Thomas agreed and encouraged the rest of the disciples to go with Jesus:[88] "Thomas therefore, who is called Didymus, said to his fellow disciples, 'Let us also go that we may die with Him.'"

Shortly before Jesus' crucifixion, Thomas revealed his lack of understanding of Jesus' mission despite the fact that he had been with Jesus as one of the Twelve. At the Last Supper, Jesus said to His disciples,[89] "'Let not your heart be troubled; believe in God, believe also in Me. In My Father's house are many mansions; if it were not so, I would have told you. I go to prepare a place for you. And if I go and prepare a place for you, I will come again and receive you to Myself; that where I am there you may be also. And where I go you know, and the way you know.'" Thomas though questioned Jesus. "Thomas said to Him, 'Lord, we do not know where You are going, how do we know the way?' Jesus said to him, 'I am the way and the truth, and the life, no one comes to the Father, but through Me.'"[90]

Thomas was not with the disciples when Jesus appeared to them after His resurrection. The other disciples later said to Thomas,[91] "'We have seen the Lord.' So he said to them, 'Unless I see in His hands the print of the nails, and put my finger into the print of the nails, and put my hand into His side, I will not believe.'" A week later, Thomas was with the disciples

---

86. John 11:5–8, NASB.
87. John 11:14a–15, NASB.
88. John 11:16, NASB.
89. John 14:1–4, NKJV.
90. John 14:5–6, NASB.
91. John 20:25, NKJV.

when Jesus again appeared to them. After Jesus said to Thomas:[92] "Reach your finger here, and look at My hands; and reach your hand here, and put it into My side. Do not be unbelieving, but believing." Thomas then said to Jesus:[93] ". . . My Lord and my God." Jesus replied to Thomas:[94] ". . . Thomas, because you have seen Me, you have believed? Blessed are those who have not seen and yet have believed."

Later, Thomas was with six of the disciples when Jesus appeared to them at the Sea of Galilee where they were fishing. "After these things Jesus showed Himself again to the disciples at the Sea of Tiberias, and in this way He showed Himself: Simon Peter, and Thomas called the twin, Nathanael of Cana in Galilee, and the sons of Zebedee, and two others of His disciples were together."[95] The disciples had caught nothing until Jesus, whom they did not recognize, told them to cast their net on the right-hand side of the boat. The disciples did so, and after then catching more fish than they could bring in, John said to Peter,[96] ". . . It is the Lord.!"

After Jesus' ascension into heaven, Thomas was in Jerusalem with the other disciples to choose a disciple to replace Judas Iscariot. "Then they returned to Jerusalem from the mount called Olivet, which is near Jerusalem, a Sabbath day's journey. And when they had entered, they went up into the upper room, where they were staying: Peter, James, John, and Andrew; Philip and Thomas; Bartholomew and Matthew; James the son of Alphaeus and Simon the Zealot; and Judas the son[97] of James."[98] Matthias became the twelfth disciple who joined the eleven to take the place of Judas Iscariot. "And they cast their lots, and the lot fell on Matthias. And he was numbered with the eleven apostles."[99]

Although Thomas had doubted Jesus resurrection, after he witnessed that fact for himself and had seen Jesus' ascension into heaven, Thomas became a most faithful and aggressive follower of the Lord. He was one of the few who carried the message of salvation to foreign lands outside the

---

92. John 20:27, NKJV.
93. John 20:28, NKJV.
94. John 20:29, NKJV.
95. John 21:1–2, NKJV.
96. John 21:7, NKJV.
97. Or brother.
98. Acts 1:13, NKJV.
99. Acts 1:26, NKJV.

The Remaining Eight Disciples

Roman empire. He sent Jude Thaddeus to Edessa,[100] established the first Christian Church in Babylon, and then, according to one historian, was led by the Holy Spirit to India.[101] Eusebius reported that Thomas was chosen for Parthia, which is now Iran,[102] and affirmed that Syrian Christians of Malabar, India, who call themselves the Christians of St. Thomas, defended their claim that Thomas took Christianity to India.[103]

Thomas also suffered a martyr's death. He is reported to have been pierced with a lance at a place near Madras, India; his remains reportedly were later moved from India to Edessa and then to Italy.[104]

VIII. Judas Iscariot, the Betrayer

Judas Iscariot was one of the Twelve until Jesus crucifixion. "And He appointed the twelve: . . . and Judas Iscariot, who also betrayed Him."[105] There is a question why Jesus chose Judas Iscariot because Jesus knew from the beginning that Judas would betray Him.[106] Jesus said to His disciples:[107] "'But there are some of you who do not believe.' For Jesus knew from the beginning who they were who did not believe, and who would betray Him." Jesus later responded to His disciples,[108] "'Did I Myself not choose you, the twelve, and yet one of you is a devil?' Now He meant Judas, the son of Simon Iscariot, for he, one of the twelve, was going to betray Him."

---

100. Eusebius, *Ecclesiastical History*, 30. Eusebius reported in *The History of the Church*, 37, that Thomas was moved by inspiration to send Thaddaeus to Edessa as preacher and evangelist for the teaching about Christ.

101. McBirnie, *The Search for the Twelve Apostles*, 118.

102. Eusebius, *The History of the Church*, 65.

103. Eusebius, *The History of the Church*, 423.

104. McBirnie, *The Search for the Twelve Apostles*, 122, 124–25.

105. Mark 3:13–19, NASB.

106. Jesus knew Judas' heart and knew he would betray Him, but Jesus' appointing Judas as a disciple fulfilled the Scriptures. As recorded in Psalms 41:9, NASB, "Even my close friend, in whom I trusted, who ate my bread, has lifted up his heel against me." However, Jesus quoted the Scriptures somewhat differently, as He did not trust Judas. John quoted Jesus at John 13:18, NASB, as follows: "I do not speak of all of you. I know the ones I have chosen; but it is that the Scripture may be fulfilled, 'He who eats My bread has lifted up his heel against Me.'" Jesus did not add the quote from the Scriptures: ". . . my close friend, in whom I trusted."

107. John 6:64, NKJV.

108. John 6:70–71, NASB.

Judas Iscariot was the treasurer for the Twelve; as such, he was concerned about money, but he was also a thief. When Mary, the sister of Martha and Lazarus, took some expensive perfume to anoint Jesus' feet, Judas criticized her. As recorded in John,[109] "Then Mary took a pound of very costly oil of spikenard, anointed the feet of Jesus, and wiped His feet with her hair. And the house was filled with the fragrance of the oil. But one of His disciples, Judas Iscariot, Simon's son, who would betray Him, said 'Why was this fragrant oil not sold for three hundred denarii, and given to the poor people?' This he said, not that he cared for the poor, but because he was a thief, and had the money box, and he used to take what was put in it. But Jesus said, 'Let her alone, she has kept this for my burial. For the poor you have with you always, but Me you do not have always.'"

Just prior to the Passover meal, at the Last Supper, Judas Iscariot left the group to betray the Lord. "Then Judas Iscariot, who of the twelve, went to the chief priests to betray Him to them."[110] Matthew records the event as follows:[111] "Then one of the twelve, called Judas Iscariot, went to the chief priests and said, 'What are you willing to give me if I deliver Him to you?' And they counted out to him thirty pieces of silver. So from that time he sought opportunity to betray Him." Luke also reported the tragedy: "Satan entered into Judas who was called Iscariot, belonging to the number of the twelve. And he went away and discussed with the chief priests and officers how he might betray Him to them. And they were glad, and agreed to give him money. And he consented, and began seeking an opportunity to betray Him to them apart from the multitude."[112]

During the Passover meal, Jesus informed the disciples that one of them would betray Him. "And as they were reclining at the table and eating Jesus said, 'Truly I say to you that one of you will betray me–one who is eating with Me.' They began to be grieved and to say to Him one by one, 'Surely not I?' And He said to them, 'It is one of the twelve, one who dips with Me in the bowl. For the Son of Man is to go just as it is written of Him; but woe to that man by whom the Son of Man is betrayed! It would have been good for that man if he had not been born.'"[113]

---

109. John 12:3–8, NKJV.
110. Mark 14:10, NKJV.
111. Matt 26:14–16, NKJV.
112. Luke 22:3–6, NASB.
113. Mark 14:21, NASB. See also Luke 22:21–22.

The Remaining Eight Disciples

Judas tried to assure Jesus that he was not that person. As recorded in Matthew,[114] "Then Judas, who was betraying Him, answered and said, 'Rabbi, is it I?' He said to him, 'You have said it.'" John reported that when the disciples asked who would betray Him, Jesus revealed that the betrayer was Judas but that the disciples did not understand. As written in John,[115] "Jesus answered, 'It is he to whom I shall give a piece of bread when I have dipped it.' And having dipped the bread, He gave it to Judas Iscariot, the son of Simon. Now after the piece of bread, Satan entered him. Then Jesus said to him, 'What you do, do quickly.' But no one at the table knew for what reason He said this to him. For some thought, because Judas had the money box, that Jesus had said to him, 'Buy those things we need for the feast,' or that he should give something to the poor. Having received the piece of bread, he then went out immediately. And it was night. So when he had gone out, Jesus said, 'Now is the Son of Man glorified, and God is glorified in Him.'"

After Jesus had prayed in the Garden of Gethsemane, Jesus knew Judas would be bringing the guards to arrest Him. He said to his disciples–Peter, James, and John–who had gone with Him away from the other disciples:[116] "'Arise let us be going; behold, the one who betrays Me is at hand!' And while He was still speaking, behold, Judas, one of the twelve, came up accompanied by a great multitude with swords and clubs, from the chief priests and elders of the people. Now he who was betraying Him gave them a sign, saying, 'Whomever I shall kiss, He is the one; seize Him.' And immediately he went to Jesus and said, 'Hail, Rabbi!' and kissed Him. And Jesus said to him, 'Friend, do what you have come for.' Then they came and laid hands on Jesus and seized Him."

Judas later regretted his action but rather than asking forgiveness, he took his life. "Then Judas, His betrayer, seeing that He had been condemned, was remorseful and brought back the thirty pieces of silver to the chief priests and elders, saying, 'I have sinned by betraying innocent blood.' And they said, 'What is that to us? You see to it!' Then he threw down the pieces of silver in the temple and departed, and went and hanged himself. But the chief priests took the silver pieces and said, 'It is not lawful to put them into the treasury, because they are the price of blood.' And they counseled together and bought with them the potter's field to bury strangers in.

---

114. Matt 26:25, NKJV.
115. John 13:26-31, NKJV.
116. Matt 26:46-50, NASB.

Therefore that field has been called the Field of Blood to this day. Then was fulfilled what was spoken through Jeremiah the prophet, saying, 'And they took the thirty pieces of silver, the value of Him who was priced, whom they of children of Israel priced, and gave them for the potter's field, as the Lord directed me.'"[117]

Peter also betrayed Jesus, but while he was overcome with grief, he did not take his life; rather he asked forgiveness and lived to see Jesus resurrected. Further, after receiving the Holy Spirit at Pentecost, Peter became a fearless preacher and a leader in the early church. In contrast, Judas did not turn to the Lord for forgiveness. His lack of belief led to his destruction. A question remains whether, had Judas Iscariot asked for forgiveness and had lived to see Jesus resurrected, he too might have become a witness for the Lord.

After Jesus ascension, the remaining eleven disciples met and chose a disciple to replace Judas Iscariot. As recorded in Acts,[118] "And at this time Peter stood up in the midst of the brethren (a gathering of about one hundred and twenty persons were there together), and said, 'Brethren, the Scripture had to be fulfilled, which the Holy Spirit foretold by the mouth of David concerning Judas, who became a guide to those who arrested Jesus. For he was counted among us and received his portion in this ministry.'" Peter referred to the Field of Blood that was acquired with the thirty pieces of silver and quoted Psalms:[119] "For it is written in the book of Psalms: Let his dwelling place be desolate, And let no one dwell in it'; and 'Let another take his office.'"[120] Peter then declared that they must appoint a disciple to replace Judas Iscariot–that person was Matthias.

IX. Matthias, the Chosen Successor

Matthias was chosen by lot for the apostleship to take the place of Judas Iscariot.[121] Following Jesus' resurrection and prior to Pentecost, the remaining eleven disciples decided they must find another to replace Judas

---

117. Matt 27:3–10, NKJV. The Field of Blood that was purchased with the thirty pieces of silver is located just outside the Jerusalem old city in the Valley of Hinnon near the Kidron Valley.

118. Acts 1:16–17, NASB.

119. Psalms 69:25, 109:8.

120. Acts 1:20, NKJV.

121. Eusebius, *The History of the Church*, 35.

The Remaining Eight Disciples

Iscariot. The eleven decided to nominate two men: Joseph, called Barsabbas, and Matthias. They then prayed:[122] "Lord, you know everyone's heart. Show us which of these two you have chosen to take over this apostolic ministry, which Judas left to go where he belongs. Then they cast lots, and the lot fell to Matthias; so he was added to the eleven apostles."

Little is known about Matthias, but he may have been one of the seventy persons, referred to in Chapter 1, that Jesus also appointed early in His ministry to help spread His message. As recorded in Luke,[123] "After this the Lord appointed seventy others also, and sent them two and two before His face into every city and place where He Himself was about to go." Eusebius affirmed that no list of the seventy has ever been found, but he did state there is evidence Matthias and the other man honored like him in the drawing of lots had been called to be among the seventy.[124]

One historian credited Matthias, along with Thaddaeus, Bartholomew, Simon the Zealot, and Andrew, with evangelizing Armenia.[125] He also stated that Matthias may have been at first a disciple of John the Baptist and would have been in Jerusalem on the day of Pentecost.[126] This historian referred to ancient church tradition that presumes Matthias suffered martyrdom either by lance or by an axe either in Judea, Colchis, or Sebastopol in 64 AD and that early church writers contend his body was in Jerusalem but later taken to Rome and then transported to Trier, Germany.[127] Another historian reported that Matthias was stoned at Jerusalem and then beheaded.[128] In whatever context, Matthias suffered a martyr's death for his faithful service in spreading the message of salvation.

Some contend that the apostle Paul should be considered as the twelfth disciple to replace Judas Iscariot because Jesus Himself chose Paul to be one of His followers, whereas Matthias acquired his status as a disciple from the eleven when they drew lots to decide who should replace Judas Iscariot. To counter this argument, one must consider the requirements Peter set out for a twelfth disciple. Luke recorded Peter's words regarding

---

122. Acts 1:21–26.
123. Luke 10:1, NKJV.
124. Eusebius, *This History of the Church*, 29–30.
125. McBirnie, *The Search for the Twelve Apostles*, 184.
126. McBirnie, *The Search for the Twelve Apostles*, 188–89.
127. McBirnie, *The Search for the Twelve Apostles*, 186.
128. Foxe, *Fox's Book of Martyrs*, 13.

a successor for Judas Iscariot as follows:[129] "It is therefore necessary that of the men who have accompanied us all the time that the Lord Jesus went in and out among us—beginning with the baptism of John, until the day that He was taken up from us—one of these should become a witness with us of His resurrection."

Matthias would have met the requirements Peter set out, and Paul did not. Eusebius stated that Matthias probably was one of the seventy[130] and, as noted above, he may have been a disciple of John the Baptist.[131] Additionally, Paul did not consider himself as one of the Twelve; he never claimed to be one of the Twelve. As Paul stated to the Corinthians, the resurrected Christ appeared "... to the twelve ..."[132] and "... and last of all, as it were to one untimely born, He appeared to me also."[133]

Paul had a distinctive calling but to a different people. Although Paul also preached to the Jewish people, his special calling was to establish the first Gentile churches across the Roman empire. Paul's message was separate and distinct from Peter's and from the other eleven. The story of Paul's life follows.

---

129. Acts 1:21–22, NASB.
130. Eusebius, *This History of the Church*, 392.
131. McBirnie, *The Search for the Twelve Apostles*, 188.
132. 1 Cor 15:5.
133. I Cor 15:8, NASB.

4

Paul (Saul of Tarsus)

PAUL, WHO WAS FIRST called Saul, was a devout Jew, born about 4 BC in Tarsus, the capital of the province of Cilicia.[1] His parents apparently moved to Jerusalem when he was young; thus, Jerusalem would have been his boyhood home. Still, because Paul was born in Cilicia, and Cilicia was part of the Roman empire, Paul had Roman citizenship. As noted below, his Roman citizenship later proved to be advantageous in his ministry to the Gentiles.

Paul studied under Gamaliel, who lived in Jerusalem and was the leading rabbi and teacher at that time. After Paul's later conversion, Paul left Jerusalem, but following his return there later, he to related to James[2] and the elders at Jerusalem ". . . those things which God had done among the Gentiles through his ministry, . . ."[3] and stated to them: "I am indeed a Jew, born in Tarsus of Cilicia, but brought up in this city at the feet of Gamaliel, taught according to the strictness of our fathers' law, and was zealous for

---

1. Cilicia, a Roman province and seat of the ancient kingdom of Armenia, was located in the southern part of what is now Turkey. Tarsus was a city in historic Cilicia.

2. This James was the half-brother of Jesus and at that time was the bishop of the church in Jerusalem. Discussion in Acts 21:18.

3. Acts 21:19b, NKJV.

God, just as you all are today."[4] Paul informed believers at Philippi[5] that he was "... circumcised the eighth day, of the nation of Israel, of the tribe of Benjamin, a Hebrew of Hebrews, as to the Law a Pharisee; as to zeal, a persecutor of the church; as to the righteousness which is in the Law, found blameless." Paul later related to members of the church at Galatia his earlier life in Jerusalem:[6] "For you have heard of my former manner of life in Judaism, how I used to persecute the church of God beyond measure, and tried to destroy it; and I was advancing in Judaism beyond many of my contemporaries among my countrymen, being more extremely zealous for my ancestral traditions."

As a strict Jew living in Jerusalem, Saul witnessed the slaying of Stephen and was at that time in agreement with the stoning. As recorded in Acts:[7] "And when they had driven him out of the city, they began stoning him, and the witnesses laid aside their robes at the feet of a young man named Saul. And they went on stoning Stephen as he called upon the Lord and said, 'Lord Jesus, receive my spirit!' And falling on his knees, he cried out with a loud voice, 'Lord, do not hold this sin against them!' And having said this, he fell asleep. And Saul was in hearty agreement with putting him to death. And on that day a great persecution arose against the church in Jerusalem; and they were all scattered throughout the regions of Judea

---

4. Acts 22:3b, NKJV. Luke referred to Gamaliel as a Pharisee and a teacher of the Law "... who was held in respect by all the people..." Acts 5:34, NKJV.

Luke later referred to Gamaliel as having defended the early believers in Jerusalem; Gamaliel probably saved the lives of Peter and John. As recorded in Acts 5, the sect of the Sadducees had brought Peter and John before the Sanhedrin wherein they were told to cease preaching about Jesus. When Peter and John continued their preaching, the Jewish leaders again brought them before the Sanhedrin and reminded them of earlier instructions that they were to cease proclaiming Jesus to the people. After Peter and John once again refused to stop preaching despite the threats, and Peter responded, as recorded at Acts 5:29b, NKJV: "We ought to obey God rather than men," Luke reported that the Jewish rulers intended to put Peter and John to death. However, Gamaliel stood up to support Peter and John, stating: "... I say to you, stay away from these men and let them alone, for if this plan or action should be of men, it will be overthrown; but if it is of God, you will not be able to overthrow them, or else you may even be found fighting against God." Acts 5:38-39, NASB. Based on Gamaliel's advice, the Jewish rulers released Peter and John, both of whom "... did not cease teaching and preaching Jesus as the Christ." Acts 5:42b, NKJV. Obviously, the teaching and preaching from Peter and John was of God, and not of men, as there now are about 2.5 billion Christians in the world.

5. Phil 3:5-6, NASB.
6. Gal 1:13-14, NASB.
7. Acts 7:58-60; 8:1-3, NASB.

Paul (Saul of Tarsus)

and Samaria, except the apostles . . . But Saul began ravaging the church, entering house after house; and dragging off men and women, he would put them in prison." Later, after Paul was converted, he acknowledged that he had "ravaged the church" and that he had approved of Stephen's martyrdom. Luke reported that Paul had said: ". . . 'Lord, they know that in every synagogue I imprisoned and beat those who believed on You. And when the blood of Your martyr Stephen was shed, I also was standing by consenting to his death, and guarding the clothes of those who were killing him.'"[8]

Saul continued to persecute the followers of Jesus until he met the Lord on his way to Damascus.[9] As recorded in Acts:[10] "Meanwhile Saul was still breathing out murderous threats against the Lord's disciples. He went to the high priest and asked him for letters to the synagogues in Damascus, so that if he found any who belonged to the Way, whether men or women, he might take them as prisoners to Jerusalem. As he neared Damascus on his journey, suddenly a light from heaven flashed around him. He fell to the ground and heard a voice say to him, 'Saul, Saul, why do you persecute Me?' 'Who art You, Lord?' Saul asked. 'I am Jesus, whom you are persecuting,' he replied. 'Now get up and go into the city, and you will be told what you must do.' The men traveling with Saul stood there speechless; they heard the sound but did not see anyone. Saul got up from the ground, but when he opened his eyes he could see nothing. So they led him by the hand into Damascus. For three days he was blind, and did not eat or drink anything. In Damascus, there was a certain disciple named Ananias. The Lord called him in a vision, 'Ananias.' 'Yes, Lord,' he answered. The Lord told him, 'Go to the house of Judas on Straight Street and ask for a man from Tarsus, named Saul, for he is praying. In a vision he has seen a man named Ananias come and place his hands on him to restore his sight.' 'Lord,' Ananias answered, 'I have heard many reports about this man and all the harm he has done to Your holy people in Jerusalem. And he has come here with authority from the chief priests to arrest all who call on Your name.' But the Lord said to Ananias, 'Go! This man is My chosen

---

8. Acts 22:19–20, NKJV.

9. Damascus is the capital of Syria. It is questionable why Saul was traveling there to persecute the early Christians as it was recorded that after Stephen's slaying, and except for the apostles, Jesus' followers were ". . . scattered throughout the regions of Judea and Samaria." See Acts 8:1b, NKJV. There is no mention of Syria; thus, some contend the reference to "Damascus" was to a refuge called Damascus.

10. Acts 9:1–18, NIV. See also Acts 22:1–21. The followers and believers of Jesus were first called the Way.

instrument to proclaim My name to the Gentiles, and their kings, and to the people of Israel. I will show him how much he must suffer for My name.' Then Ananias went to the house and entered it. Placing his hands on Saul, he said, 'Brother Saul, the Lord—Jesus, who appeared to you on the road as you were coming here—has sent me so you may see again and be filled with the Holy Spirit.' Immediately something like scales fell from Saul's eyes, and he could see again. He got up and was baptized, and after taking some food, he regained his strength."

Following Ananias laying hands on Paul and Paul then being filled with the Holy Spirit, Paul, a devout Jew, also became a devout Christian. He was baptized, stayed for several days with the disciples who were at Damascus, and then he immediately ". . . preached the Christ in the synagogues, that He is the Son of God."[11]

Paul informed the Philippians of his undivided devotion to Jesus whom he called the Christ.[12] "But whatever things were gain to me, those things I have counted as loss for the sake of Christ. More than that, I count all things to be loss in view of the surpassing value of knowing Christ Jesus my Lord, for whom I have suffered the loss of all things, and count them but rubbish in order that I may gain Christ, and may be found in Him, not having a righteousness of my own derived from the Law, but that which is through faith in Christ, the righteousness which comes from God on the basis of faith, that I may know Him, and the power of His resurrection and the fellowship of His sufferings, being conformed to His death; in order that I may attain to the resurrection from the dead. Not that I have already become perfect, but I press on in order that I may lay hold of that for which also I was laid hold of by Christ Jesus. Brethren, I do not regard myself as having laid hold of it yet; but one thing I do: forgetting what lies behind and reaching forward to what lies ahead, I press on toward the goal for the prize of the upward call of God in Christ Jesus." Paul told the believers at Philippi:[13] "Therefore also God highly exalted Him, and bestowed on Him the name which is above every name, that at the name of Jesus every knee should bow, of those who are in heaven, and on earth, and under the earth, and that every tongue should confess that Jesus Christ is Lord, to the glory of God the Father." As Eusebius confirmed, Paul brought the message of

---

11. Acts 9:20, NKJV. See also Acts 9:17:19.

12. Phil 3:8–14, NASB.

13. Phil 2:9–11, NASB.

Paul (Saul of Tarsus)

salvation to the Gentiles ". . . in the power of Christ, who had said to them:" 'Go and make disciples of all the nations in my name.'"[14]

Paul acknowledged that he ". . . was unknown by face to the churches of Judea which were in Christ."[15] Nonetheless, Paul referred to himself as an apostle and affirmed that status in a letter to the church in Corinth:[16] "Am I not an apostle? Am I not free? Have I not seen Jesus our Lord? Are you not my work in the Lord? If I am not an apostle to others, yet doubtless I am to you. For you are the seal of my apostleship in the Lord."

Unfortunately, Paul continued to have problems with Jesus' followers. They did not trust him until Barnabas described Paul's conversion to them. As recorded in Acts, when Paul tried to associate with the disciples in Jerusalem, ". . . they were all afraid of him, not believing that he was a disciple. But Barnabas took hold of him and brought him to the apostles and described to them how he had seen the Lord on the road, and that He had talked to him, and how at Damascus he had spoken out boldly in the name of Jesus."[17] After that, Paul ". . . was with them at Jerusalem, coming in and going out. And he spoke boldly in the name of the Lord Jesus . . ."[18]

Peter carried the gospel to the Jewish people, Paul to the Gentiles. Paul wrote to the believers at Galatia:[19] "As for those who were held in high esteem—whatever they were makes no difference to me; God does not show favoritism—they added nothing to my message. On the contrary, they recognized that I had been entrusted with the task of preaching the gospel to the uncircumcised, just as Peter had been to the circumcised. For God, who was at work in Peter as an apostle to the circumcised, was also at work in me as an apostle to the Gentiles. James, Cephas and John, those esteemed as pillars, gave me and Barnabas the right hand of fellowship when they recognized the grace given to me. They agreed that we should go to the Gentiles, and they to the circumcised. All they asked was that we should continue to remember the poor, the very thing I had been eager to do all along."

Eusebius referred to Philip the Evangelist as the first person to bring the message of salvation to the Gentiles, that occasioned by Philip's witness

---

14. Eusebius, *The History of the Church*, 68, quoting Matt 28:19.
15. Gal 1:22, NKJV.
16. 1 Cor 9:1–2, NKJV.
17. Acts 9:26–27, NASB.
18. Acts 9:28–29b, NKJV.
19. Gal 2:6–10, NIV.

to an Ethiopian.[20] According to Eusebius, the Ethiopian then was "... the first to go back to his native land and preach the gospel of the knowledge of the God of the universe ...." Eusebius affirmed this encounter was the first stage in "... the life-giving sojourn of our Savior among men."[21] He then asserted that the "... next stage began when Paul ... was appointed an apostle ...."[22] Luke affirmed in Acts that Paul was filled with the Holy Spirit:[23] "Then Saul, who also is called Paul, filled with the Holy Spirit ..."

Paul founded many churches in Asia Minor and in Europe.[24] As recorded in Acts, he carried the Gospel to Macedonia, Syria, Greece, Ephesus, Caesarea, Antioch, Derbe, Lystra, Thessalonica, Corinth, Galatia, Spain, and Rome, among others.[25] Paul recorded in his Epistle to the Galatians that he brought the message of salvation to Arabia and Damascus,[26] and to the regions of Syria and Cilicia.[27] Further, in his letter to the believers in Rome, Paul referred to his travels to Macedonia, to Achaia, which is now called Greece, and to Spain.[28]

Paul traveled about 13,000 miles, much of it on foot, to spread the message of salvation. At various times, Paul took with him on his missionary

---

20. Philip brought the message first to the Gentiles when he met with the Ethiopian. See Acts 8:26–39. Discussion in Chapter 5 on the life of Philip the Evangelist.

21. Eusebius, *The History of the Church*, 37–38.

22. Eusebius, *The History of the Church*, 39. Eusebius stated that Paul received "... his call through a vision and the heavenly voice that accompanied the revelation ..." and referred to Paul as "... the chosen vessel–neither from men nor through men, but through revelation of Jesus Christ Himself and God the Father who raised Him from the dead ...." Eusebius, *The History of the Church*, 39.

23. Acts 13:9a, NKJV.

24. Eusebius recorded, in *The History of the Church*, 83, that Paul founded the church at Ephesus.

25. Acts 18.

26. Gal 1:17.

27. Gal 1:21.

28. Rom 15:24, 26.

journeys Barnabas, John Mark,[29] Titus,[30] Timothy,[31] Silas,[32] also called Silvanus,[33] Luke,[34] and at one time Aquila and his wife Priscilla.[35]

On his first missionary journey, which occurred in about 46-48 AD,[36] Paul was accompanied by Barnabas and for a short time, John Mark. After returning from that first missionary journey, Luke reported in Acts:[37] "And Barnabas and Saul returned from Jerusalem when they had fulfilled their mission, taking along with them John, who was also called Mark." Paul, Barnabas, and John Mark carried the gospel to Seleucia, a seaport in Syria. The trio then left Seleucia and sailed to Cyprus.[38] They landed at Salamis, which was a city on the east coast of Cyprus, and ". . . they preached the word of God in the synagogues of the Jews."[39] Then Paul, Barnabas, and John Mark ". . . set sail from Paphos . . . and . . . came to Perga in Pamphylia . . ." where ". . . John, departing from them, returned to Jerusalem."[40] It is unclear why John Mark deserted Paul and Barnabas at Perga in Pamphylia,[41] but it later led to a major disagreement between Paul and Barnabas.

---

29. Acts 13:46, 50; 15: 2, 22, 37-38; Gal 2:1.

30. Referred to in Gal 2:1. Eusebius is recorded in *The History of the Church*, 67, as affirming that Titus was credited as being the first bishop appointed to the churches of Crete.

31. Referred to in 2 Cor 1:1, Phil 1:1, 1 Thess 1:1, 2 Thess 1:1, 1 Tim 1:2, 2 Tim 2:1, Phlm 1:1. Eusebius recorded in *The History of the Church*, 67, that Timothy was stated to have been the first bishop appointed to the see, or diocese, of Ephesus.

32. Acts 15:22; 17:10, 15.

33. 1 Thess 1:1, 2 Thess 1:1.

34. Luke refers to his accompanying Paul on his third missionary journey in Acts 20:6, 13; 21:1. Silas and Timothy apparently were also with Paul on this journey.

35. Acts 18:18.

36. Acts 13 to 15:35.

37. Acts 12:25, NASB.

38. Acts 13:4.

39. Acts 13:5, NKJV.

40. Acts 13:13, NKJV. Paphos was a coastal city in Cyprus; Perga was the capital of Pamphylia, which was a province in Asia Minor.

41. Some have suggested that Mark did not, at that time, fully accept Paul's doctrine of salvation by grace through faith alone. See discussion in McBirnie, *The Search for the Twelve Apostles*, 194. McBirnie stated that at that time Mark was still a devout Jew and perhaps unable to accept the doctrine of faith for salvation. Additionally, Mark was young then and may not have been strong enough for another strenuous journey. As Barnabas' cousin, he may also have been disturbed because Paul had by then replaced Barnabas as the leader of the Gentile mission.

From Pamphylia, Paul and Barnabas traveled to Antioch in what was then Galatia, now Turkey, but then proceeded back to Jerusalem where Paul faced the Council in Jerusalem regarding the issue of whether the Gentile believers should be circumcised.

Paul earlier reflected that he and Peter had opposing views on his carrying the message of salvation to the Gentiles. Paul explained this disagreement to the Gentiles at Galatia while pointing out to them that they were saved by the grace of God. "Now when Peter came to Antioch, I withstood him to his face, because he was to be blamed; for before certain men came from James, he would eat with the Gentiles; but when they came, he withdrew and separated himself, fearing those who were of the circumcision. And the rest of the Jews also played the hypocrite with him, so that even Barnabas was carried away by their hypocrisy. But when I saw that they were not straightforward about the truth of the gospel, I said to Peter before them all, 'If you, being a Jew, live in the manner of Gentiles and not as the Jews, why do you compel Gentiles to live like Jews? We who are Jews by nature, and not sinners of the Gentiles, knowing that a man is not justified by the works of the law but by faith in Jesus Christ, even we have believed in Christ Jesus, that we might be justified by faith in Christ and not by the works of the law; for by the works of the law no flesh shall be justified . . . For I through the Law died to the law that I might live to God. I have been crucified with Christ; it is no longer I who live, but Christ lives in me; and the life which I now live in the flesh I live by faith in the Son of God, who loved me, and gave Himself for me. I do not set aside the grace of God; for if righteousness comes through the law, then Christ died in vain.'"[42] Paul told the Galatians,[43] "Even so Abraham believed God, and it was reckoned to him as righteousness. Therefore, be sure that it is those who are of faith who are sons of Abraham." With respect to Peter's initial agreement with the Jewish believers that the Gentile believers should be circumcised, Paul wrote in his letter to the Galatians, "Behold I, Paul, say to you that if you receive circumcision, Christ will be of no benefit to you."

Although Peter earlier had disagreements with Paul on the question of circumcision for the Gentiles, Peter later agreed with Paul that Gentile believers need not be circumcised, and at the Council of Jerusalem,[44] Peter supported Paul in his mission to the Gentiles. Luke recorded Peter's

---

42. Gal 2:11–21, NKJV.
43. Gal 3:7–8, NASB.
44. Acts 15.

response to the debate on the issue of circumcision of the Gentile believers as follows. "And the apostles and the elders came together to look into this matter, and after there had been much debate, Peter stood up and said to them, 'Brethren, you know that in the early days God made a choice among you, that by my mouth the Gentiles should hear the word of the gospel and believe, and God, who knows the heart, bore witness to them, giving them the Holy Spirit, just as He also did to us; and He made no distinction between us and them, cleansing their hearts by faith. Now therefore why do you put God to the test by placing upon the neck of the Gentiles a yoke which neither our fathers nor we have been able to bear? But we believe that we are saved through the grace of the Lord Jesus, the same way as they also are.'"[45] Peter also later referred to Paul as ". . . our beloved brother Paul, according to the wisdom given to him."[46]

Before Paul began his second missionary journey, Paul had a disagreement with Barnabas about John Mark that led to Barnabas' failure to accompany Paul on any more of the missionary journeys.[47] Luke recorded in the book of Acts the disagreement between Paul and Barnabas after Mark left them:[48] "But Paul and Barnabas stayed in Antioch, teaching and preaching, with many others also, the word of the Lord. And after some days Paul said to Barnabas, 'Let us return and visit the brethren in every city in which we proclaimed the word of the Lord, and see how they are.' And Barnabas was desirous of taking John, called Mark, along with them also. But Paul kept insisting that they should not take him along who had deserted them in Pamphylia and had not gone with them to the work. And there arose such a sharp disagreement that they separated from one another, and Barnabas took Mark with him and sailed away to Cyprus. But Paul chose Silas and departed, being committed by the brethren to the grace of

---

45. Acts 15:7–11, NASB.

46. 2 Pet 3:15, NKJV.

47. Paul wanted Barnabas to accompany him, but because of the disagreement when Barnabas wanted John Mark to go as well, and Paul refused to permit John Mark to join them, Barnabas traveled with John Mark to Cyprus, and Silas accompanied Paul. Following the disagreement about John Mark, Barnabas never again traveled with Paul although John Mark did later rejoin Paul. See Acts 15:36–41 and 2 Tim 4:11. Perhaps the disagreement had some favorable results in that it led to a more expansive spread of the Gospel with Barnabas and John Mark going to Cyprus and Paul and Silas journeying to Syria and Cilicia.

48. Acts 15:34–41, NASB.

the Lord. And he was traveling through Syria and Cilicia, strengthening the churches."

Paul began his second missionary journey at Jerusalem;[49] this second journey occurred from about 49 or 51 AD to approximately 53 AD. Paul traveled from Jerusalem to Damascus, then to Antioch in Syria, and from there to Tarsus, which was then in Cilicia; from there to Derbe, then to Lystra, Antioch, Troas, all of which are now in Turkey, and then to Macedonia, to the cities of Neapolis, Philippi, Thessalonica, and Berea. Paul was accompanied on his second missionary journey first by Silas and joined later by Timothy at Lystra[50] and then by Titus at Macedonia. Paul and Silas were attacked by mobs while in many of these towns and were forced to leave many of the cities.

While Paul and Silas were in Thessalonica, a city in Macedonia, a mob stirred up the people in that city by alleging that Silas and Paul were acting "... contrary to the decrees of Caesar, saying there is another king—Jesus."[51] Earlier, while Paul and Silas were in Philippi, they were arrested, but during their imprisonment they witnessed to other prisoners and to the jailor, who later became a believer. As recorded in the book of Acts:[52] "But at midnight Paul and Silas were praying and singing hymns to God, and the prisoners were listening to them. Suddenly there was a great earthquake, so that the foundations of the prison were shaken; and immediately all the doors were opened, and everyone's chains were loosed. And when the keeper of the prison, awaking from sleep and seeing the prison doors open, supposing the prisoners had fled, drew his sword and was about to kill himself. But Paul called with a loud voice, saying, 'Do yourself no harm, for we are all here!' Then he called for a light, ran in, and fell down trembling before Paul and Silas. And he brought them out and said, 'Sirs, what must I do to be saved?' So they said, 'Believe in the Lord Jesus and you will be saved, you and your household.'" Then they spoke the word of the Lord to him and to all who were in his house. And he took them the same hour of the night and washed their stripes. And immediately he and his family were baptized. Now when he had brought them into his house, he set food before them; and he rejoiced, having believed in God with all his household." Later the chief magistrates sent word to the keeper of the prison to let Paul and

---

49. Acts 15:36 to 18:22.
50. Timothy lived in Lystra, which was located in south central, modern day Turkey.
51. Acts 17:7, NKJV.
52. Acts 16:25–31, NKJV.

Paul (Saul of Tarsus)

Silas go, and, learning that Paul and Silas were Romans, the magistrates were afraid and begged them to leave the city.[53] Paul and Silas then visited the believers in Philippi, encouraged them, and departed for Thessalonica where some believed, but others gathered mobs and forced them to leave there also.

Silas and Paul left Thessalonica for Berea,[54] and there "... went into the synagogue of the Jews"[55] where they preached the word. Many persons in Berea believed. As recorded in Acts:[56] "... they received the word with all readiness, and searched the Scriptures daily to find out whether these things were so. Therefore many of them believed...." However, when some of the Jews of Thessalonica "... learned that the word of God was preached by Paul at Berea, they came there also and stirred up the crowds."[57] While they were preaching in Berea and when a few of the Jews of Thessalonica sought again to arrest Paul, the believers in Berea sent Paul "... away to go to the sea."[58] Paul then left Berea for Athens, Greece, but "... both Silas and Timothy remained there" until Paul later commanded them to come to him in Athens.[59]

While in Athens, Paul stood in the midst of a crowd and said: "Men of Athens, I perceive that in all things you are very religious; for as I was passing through and considering the objects of your worship, I even found an altar with this inscription: 'TO AN UNKNOWN GOD.' Therefore the One whom you worship without knowing Him, I proclaim to you: God who made the world and everything in it, since He is Lord of heaven and earth, does not dwell in temples made with hands. Nor is He worshiped with men's hands, as though He needed anything, since He gives to all life, breath, and all things. And He made from one blood every nation of man to dwell on all the face of the earth, and has determined their preappointed times, and the boundaries of their dwellings so that they should seek the Lord, in the hope that they might grope for Him and find Him, though He is not far from each

---

53. Acts 16:34–40.
54. Berea is a city in Macedonia, in northern Greece.
55. Acts 17:10, NKJV.
56. Acts 17:11–12a, NKJV.
57. Acts 17:12–13, NKJV.
58. Acts 17:14, NKJV.
59. Acts 17:14–15, NKJV.

one of us; for in Him we live and move and have our being, as also some of your own poets have said, 'For we also are His offspring.'"[60]

After Paul left Athens, he went to Corinth where Silas and Timothy joined him.[61] Paul supported himself through continuing his trade as a tentmaker, and at Corinth, ". . . he found a certain Jew named Aquilla, a native of Pontus, having recently come from Italy with his wife Priscilla, because Claudius had commanded all the Jews to leave Rome. He came to them, and because he was of the same trade, he stayed with them and they were working; for by trade they were tent-makers."[62]

While in Corinth, Paul visited every synagogue to try to convince the Jews and the Greeks that Jesus was the Christ. However, some of the Jews resisted him. As recorded in the book of Acts:[63] "And he was reasoning in the synagogue every Sabbath and trying to persuade Jews and Greeks, but when Silas and Timothy came down from Macedonia, Paul began devoting himself completely to the Word, solemnly testifying to the Jews that Jesus was the Christ. And when they resisted and became abusive, he shook out his garments and said to them, 'Your blood be upon your own heads! I am innocent of it. From now on I shall go to the Gentiles.'" From Corinth, Paul, Silas, and Timothy traveled to Ephesus and from there to Caesarea on their return to Jerusalem.

Prior to his crucifixion, Jesus had stated to the Jews:[64] "And I have other sheep, which are not of this fold; I must bring them also, and they shall hear My voice; and they shall become one flock with one shepherd." Paul much later queried the Gentile believers in Rome:[65] "Or is He the God of the Jews only? Is He not also the God of Gentiles?" and answered: "Yes, of the Gentiles also."[66] He further stated to the believers in Rome:[67] "But now apart from the Law the righteousness of God has been manifested, being witnessed by the Law and the Prophets, even the righteousness of God through faith in Jesus Christ for all those who believe; for there is no

60. Acts 17:22–27, NKJV.
61. Acts 18:1, 5.
62. Acts 18:2–3, NASB.
63. Acts 18:4–6, NASB.
64. John 10:16, NASB.
65. Rom 3:29a, NKJV.
66. Rom 3:29b, NKJV
67. Rom 3:21–24, NASB.

distinction; for all have sinned and fall short of the glory of God, being justified as a gift by His grace through the redemption which is in Christ Jesus."

Despite Paul having been a devout Jew, even a Pharisee, after some of the Jews rejected Paul's testimony about Jesus at Corinth, Paul did carry the message of salvation principally to the Gentiles. Paul stated to the believers at Galatia that God revealed ". . . His Son to me, that I might preach Him among the Gentiles . . ."[68] Paul further stated to the church at Galatia:[69] "God shows no partiality . . .But on the contrary, seeing that I had been entrusted with the gospel to the uncircumcised, just as Peter had been to the circumcised (for He who effectually worked for Peter in his apostleship to the circumcised effectually worked for me also to the Gentiles), and recognizing the grace that had been given to me, James and Cephas and John, who were reputed to be pillars, gave to me and Barnabas the right hand of fellowship, that we might go to the Gentiles, and they to the circumcised. They only asked us to remember the poor–the very thing I also was eager to do."

Paul assured the Galatians that they were saved by faith, not by the Law, and thus were also the offspring of Abraham. "For as many as are of the works of the law are under the curse; for it is written, 'Cursed is everyone who does not continue in all things which are written in the book of the Law, to do them.' But that no one is justified by the law in the sight of God is evident, for 'the just shall live by faith.' Yet the law is not of faith, but 'the man who does them shall live by them.' Christ has redeemed us from the curse of the law, having become a curse for us (for it is written, 'Cursed is everyone who hangs on a tree'), that the blessing of Abraham might come upon the Gentiles in Christ Jesus, that we might receive the promise of the Spirit through faith."[70] Paul stated:[71] "There is neither Jew nor Greek, there is neither slave nor free, there is neither male nor female; for you are all one in Christ Jesus. And if you are Christ's, then you are Abraham's seed, and heirs according to promise."

Paul stated to the Romans:[72] "Therefore having been justified by faith, we have peace with God through our Lord Jesus Christ, through whom also we have access by faith into this grace in which we stand; and rejoice

---

68. Gal 1:16, NKJV.
69. Gal 2:6b-10, NASB.
70. Gal 3:10-14, NKJV.
71. Gal 3:28-29, NKJV.
72. Rom 5:1-8, NKJV.

in hope of the glory of God. And not only that, but we also exult in tribulations, knowing that tribulation produces perseverance; and perseverance, character; and character, hope. Now hope does not disappoint, because the love of God has been poured out in our hearts by the Holy Spirt who was given to us. For when we were still without strength, in due time Christ died for the ungodly. For scarcely for a righteous man will one die; yet perhaps for a good man someone would even dare to die. But God demonstrates His own love toward us, in that while we were still sinners, Christ died for us." He stated to the Ephesians:[73] "For by grace you have been saved through faith, and that not of yourselves; it is the gift of God."

Paul defined himself to the Corinthian believers as having become ". . . all things to all people"[74] in order to spread the word of God to all the world. Paul informed the Corinthians:[75] "For though I am free from all men, I have made myself a servant to all, that I might win the more; and to the Jews I became as a Jew, that I might win Jews; to those who are under the law, as under the law, that I might win those who are under the law; to those who are without law, as without law (not being without the law toward God, but under the law toward Christ), that I might win those who are without law; to the weak I became as weak, that I might win the weak. I have become all things to all men, that I might by all means save some. Now this I do for the gospel's sake, that I may be partaker of it with you."

Although Paul expressed to the Roman Gentiles his pride in bringing to them the Gospel of Christ, he nonetheless expressed to them his concern for the Jewish people:[76] "I am talking to you Gentiles. Inasmuch as I am the apostle to the Gentiles, I take pride in my ministry in the hope that I may somehow arouse my own people to envy and save some of them. For if their rejection brought reconciliation to the world, what will their acceptance be but life from the dead?" Although Paul brought the saving Gospel to the Gentiles, he also related to the Gentile believers that God had not forgotten the Jews. In his letter to the believers in Rome, Paul avowed to the Gentile followers of Jesus:[77] "God has not rejected His people whom He foreknew."

---

73. Eph 2:8, NKJV.
74. I Cor 9:22, NIV.
75. I Cor 9:19–23, NKJV.
76. Rom 11:13–15, NIV.
77. Rom 11:2, NASB.

Paul (Saul of Tarsus)

Paul further stated to them:[78] "I do not want you to be ignorant of this mystery, brothers and sisters, so that you may not be conceited. Israel has experienced a hardening in part until the full number of the Gentiles has come in, and in this way all Israel will be saved. The deliverer will come from Zion, he will turn godliness away from Jacob. And this is My covenant with them when I take away their sins." Paul affirmed to the believers in Rome:[79] "Just as you who were at one time disobedient to God have now received mercy as a result of their disobedience, so they too have now become disobedient in order that they may now receive mercy as a result of God's mercy to you. For God has bound everyone to disobedience so that he may have mercy on them all." Luke recorded Jesus' words in his Gospel: "Jerusalem will be trampled on by the Gentiles until the times of the Gentiles are fulfilled."[80] This prophecy, which is a difficult prediction to understand, is discussed in more detail in Chapter 6.

Paul was in Antioch in Syria when he began his third missionary journey,[81] which occurred around 54 to 58 AD and was a return to the cities Paul had visited on his first missionary journey. Paul traveled from Antioch to Tarsus, in what was then Cilicia and now Turkey, to Derbe, Lystra, Iconium in Galatia (now Turkey) to Antioch in Asia Minor and then to Ephesus where he stayed for about three years. After that, Paul traveled to Smyrna, Perganum, Troas, and Macedonia–to the cities of Neapolis, Philippi, Thessalonica, and Berea. From Macedonia, Paul and his companions continued on to Corinth where Paul wrote his Epistle to the Romans. Paul later retraced his journey from Corinth back through Macedonia to Berea, Thessalonica, and Philippi, going then to Miletus in Turkey, sailing by Rhodes to Patara in Asia Minor, then continuing across the Mediterranean Sea to Tyre in Syria and then to Caesarea. From Caesarea, Paul and his companions returned to Jerusalem where Paul was arrested.

Silas was not with Paul on his third journey, but, during part of that journey, Timothy accompanied him, along with Erastus, who was a treasurer in Corinth and a believer.[82] Luke, the physician, also apparently accompanied Paul on the third missionary journey, at least from Troas. Luke refers in the book of Acts to their waiting for others in Troas and then

---

78. Rom 11:25–27, NIV.
79. Rom 11:30–31, NIV.
80. Luke 21:24b, NIV.
81. Acts 18:23 to 21:17.
82. See Rom 16:23.

sailing from Philippi. Luke also recorded that they stayed with Philip, the Evangelist, when they arrived at Caesarea, near the end of their journey.[83]

Following the end of the third missionary journey and then his arrest in Jerusalem, Paul claimed his Roman citizenship. He was then sent as a prisoner to Rome, rather than remaining as one in Jerusalem. Paul traveled as a prisoner with the group accompanying him, from Jerusalem to Patara, to Crete, from there to Malta, then to Syracuse in Sicily, and from there to Puteoli in Italy. The group then completed their journey to Rome where Paul lived for at least two years and witnessed to many. Paul was allegedly beheaded by the Roman emperor Nero in Rome, presumably in about 68 AD, or sometime between 64 to 69 AD.

Paul wrote, or is credited with writing, thirteen, and by some fourteen, of the twenty-seven books of the New Testament.[84] Paul referred to the favorable response to his letters that comprise so much of the New Testament:[85] "'For his letters,' they say, 'are weighty and strong' . . ." However, Paul attributed to himself as not being impressive, stating of the public's perception of him: ". . . but his bodily presence is weak, and his speech contemptible.'"[86]

Paul never boasted of his many accomplishments in preaching and spreading the gospel. He stated to the Corinthian believers: ". . . Let the one who boasts boast in the Lord. For it is not the one who commends himself who is approved, but the one whom the Lord commends."[87] He

---

83. See Acts 20:5–6, 21:8. Luke records in Acts 21:8 that they stayed with Philip the Evangelist, whom Luke said was "one of the seven," apparently referring to the Twelve choosing seven deacons to minister to believers in the early church in Jerusalem. See Acts 6:1–7, which is quoted in Chapter 1 in reference to deacons being chosen in the early church in Jerusalem. Philip the Apostle was one of the twelve disciples; he would not then have been "one of the seven," as was Philip the Evangelist. Consequently, Philip the Apostle and Philip the Evangelist were different persons.

84. The thirteen are: Romans, 1 and 2 Corinthians, Galatians, Ephesians, Philippians, Colossians, 1 and 2 Thessalonians, 1 and 2 Timothy, Titus, and Philemon although some contend Paul's assistants, Timothy and Titus, may have written, or helped write, some of these books. Discussion in Chapter 5. The fourteenth book is Hebrews, which some deny was written by Paul.

Eusebius stated that Paul ". . . was obviously and unmistakably the author of the fourteen epistles," but asserted that ". . . we must not shut our eyes to the fact that some authorities have rejected the Epistle to the Hebrews, pointing out that the Roman Church denies that it is the work of Paul." See Eusebius, *The History of the Church*, 66.

85. 2 Cor 10:10a, NKJV.

86. 2 Cor 10:10b, NKJV.

87. 2 Cor 10:17–18, NIV.

Paul (Saul of Tarsus)

also referred to a thorn in the flesh that he thought God had given him to prevent him from boasting:[88] "And because of the surpassing greatness of the revelations, for this reason, to keep me from exalting myself, there was given me a thorn in the flesh, a messenger of Satan to buffet me–to keep me from exalting myself! Concerning this I entreated the Lord three times that it might depart from me. And He has said to me, 'My grace is sufficient for you for power is perfected in weakness.' Most gladly, therefore, I will rather boast about my weaknesses, that the power of Christ may dwell in me. Therefore, I am well content with weaknesses, with insults, with distresses, with persecutions, with difficulties, for Christ's sake; for when I am weak, then I am strong."

Paul affirmed to the believers at Corinth:[89] "And so it was with me, brothers and sisters. When I came to you, I did not come with eloquence or human wisdom as I proclaimed to you the testimony about God. For I resolved to know nothing while I was with you except Jesus Christ and Him crucified. I came to you in weakness with great fear and trembling. My message and my preaching were not with wise and persuasive words, but with a demonstration of the Spirit's power, so that your faith might not rest on human wisdom, but on God's power. We do, however, speak a message of wisdom among the mature, but not the wisdom of this age or of the rulers of this age, who are coming to nothing. No, we declare God's wisdom, a mystery that has been hidden and that God destined for our glory before time began. None of the rulers of this age understood it; for if they had, they would not have crucified the Lord of glory. However, it is written: 'What no eye has seen, what no ear has heard, and what no human mind has conceived'—the things God has prepared for those who love Him—these are the things God has revealed to us by His Spirit.'"

Still, Paul recognized his calling, as well as his unrivaled ability to spread the gospel, stating to the believers at Corinth: "I not think I am in the least inferior to those "super-apostles." I may indeed be untrained as a speaker, but I do have knowledge. We have made this perfectly clear to you in every way."[90] He furthered stated to the Corinthians:[91] "I ought to have been commended by you, for I am not in the least inferior to the "super-apostles," even though I am nothing."

88. 2 Cor 12:7–10, NASB.
89. 1 Cor 2:1–9, NIV.
90. 2 Cor 11:5–6, NIV.
91. 2 Cor 12:11b, NIV.

Paul was concerned that some in the church were not following the true Gospel, which he affirmed he had received from God. He reported to the churches in Galatia:[92] "I am astonished that you are so quickly deserting the one who called you to live in the grace of Christ and are turning to a different gospel—which is really no gospel at all. Evidently some people are throwing you into confusion and are trying to pervert the gospel of Christ. But even if we or an angel from heaven should preach a gospel other than the one we preached to you, let him be under God's curse! As we have already said, so now I say again: If anybody is preaching to you a gospel other than what you accepted, let him under God's curse! Am I now trying to win the approval of human beings, or of God? Or am I trying to please people? If I were still trying to please people, I would not be a servant of Christ. I want you know, brothers and sisters, that the gospel I preached is not of human origin. I did not receive it from any man, nor was I taught it; rather, I received it by revelation from Jesus Christ."

Some Greeks believed after Paul preached to them at Athens. As noted previously, Paul proclaimed to the Greeks at Athens: "People of Athens! ...The God who made the world and everything in it is the Lord of heaven and earth and does not live in temples built by human hands. And He is not served by human hands, as if he needed anything. Rather, He Himself gives everyone life and breath and everything else . . . For in Him we live and move and have our being. As some of your own poets have said, 'We are His offspring.'"[93]

Paul carried the Gospel of Christ to the world despite his many sufferings. Paul spoke of some of his sufferings in a letter to the followers of Jesus at Corinth, stating to the Corinthian believers:[94] "Five times I received from the Jews thirty-nine lashes. Three times I was beaten with rods, once I was stoned, three times I was shipwrecked, a night and a day I have spent in the deep. I have been on frequent journeys, in dangers from rivers, dangers from robbers, dangers from my countrymen, dangers from the Gentiles, dangers in the city, dangers in the wilderness, dangers on the sea, dangers among false brethren; I have been in labor and hardship, through many sleepless nights, in hunger and thirst, often without food, in cold and exposure. Apart from such external things, there is the daily concern for all the

---

92. Gal 1:6–12, NIV.
93. Acts 17:22b-28, NIV.
94. 2 Cor 12:24-28, NASB.

churches." However, Paul informed the Philippians:[95] "I can do all things through Christ who strengthens me."

Although Paul suffered greatly physically because of his spreading the Gospel to the Gentiles, he counted that as nothing. As he stated in his letter to the Romans:[96] "The Spirit Himself bears witness with our spirit that we are children of God, and if children, heirs also, heirs of God and fellow heirs with Christ, if indeed we suffer with Him in order that we may also be glorified with Him. For I consider that the sufferings of this present time are not worthy to be compared with the glory that is to be revealed to us... And we know that God causes all things to work together for good to those who love God, to those who are called according to His purpose." He told the believers at Rome:[97] "What then shall we say to these things? If God is for us, who is against us? He who did not spare His own Son, but delivered Him up for us all, how will He not also with Him freely give us all things? Who will bring a charge against God's elect? God is the one who justifies; who is the one who condemns? Christ Jesus is He who died, yes, rather who was raised, who is at the right hand of God, who also intercedes for us. Who shall separate us from the love of Christ? Shall tribulation, or distress, or persecution, or famine, or nakedness, or peril, or sword? Just as it is written, 'For Thy sake we are being put to death all day long; We were considered as sheep to be slaughtered.' But in all these things we overwhelmingly conquer through Him who loved us, For I am convinced that neither death, nor life, nor angels, nor principalities, nor things present, nor things to come, nor powers, nor height nor depth, nor any other created thing, shall be able to separate us from the love of God, which is in Christ Jesus our Lord."

As noted previously, when Paul returned to Jerusalem after his third missionary journey, he was arrested there,[98] but because he was a Roman citizen, he appealed to Caesar and was sent a prisoner to Rome.[99] Paul remained a prisoner in Rome for a few years,[100] and at first he was "under no restraint and preached the word of God without hindrance."[101] Luke

---

95. Phil 4:13, NKJV.
96. Rom 8:16–18, 28, NASB.
97. Rom 8:31–39, NASB.
98. Acts 21:26–30.
99. Acts 22:25b–29; 26:32.
100. Acts 28:30.
101. Eusebius, *The History of the Church*, 57.

reported:[102] "He stayed two full years in his own rented quarters, and was welcoming all who came to him, preaching the kingdom of God, and teaching concerning the Lord Jesus Christ with all openness, unhindered."

While he was imprisoned and awaiting execution, Paul wrote in his second letter to Timothy that ". . . I am already being poured out . . . and the time of my departure has come."[103] Paul assured Timothy that the Lord would deliver him[104] ". . . from every evil work . . ." and would preserve him ". . . for His heavenly kingdom." As Paul neared death, he reminded Timothy to never ". . . be ashamed of the testimony of our Lord"[105] and stated to him:[106] "For this reason I also suffer these things; nevertheless, I am not ashamed, for I know whom I have believed and am persuaded that He is able to keep what I have committed to Him until that Day."

Paul made the following statements to the Thessalonians, in a letter to them that he wrote in about 51 AD, or approximately twenty years after Jesus' crucifixion, as a comfort to them; it is a comfort to Christians today: "For this we say to you by the words of the Lord, that we who are alive, and remain until the coming of the Lord, shall not precede those who have fallen asleep. For the Lord Himself will descend from heaven with a shout, with the voice of the archangel, and with the trumpet of God and the dead in Christ shall rise first. Then we who are alive and remain shall be caught up together with them in the clouds to meet the Lord in the air, and thus we shall always be with the Lord."[107]

In his last Epistle, which was addressed to Timothy whom he called his "beloved son," Paul stated:[108] "At my first defense, no one came to my support, but everyone deserted me. May it not be held against them. But the Lord stood at my side and gave me strength, so that through me the message might be fully proclaimed and all the Gentiles might hear it. And I was delivered from the lion's mouth. The Lord will rescue me from every evil attack and will bring me safely to His heavenly kingdom. To Him be glory for ever and ever. Amen." Paul recorded these last words in his second letter to Timothy, which he wrote to instruct Timothy to greet other believers

---

102. Acts 28:30–31, NASB.
103. 2 Tim 4:6, NASB.
104. 2 Tim 4:18, NKJV.
105. 2 Tim 1:8, NASB.
106. 2 Tim 1:12, NKJV.
107. 1 Thess 4:15–17, NASB.
108. 2 Tim 4:16–18, NIV.

Paul (Saul of Tarsus)

and to pass to them the requirement that they continue Jesus' command to carry forward the message of salvation.

As noted previously, it is recorded that in the reign of Nero, Paul was beheaded in Rome.[109] Paul indicated that only Luke was with him just prior to his death. Like Jesus, Paul died almost alone. Still, Paul was secure in the comfort of the Lord; he stated to Timothy at the end of his ministry: "I have fought the good fight, I have finished the course, I have kept the faith; in the future there is laid up for me the crown of righteousness which the Lord, the righteous judge, will award to me on that day; and not only to me, but also to all who have longed for His appearing."[110]

As noted in Chapter 3, some contend Paul should have been the twelfth disciple to succeed Judas Iscariot because God personally called Paul to His ministry. Whether or not Paul can be considered to be the twelfth disciple, he was probably the most important person in bringing the message of salvation to the world and thereby making Christianity a universal religion. Without Paul's ministry to the Gentiles, Christianity may have been only a small and insignificant and perhaps later discarded branch of Judaism. Still, undoubtedly, even without Paul, through the other early followers of Jesus, God would have found a way to bring the message of salvation to the world. Nonetheless one can never discount the efforts of Paul, who has been called the greatest Christian who ever lived.

---

109. Eusebius, *The History of the Church*, 62.
110. 2 Tim 4:7–8, NASB.

5

Other God-Fearing Followers of Jesus

I. James, Half-Brother of Jesus and Bishop of Jerusalem Church
II. Philip, the Evangelist
III. Luke, the Beloved Physician
IV. John Mark, Author of the Gospel of Mark
V. Barnabas, the Son of Encouragement
VI. Timothy, Beloved Companion of Paul
VII. Silas, Follower with Paul
VIII. Titus, Child of the Faith
IX. Erastus, Treasurer in Corinth and Minister to Paul
X. Linus, Second Bishop of Roman Church
XI. Aquila and Priscilla, Tent Makers and Companions to Paul
XII. Apollos, Jewish Christian from Alexandria
XIII. Women who Followed Jesus
   A. Women who Assisted Jesus During His Ministry
   B. Women Leaders in the Early Church

MANY OTHER FOLLOWERS OF Jesus devoted their lives to spreading the message of salvation. Among these were James, the half-brother of Jesus who was the first bishop of the church in Jerusalem, and Paul's companions and fellow workers. These included Luke, the beloved physician who wrote the Gospel of Luke and the book of Acts, John Mark, the author of the Gospel of Mark, and Barnabas, Timothy, Titus, Erastus, to include Linus, who

Other God-Fearing Followers of Jesus

became the second bishop of the Roman church after Peter was martyred, as well as Aquilla and Priscilla, who were tentmakers like Paul. Additionally, there were many faithful and devoted women, who like Priscilla, were leaders and teachers in the early church and instrumental in carrying the Gospel to the world. This chapter sets out the involvement of these courageous and devout believers in their fearless work for the Lord.

I. James, Half-Brother of Jesus and Bishop of Jerusalem Church

James, the half-brother of Jesus,[1] who, along with Peter and John, was listed as a pillar of the early church[2] and who was appointed the first bishop of the church in Jerusalem, was called James the Righteous and James the Just.[3] James originally did not believe in the divinity of Jesus; he along with others who knew Jesus in the years prior to His ministry, attributed no special status to Jesus.[4] Although many who listened to Jesus preach in the synagogue and were astonished at His wisdom, apparently among these Jesus' half-brother, James,[5] these nonbelievers nevertheless discredited Jesus as having any miraculous powers, many referring to Jesus as the son of a carpenter.[6] Jesus responded to these unbelievers that: ". . . A prophet is not without honor except in his own country and in his own house."[7]

It undoubtedly was difficult also for James to relate to his brother as being a prophet and one with God. As recorded in John,[8] "For even His brothers did not believe in Him." Jesus also spoke out against any special distinction for James because of his being a brother. As Matthew recorded:[9]

1. See Matt 13:55 and Mark 6:1–3.

2. Gal 2:9.

3. See Eusebius, *The History of the Church*, 36 and Eusebius, *Ecclesiastical History*, 59.

4. Matthew set out in his Gospel questions some of the Jews asked about Jesus: "Is not this the carpenter's son? Is not his mother called Mary, and His brothers, James and Joseph and Simon and Judas?" Matt 13:55, NASB.

5. See Matt 13:46–47 and John 7:5

6. Mark 6:1–3.

7. Matt 13:57, NKJV. Jesus did not perform many miracles in his hometown ". . . because of their unbelief." Matthew 13:58, NKJV. As a result of the Nazarenes not accepting Jesus' divinity, Jesus left Nazareth and preached most of His three-year ministry in Capernaum and along the Sea of Galilee.

8. John 7:5, NKJV.

9. Matt 12:46–50, NASB. See also Mark 3:31–35 and Luke 8:19–21.

"While He was still speaking to the multitudes, behold, His mother and brothers were standing outside, seeking to speak to Him. And someone said to Him, 'Behold, Your mother and Your brothers are standing outside seeking to speak to You.' But He answered the one who was telling Him and said, 'Who is My mother and who are My brothers?' And stretching out His hand toward His disciples, He said, "Behold, My mother and My brothers! For whoever does the will of My Father who is in heaven, he is My brother and sister and mother."' Additionally, when Jesus was on the cross at His crucifixion, He referred to the disciple John as being His mother's son who was to care for her:[10] "When Jesus therefore saw His mother, and the disciple whom He loved standing nearby, He said to His mother, 'Woman, behold, your son!' Then He said to the disciple, 'Behold, your mother!' And from that hour the disciple took her into his own household."

Some have contended that Jesus' instruction to John to care for His mother, Mary, indicates Jesus had no siblings and that James was either Joseph's son from a prior marriage or was Jesus' cousin. Perhaps though Jesus was concerned that James and His other siblings did not believe in His divinity at the time of His crucifixion. In contrast, John, the beloved disciple, not only believed, he also was with Jesus when He was crucified while others had left Jesus to die alone. It is also probable that because Jesus knew of the forthcoming destruction of Jerusalem, He wanted His mother removed from Jerusalem and knew that his half-brothers would remain there. Jesus foresaw the destruction of Jerusalem that followed James' death and would not have wanted His mother to remain in Jerusalem with James or any of Jesus' other siblings. Because John took Mary with him to Ephesus, she escaped the destruction and tragedy when Jerusalem fell to the Romans beginning in 70 AD. Still, Jesus had great love for James; He appeared to James alone after His resurrection[11] and apparently instructed James for the special role James was to play as head of the first church of the believers in Jerusalem. James remained in Jerusalem as the head of the Jerusalem church and later suffered a grievous martyr's death there.

James obviously came to know that his half-brother, Jesus, was the Christ shortly after Jesus' resurrection. Luke recorded in Acts that after Jesus' resurrection, Mary, the mother of Jesus, and Jesus' brothers were ". . . all with one mind, . . ." with the eleven disciples[12] ". . . continually devoting

---

10. John 19:26–27, NASB. Joseph undoubtedly would no longer have been alive.
11. 1 Cor 15:7.
12. Prior to their choosing Matthias to succeed Judas Iscariot.

Other God-Fearing Followers of Jesus

themselves to prayer."[13] Paul reported in a letter to the Corinthians that after Jesus appeared to the disciples, He also appeared ". . . to more than five hundred brethren at one time"[14] and ". . . then He appeared to James, then to all the apostles."[15] James assuredly was present at Pentecost and would have received the Holy Spirit along with the then confident believers in Christ.[16]

James was appointed the first bishop of the church in Jerusalem because of his great faith and righteousness. In referring to James as "the brother of the Lord," Eusebius affirmed that ". . . this James, whom the early Christians surnamed the Righteous because of his outstanding virtue, was the first, as the records tell us, to be elected to the episcopal throne of the Jerusalem church."[17] Eusebius quoted Clement[18] as stating: "Peter, James, and John, after the Ascension of the Saviour, did not claim pre-eminence because the Saviour had specially honoured them, but chose James the Righteous as Bishop of Jerusalem." Eusebius also quoted Hegesippus as stating, in the fifth book of his commentaries, that James was surnamed the Just.[19] Eusebius further reported that James ". . . was the first to receive from the Saviour and His apostles the episcopacy of the Jerusalem church," and, in stating that James ". . . was called Christ's brother," referred to the "throne of James" that Eusebius avowed had "been preserved" until his writing.[20]

Paul referred to having visited James, whom he called an apostle, when he was in Jerusalem probably after his first missionary journey. In his letter to the Gentile believers at Galatia, Paul stated:[21] ". . . nor did I go

---

13. Acts 1:14.

14. 1 Cor 15:5.

15. 1 Cor 15:7. Jesus appeared to demonstrate a special love for James as Paul pointed out Jesus' special appearance to James, His half-brother.

16. See Acts 2:1.

17. Eusebius, *The History of the Church*, 36.

18. Clement, *Outlines*, Book VI.

19. Eusebius, *Ecclesiastical History*, 59. Thus, James the brother of Jesus, was called both James the Righteous and James the Just.

Hegesippus was a second century Jewish Christian who wrote about the history of the early church.

20. Eusebius, *The History of the Church*, 234. Eusebius was referring to his writings. Thus, even though Jerusalem had been destroyed long before Eusebius wrote of the early church history there, the *"throne of James"* nonetheless would have been preserved for at least nearly 300 years after Christ's resurrection in that Eusebius wrote of the early church about 300 years after Jesus' resurrection. Eusebius became the bishop of Caesarea in about 314 AD.

21. Gal 1:17-19, NASB.

up to Jerusalem to those who were apostles before me; but I went away to Arabia, and returned once more to Damascus. Then three years later I went up to Jerusalem to become acquainted with Cephas [Peter] and stayed with him fifteen days. But I did not see any other of the apostles except James, the Lord's brother." Paul referred to James as a "pillar" in the early church and reported to the Galatians that "... recognizing the grace that had been given to me, James and Cephas and John, who were reputed to be pillars, gave to me and Barnabas the right hand of fellowship, that we might go to the Gentiles, and they to the circumcised."[22] Paul further stated:[23] "They desired only that we should remember the poor, the very thing which I also was eager to do."

Luke records in Acts that Peter wanted James informed about "... how the Lord had led him [Peter] out of prison..." after Herod had arrested him following Herod having "... had James the brother of John put to death with a sword."[24] Peter obviously then had great respect for James, deservedly so as he was the half-brother of Jesus and the first bishop of the early church in Jerusalem.

Luke reported that James the Righteous came to Paul's defense when "... some men came down from Judea and began teaching the brethren, 'Unless you are circumcised according to the custom of Moses, you cannot be saved.'"[25] The Gentile believers "... determined that Paul and Barnabas and certain others of them should go up to Jerusalem, to the apostles and elders, about this question."[26]

Paul and Barnabas then traveled to Jerusalem to discuss the issue and found that James supported them. Luke recorded the discourse:[27] "The whole assembly became silent as they listened to Barnabas and Paul telling about the signs and wonders God had done among the Gentiles through them. When they finished, James spoke up, 'Brothers,' he said, 'listen to me. Simon described to us how God first intervened to choose a people for His name from the Gentiles. The words of the prophets are in agreement with this, as it is written 'After this I will return and rebuild David's fallen tent. Its ruins I will rebuild, and I will restore it, that the rest of mankind

22. Gal 2:9, NASB.
23. Gal 2:10, NKJV.
24. Acts 12:2.
25. Acts 15:1, NASB.
26. Acts 15:2b, NKJV.
27. Acts 15:12–22, NIV.

may seek the Lord, even all the Gentiles who bear My name,' says the Lord, who does these things—things known from long ago. It is my judgment, therefore, that we should not make it difficult for the Gentiles who are turning to God. Instead we should write to them, telling them to abstain from food polluted by idols, from sexual immorality, and from the meat of strangled animals and from blood. For the law of Moses has been preached in every city from the earliest times and is read in the synagogues on every Sabbath.' Then the apostles and elders, with the whole church, decided to choose some of their own men and send them to Antioch with Paul and Barnabas. They chose Judas (called Barsabbas) and Silas, men who were leaders among the believers."

Luke reported that, after James' statements, the Jewish believers prepared a letter and sent it to the Gentile believers at Antioch, who, when reading the letter ". . . rejoiced because of its encouragement."[28] Luke also recorded that Paul met again with James after Paul's final return to Jerusalem following his third missionary journey.[29]

In the Epistle of James,[30] James humbly referred to himself as ". . . a servant of God and of the Lord Jesus Christ."[31] James wrote his epistle: "To the twelve tribes scattered among the nations."[32] He apparently wanted to prepare the Jewish believers who were scattered throughout the then world to be patient in their waiting for Jesus' return. James stated to the tribes[33] "Be patient, therefore, brethren, until the coming of the Lord. Behold, the farmer waits for the precious produce of the soil, being patient about it, until it gets the early and late rains, You too be patient; strengthen your hearts, for the coming of the Lord is at hand."

James also admonished the Jewish followers of Jesus that ". . . faith without deeds is useless."[34] He affirmed:[35] "As the body without the spirit is

28. Acts 15:31. Luke reported that Judas and Silas ". . . who themselves were prophets, said much to encourage and strengthen the believers." Acts 15:32, NIV.

29. Acts 21:18. As noted previously, Paul was later arrested and then was sent to Rome where he was martyred a few years later.

30. James, the half-brother of Jesus, is credited by most as the author of the Epistle of James.

31. Jas 1:1, NIV. Perhaps James thought he could not claim status as a brother of Jesus because he did not originally believe that Jesus was the Christ.

32. Jas 1:1, NIV.

33. Jas 5:7–8, NASB.

34. Jas 2:20, NIV.

35. Jas 2:26, NIV. James responded to some who would say: "You have faith; I have

dead, so faith without deeds is dead." James was explaining to the Jewish believers that if they had true faith in Jesus, that faith would be demonstrated by good works. Paul apparently agreed as he stated to the believers at Ephesus:[36] "For we are His workmanship, created in Christ Jesus for good works, which God prepared beforehand, that we should walk in them." Paul also declared to the Gentile believers at Corinth:[37] "Therefore if anyone is in Christ, the new creature has come. The old is gone, the new is here!"

James suffered a very violent death when he was bishop of the church in Jerusalem. Eusebius speculated that some of the Jews were of the opinion the cause of the siege of Jerusalem, and what "happened to them," occurred because of the martyrdom of James and how "... admirable a man ... was James and so celebrated among all for his justice ..."[38] Eusebius referred to Josephus' conclusion that "... these things happened to the Jews to avenge James the Just, who was the brother of him that is called Christ, and whom the Jews had slain, notwithstanding his pre-eminent justice."[39]

Eusebius recorded James' death as occurring about AD 69 and as having come about when James was "... thrown down from [a] parapet and beaten to death with a fuller's club."[40] Eusebius quoted Hegesippus, whom he said "... belonged to the first generation after the apostles,[41] as stating that because James was still alive after his fall, the Jewish Scribes and Pharisees, who had made James stand on the Temple parapet and then threw him down, began to stone him. Hegesippus recorded that James had turned and knelt, uttering the words: "I beseech Thee, Lord God and Father, forgive them; they do not know what they are doing." Eusebius reported that one of the Jews then took a club and "... brought it down on the head of the Righteous one."[42] Eusebius also quoted Hegesippus as stating that James was buried on the spot, by the Sanctuary, and that his headstone was still

---

deeds." He stated: "Show me your faith without deeds, and I will show you my faith by my deeds. Jas 2:18, NIV.

36. Eph 2:10, NASB.
37. 2 Cor 5:17, NIV.
38. Eusebius, *Ecclesiastical History*, 61.
39. Eusebius referred to Josephus' 20th book of his *Antiquities*.
40. Eusebius, *The History of the Church*, 36. Eusebius recorded that these were the words of Clement who wrote around 100 AD and thus was directly involved in the events following Jesus' resurrection and ascension. He asserted that Clement would have known of the circumstances relating to James' death. See Eusebius, *The History of the Church*, 58.
41. Eusebius, *The History of the Church*, 59.
42. Eusebius quoting Hegesippus in *The History of the Church*, 60.

Other God-Fearing Followers of Jesus

there "by the Sanctuary" at the time of Hegesippus. Eusebius additionally quoted Hegesippus as stating: "He [James] has proved a true witness to Jews and Gentiles alike that Jesus is the Christ."[43] According to Eusebius, the siege of Jerusalem immediately followed James' death.[44]

II. Philip, the Evangelist

Philip, the Evangelist, lived in an ancient city near Caesarea. As discussed in Chapter 1, Philip was one of seven deacons appointed to take care of the poor in Jerusalem. These first seven deacons were chosen to oversee contributions for the poor believers in Jerusalem.[45] As recorded in the book of Acts,[46] the twelve disciples ". . . summoned the congregation"[47] in Jerusalem, telling the members to "'. . . select from among you, brethren, seven men of good reputation, full of the Spirit and of wisdom, whom we may put in charge of this task'. . . and they chose Stephen, a man full of faith and of the Holy Spirit, and Philip . . . ." The seven deacons, which included Philip the Evangelist, were brought before the twelve disciples. The Twelve would have included Philip the Apostle, as distinguished from Philip the Evangelist. The disciples prayed with the seven deacons and then ". . . *laid their hands on them.*"[48]

After believers left Jerusalem following James' death, Philip the Evangelist spread the gospel to Samaria where he was reported to have performed miracles. As recorded in the book of Acts: "Therefore, those who had been scattered went about preaching the Word. And Philip went down to the

---

43. Eusebius quoting Hegesippus in *The History of the Church*, 60.

An ossuary, which is a container in which bones of a deceased person are deposited a year after the initial burial, was found in the Kidron Valley, which separates the Mount of Olives and the Temple Mount. This is where James was martyred. The ossuary had the inscription "James, the son of Joseph, and brother of Jesus," written on the box in Aramaic, the language that replaced Hebrew as the language of the Jews in the sixth century and that was Jesus' language. The original contention that the ossuary was a forgery has never been proven, and many claim it is authentic. Actually, the antiquity of the ossuary has been proven. It is a limestone box that dates back to the first century. The ossuary was last reported to be in possession of the Israel Antiquities Authority.

44. Titus, a later Roman emperor, began the destruction of Jerusalem in 70 AD.
45. Acts 6:1–6.
46. Acts 6:5b.
47. Acts 6:2a, 3, 5b, NASB.
48. Acts 6:6b, NIV.

city of Samaria and began proclaiming Christ to them. And the multitudes with one accord were giving attention to what was said by Philip, as they heard and saw the signs which he was performing."[49] As further reported in Acts:[50] "But when they believed Philip as he proclaimed the good news of the kingdom of God, and the name of Jesus Christ, they were baptized, both men and women. Simon[51] himself believed and was baptized. And he followed Philip everywhere, astonished by the great signs and miracles he saw."

Eusebius recorded that, after Stephen's martyrdom, some of the Jewish leaders began persecution of the Jerusalem church. The Jewish followers of Jesus had not ventured to share the Gospel with the Gentiles, proclaiming it to be for Jews alone. Later, though, Eusebius reported that Jesus' followers, including the Jewish believers, were dispersed to Samaria, Phoenicia, Cyprus, and Antioch and did then carry the gospel to the Gentiles.

Eusebius pointed to Philip as having been the first to have shared the Gospel with a Gentile. This Gentile was an Ethiopian who is reported to have started the church in Ethiopia. Eusebius reported that the Ethiopian "... is believed to have been the first to go back to his native land and preach the gospel of the knowledge of the God of the universe . . ."[52] in fulfilment of the prophecy: "Ethiopia shall soon stretch out her hands unto God."[53]

As recorded in the book of Acts:[54] "Now an angel of the Lord spoke to Philip, saying, 'Arise and go toward the south along the road which goes down from Jerusalem to Gaza.' This is desert. So he arose and went. And behold, a man of Ethiopia, a eunuch of great authority under Candace, the queen of the Ethiopians, who had charge of all her treasury; and had come to Jerusalem to worship, was returning. And sitting in his chariot, he was reading Isaiah the prophet. Then the Spirit said to Philip, 'Go near and overtake this chariot.' So Philip ran to him, and heard him reading the prophet Isaiah, and said, 'Do you understand what you are reading?' And he said, 'How can I, unless someone guides me?' And he asked Philip to come up and sit with him. The place in the Scripture which he read was this: 'He was led as a sheep to the slaughter; And as a lamb before its shearer is silent,

---

49. Acts 8:4–6, NASB. This Philip was Philip the Evangelist.

50. Acts 8:12–13, NIV.

51. This Simon was an individual who had practiced sorcery in the city but who was converted when he heard Philip and witnessed his miracles. See Acts 8:8–13.

52. Eusebius, *The History of the Church*, 37–38.

53. Ps 68:31b, KJV.

54. Acts 8:26–40, NKJV.

Other God-Fearing Followers of Jesus

so He opened not His mouth. In His humiliation His judgment was taken away, And who will declare His generation? For His life is taken from the earth.' So the eunuch answered Philip, and said, 'I ask you, of whom does the prophet say this, of himself or of some other man?' Then Philip opened his mouth, and beginning at this Scripture, preached Jesus to him. Now as they went down the road, they came to some water. And the eunuch said, 'See, here is water. What hinders me from being baptized?' Then Philip said, 'If you believe with all your heart, you may.' And he answered and said, 'I believe that Jesus Christ is the Son of God.' So he commanded the chariot to stand still. And both Philip and the eunuch went down into the water, and he baptized him. Now when they came up out of the water, the Spirit of the Lord caught Philip away, so that the eunuch saw him no more; and he went on his way rejoicing. But Philip was found himself at Azotus. And passing through, he preached in all the cities till he came to Caesarea."[55]

Philip was married and had four daughters, all of whom were unmarried, but all endowed with a prophetic gift.[56] The book of Acts records that Paul and Luke visited Philip the evangelist and his daughters in Caesarea. Luke recorded in Acts:[57] "And the next day we departed and came to Caesarea; and entering into the house of Philip the evangelist, who was one of the seven; we stayed with him. Now this same man had four virgin daughters who were prophetesses."

Eusebius thought that Philip the Apostle and Philip the Evangelist were the same person.[58] However, Luke's reference in the book of Acts to a Philip who was one of "seven" chosen by the "twelve" disciples as one of the first deacons and Philip the Apostle being one of the twelve disciples, clearly refutes this assumption.[59] Some, possibly in error, reported that Philip the Apostle resided at Hierapolis in Turkey and that he suffered a

---

55. Azotus was one of the principal cities of the Philistines. Azotus is the Hebrew name for Ashdod, which is the currently used Greek name for the city. It is located near Tel Aviv, northeast of Gaza.

56. Eusebius, *The History of the Church*, 94. Eusebius referred to the daughters as prophetesses.

57. Acts 21:8–9, NASB.

58. Discussion in Eusebius, *The History of the Church*, 94.

59. See Acts 6. In Acts 6:2–6, Luke records Philip the Evangelist as having been chosen by the Twelve. In Acts 21:8, Luke refers to Paul and himself staying with Philip the Evangelist who Luke states was of the "seven." Philip the Apostle was one of the "twelve." As one of the "twelve," Philip the Apostle would have chosen Paul the Evangelist to be one of the "seven." Thus, the historians who treat Philip the Apostle and Philip the Evangelist as the same person are clearly wrong.

martyr's death there.[60] Undoubtedly it was Philip the Evangelist who resided at Hierapolis and who suffered the martyr's death, according to reports, by being pierced through the thighs and hung upside down.[61] There has been much confusion about the two Philips and it is not possible then to know which of the two was buried at Hierapolis. It has been reported that "Philip," which is alleged to be Philip the Apostle, was initially buried at Hierapolis, but that his body was later taken from Hierapolis to Constantinople and then subsequently interred in a church in Rome.[62] This body must be that of Philip the Evangelist.

III. Luke, the Beloved Physician

Little is recorded or known about the birth, life or death of Luke. He apparently either was born in the Greek city of Antioch or had family members there.[63] From the only three references to him by name in the Bible,[64] it is evident Luke was a disciple of Paul, a physician, and a Gentile.[65] Eusebius

---

60. See Eusebius, *The History of the Church*, 171.

61. See McBirnie, *The Search for the Twelve Apostles*, 102-3, where McBirnie reports that Philip may have been martyred by being pierced through the thighs and hung upside down. Both Eusebius and McBirnie assumed this was Philip the Apostle because they thought he and the Philip, who was called the Evangelist, were one and the same.

62. McBirnie, *The Search for the Twelve Apostles*, 101. McBirnie assumes though that this Philip was Philip the Apostle. The body interred in a church in Rome is thought to be the body of Philip the Apostle but probably is the body of Philip the Evangelist with the location of the body of Philip being unknown.

Philip the Apostle may not have suffered a martyr's death. As noted in Chapter 3, Philip the Apostle is reported to have accompanied Joseph of Arimathea, Lazarus and the Marys to France to spread the Gospel and later to have sent Joseph of Arimathea to England to spread the Gospel there. Philip the Apostle may have accompanied Joseph of Arimathea to England and either lived there or in France and died a natural death. At any rate, there is confusion regarding the later life of Philip the Apostle because he obviously was not Philip the Evangelist as many had thought. (Further discussion below of Lazarus and the Marys traveling to France.)

63. Eusebius, *The History of the Church*, 67.

The name "Christian," which was given later to Jesus' followers, first appeared at the church at Antioch. The Antioch church flourished with "... the greatest number of teachers coming there from Jerusalem;" Barnabas and Paul were among them. See Eusebius, *Ecclesiastical History*, 39. The ruins of Antioch are near Antakya, Turkey.

64. Col 4:14, Phil 1:24, and 2 Tim 4:11.

65. Col 4:11, 14. Some have contended that Luke was also a painter. Discussion in McBirnie, *The Search for the Twelve Apostles*, 205-6.

Other God-Fearing Followers of Jesus

referred to Luke as being "... for long periods a companion of Paul" and "... closely associated with the other apostles as well."[66] Paul referred to Luke as 'the beloved physician."[67]

Eusebius reported that Luke "... has left us examples of the art of healing souls ...," which he taught "... in two divinely inspired books, the Gospel and the Acts of the Apostles."[68] Eusebius affirmed that the Gospel of Luke was the third of the four "undeniably authentic" gospels[69] and stated that Luke "... wrote for Gentile converts ..." a gospel that was "... praised by Paul."[70]

Luke stated in the introduction to the Gospel of Luke: "Inasmuch as many have undertaken to compile an account of the things accomplished among us, just as those who from the beginning were eyewitnesses and servants of the word have handed them down to us, it seemed fitting for me as well, having investigated everything carefully from the beginning, to write it out for you in consecutive order ... so that you might know the exact truth about the things you have been taught."[71] It appears then that Luke acknowledged he did not personally encounter the Lord but rather that his knowledge of Jesus' ministry was "handed down" to him by persons he quoted as having been "... eyewitnesses and servants of the word."[72]

Still, some contend that Luke may have been one of the seventy followers that Jesus appointed after He called His twelve disciples,[73] for Luke refers to them in his gospel, and the seventy are only mentioned in the Gospel of Luke. As reported in Luke:[74] "Now after this the Lord appointed seventy others, and sent them two and two ahead of Him to every city and

---

66. Eusebius, *The History of the Church*, 67.

67. Col 4:14.

68. Eusebius, *The History of the Church*, 67.

69. Eusebius, *The History of the Church*, 201.

70. Eusebius, *The History of the Church*, 201. Eusebius recorded that the Gospel of Luke was followed "last of all" by the Gospel of John.

71. Luke 1-4, NASB. Luke wrote his gospel to Theophilus and also referred to Theophilus in Acts, Luke's other book (Act 1:1). There is no record of who Theophilus was, but undoubtedly he was an influential Gentile and doubtless a follower of Jesus. The name, Theophilus, means "lover" or "friend" of God.

72. Luke 1:1-2, NIV.

73. Others contend that this "legend" is "pure conjecture;" that "... Luke himself was not an eyewitness of the ministry of Jesus." McBirnie's account in *The Search for the Twelve Apostles*, 203, is an example.

74. Luke 10:1-3, NASB.

place where He Himself was going to come. And He was saying to them, 'The harvest is plentiful, but the laborers are few; therefore beseech the Lord of the harvest to send out laborers into His harvest. Go your ways; behold, I send you out as lambs in the midst of wolves."

Luke apparently was a Gentile who became a believer and a disciple of Paul in helping Paul spread the Gospel to the Gentiles. When Paul referred in Colossians[75] to his ". . . fellow workers for the kingdom of God who are from the circumcision, . . ." he made no mention of Luke being among these workers "from the circumcision." Paul's reference following this statement to "Our dear friend Luke, the doctor . . ."[76] indicates that Luke was not "from the circumcision," and thus was not a Jew, but instead was a Gentile.

Luke referred to statements in Isaiah[77] to affirm: ". . . the Lord has commanded us. 'I have placed you as a light for the Gentiles, that you should bring salvation to the end of the earth.'"[78] Luke further confirmed:[79] ". . . that the Christ was to suffer, and that by reason of His resurrection from the dead He should be the first to proclaim the light both to the Jewish people and to the Gentiles."

Luke has provided much information about the early history of the church in the book of Acts. He reported to a Jewish Christian from Alexandria named Theophilus the events relating to the early churches—beginning in 33 AD with Christ's resurrection[80] and ending in 60 AD with a record of Paul's two-year imprisonment in Rome.[81] Luke stated in the book of Acts:[82] ". . . the first account I composed, Theophilus, about all that Jesus began to do and teach, until the day when He was taken up, after He had by the Holy Spirit given orders to the apostles whom He had chosen. To these He also presented Himself alive, after His suffering, by many convincing proofs, appearing to them over a period of forty days, and speaking of the things concerning the kingdom of God." Luke additionally affirmed in

---

75. Col 4:11, NASB.
76. Col 4:14, NIV.
77. Isa 42:6 and 49:6.
78. Acts 13:47, NASB. Isaiah recorded at Isa 42:6, NASB "And I will appoint you as a covenant to the people." Isaiah further recorded, Isa 49:6, NASB: "To raise up the tribes of Jacob, and to restore the preserved ones of Israel; I will also make You a light of the nations so that My salvation may reach to the end of the earth."
79. Acts 26:23, NASB.
80. Acts 1:1–11.
81. Acts 28:30.
82. Acts 1:1–3, NASB.

Other God-Fearing Followers of Jesus

Acts:[83] "It is therefore necessary that of the men who have accompanied us all the time that the Lord Jesus went in and out among us–beginning with the baptism of John, until the day that He was taken up from us–one of these should become a witness with us of His resurrection."

Luke wrote much of the book of Acts from his personal experiences.[84] Luke uses the word "we" occasionally to indicate that he was present with Paul in Paul's third missionary journey and was with Paul when Paul was imprisoned in Rome.[85] It is apparent that Paul had great love and respect for Luke. Paul stated in his last letter,[86] which he wrote shortly before his martyrdom in Rome: "*Only Luke is with me.*"[87]

Luke described in Acts some of his journeys with Paul as they spread the Gospel to the Gentile world. Luke apparently was with Paul prior to Paul leaving for Macedonia on Paul's third missionary journey; Luke then accompanied Paul to Macedonia. Luke reported these events in Acts:[88] "And a vision appeared to Paul in the night: a certain man of Macedonia was standing and appealing to him, and saying, 'Come over to Macedonia and help us.' And when he had seen the vision immediately we sought to go into Macedonia, concluding that God had called us to preach the gospel to them. Therefore putting out to sea from Troas, we ran a straight course to Samothrace and on the day following to Neapolis; and from there to Philippi, which is a leading city of the district of Macedonia, a Roman colony; and we were staying in this city for some days. And on the Sabbath day we went outside the gate to a riverside, where we were supposing that there would be a place of prayer; and we sat down and began speaking to the women who had assembled." One of the women was Lydia, who is discussed below in this chapter.

Luke later referred to being with Paul in Troas: "But these had gone on ahead and were waiting for us at Troas. And we sailed from Philippi after the days of Unleavened Bread, and came to them at Troas within five days; and there we stayed seven days. And on the first day of the week, when we were

---

83. Acts 1:21–22, NASB.

84. Discussion in Eusebius, *The History of the Church*, 67, and mentioned in Eusebius, *Ecclesiastical History*, 69.

85. See Acts 16:10–13; 20:5–17; 21:1–18; 27:1–31; 28:1; 10–16.

86. 2 Tim.

87. 2 Tim 4:11, NIV.

88. Acts 16:9–13, NASB. In Acts 16:15–16, Luke also uses the words "we" and "us" in describing Paul's witnessing in Macedonia.

gathered together to break bread, Paul began talking to them, intending to depart the next day, and he prolonged his message until midnight. And there were many lamps in the upper room where we were gathered together."[89]

Luke further wrote: "But we, going ahead to the ship, set sail for Assos, intending from there to take Paul on board; for thus he had arranged it, intending himself to go by land. And when he met us at Assos, we took him on board and came to Mitylene, And sailing from there, we arrived the following day opposite Chios; and the next day we crossed over to Samos; and the day following we came to Miletus. For Paul had decided to sail past Ephesus in order that he might not have to spend time in Asia, for he was hurrying to be in Jerusalem, if possible, on the day of Pentecost."[90] Luke then recorded their travels in their sailing to Jerusalem:[91] "And when it came about that we had parted from them and set sail, we ran a straight course to Cos and the next day to Rhodes and from there to Patara; and having found a ship crossing over to Phoenicia, we went aboard and set sail. And when we had come in sight of Cyprus, leaving it on the left, we kept sailing to Syria and landed at Tyre; for there the ship was to unload its cargo. And after looking up the disciples, we stayed there seven days; and they kept telling Paul through the Spirit not to set foot in Jerusalem." Luke also reported that he and Paul stayed with Philip, the Evangelist, for a few days on their way to Jerusalem: "And on the next day we departed and came to Caesarea; and entering the house of Philip the evangelist, who was one of the seven, we stayed with him."[92]

Luke, along with some of the disciples from Caesarea, accompanied Paul on the final route to Jerusalem where they met with James, the

---

89. Acts 20:5-8, NASB.

90. Acts 20:13-16, NASB. Assos was a coastal city located in what is now the western of part of Turkey. Chios and Lesbos, with Mitylene as its capital, were prefectures (administrative divisions) of Greece. They were located on an island just below and across from Assos. Samos was an island South of Chios and north of Patmos. Miletus was an ancient city in Asian Turkey.

91. Acts 21:1-4, NASB. Luke records setting sail to Cos, from there to Rhodes and then to Patara. Cos was an island in the Aegean Sea; it was a financial center in eastern Mediterranean. Rhodes is a Greek island which is located northeast of Crete. Patara was a large seaport city located in what is now Turkey, opposite the island of Rhodes. Cos was about fifty miles south of Miletus; Rhodes was fifty miles southeast of Cos; and Patara was about fifty miles east of Rhodes.

Luke also mentioned that they landed at Tyre, which is located on the Mediterranean coast of what is now southern Lebanon, just north of Israel.

92. Acts 21:8, NASB.

Other God-Fearing Followers of Jesus

bishop of the Jerusalem church, and informed him of Paul's ministry to the Gentiles: "And after these days we got ready and started on our way up to Jerusalem. And some of the disciples from Caesarea also came with us, taking us to Mnason of Cyprus, a disciple of long standing with whom we were to lodge. And when we had come to Jerusalem, the brethren received us gladly. And now the following day Paul went in with us to James, and all the elders were present. And after he had greeted them, he began to relate one by one the things which God had done among the Gentiles through his ministry."[93]

As noted previously, Paul was arrested in Jerusalem and then sent to Rome because he had appealed to Caesar as a citizen of Rome. Luke records that he accompanied Paul on this journey. "And when it was decided that we should sail for Italy, they proceeded to deliver Paul and some other prisoners to a centurion of the Augustan cohort named Julius. And embarking in an Adramyttian ship, which was about to sail to the regions along the coast of Asia, we put out to sea, accompanied by Aristarchus, a Macedonian of Thessalonica. And the next day we put in at Sidon; and Julius treated Paul with consideration and allowed him to go to his friends and receive care. And from there we put out to sea and sailed under the shelter of Cyprus because the winds were contrary. And when we had sailed through the sea along the coast of Cilicia and Pamphylia, we landed at Myra in Lycia. And there the centurion found an Alexandrian ship sailing for Italy, and he put us aboard it. And when we had sailed slowly for a good many days, and with difficulty had arrived off Cnidus, since the wind did not permit us to go farther, we sailed under the shelter of Crete off Salmone; and with difficulty sailing past it we came to a certain place called Fair Havens, near which was the city of Lasea."[94]

Luke recorded how they were later shipwrecked and feared they could not be saved: "But before very long, there rushed down from the land a violent wind, called Euraquilo; and when the ship was caught in it, and could not face the wind, we gave way to it, and let ourselves be driven along. And running under the shelter of a small island called Clauda, we were scarcely able to get the ship's boat under control . . . the next day as we were being violently storm-tossed, they began to jettison the cargo;

---

93. Acts 21:15–19, NASB.

94. Acts 27:1–8, NASB. Sidon was a famous city located upon the northern border of the land of Israel. Cilicia and Pamphylia were located in the region of Asia Minor along with Myra, which was a city in Lycia, also located in Asia Minor. Fair Havens was located in Crete, which is the largest of the Greek islands.

and on the third day they threw the ship's tackle overboard with their own hands. And since neither sun nor stars appeared for many days, and no small storm was assailing us, from then on all hope of our being saved was gradually abandoned."[95]

Luke then described how they survived the storm, were brought to the island of Malta, and eventually arrived at Rome.[96] "And at the end of three months we set sail on an Alexandrian ship which had wintered at the island, and which had the Twin Brothers for its figurehead. And after we put in at Syracuse, we stayed there for three days. And from there we sailed around and arrived at Rhegium, and a day later a south wind sprang up, and on the second day we came to Puteoli. There we found some brethren, and were invited to stay with them for seven days, and thus we came to Rome. And the brethren, when they heard about us, came from there as far as the Market of Appius and Three Inns to meet us; and when Paul saw them, he thanked God and took courage."[97] While in Rome, Paul referred to Luke as his fellow worker.[98]

There is no clear evidence of how or where Luke died. Some contend "... he died peacefully in Boeotia," which is in Greece, and "... others that he was crucified with St. Andrew at Patras or at Elaea in Peloponnesus,"[99] which are also in Greece. One historian reported that Luke was "... supposed to have been hanged on an olive tree by the idolatrous priests of Greece."[100]

IV. John Mark, Author of the Gospel of Mark

Little is known of the birth, life or death of John Mark other than he is the author of the Gospel of Mark, apparently was an early believer,[101] was the

---

95. Acts 27:14–20, NASB. Clauda was a small island located off the southwest coast of Crete.

96. Acts 27:36–44; 28:1.

97. Acts 28:11–15, NASB. Syracuse was located in what is now Sicily. Rhegium and Puteoli were located in Italy, south of Rome.

98. Phlm 1:24.

99. McBirnie, *"The Search for the Twelve Apostles,* 207.

100. Foxe, *Fox's Book of Martyrs,* 14.

101. Acts 12:25.

Other God-Fearing Followers of Jesus

son of Mary,[102] a cousin of Barnabas,[103] and lived in Jerusalem.[104] Mark was Peter's interpreter and some contend he wrote the Gospel of Mark based largely on Peter's missionary preaching to communicate "... the good news of Jesus in order to evoke and to sustain the Christian faith."[105] Eusebius reported that Mark "... followed Peter's instructions in writing the Gospel of Mark.[106] Peter referred to Mark as "my son Mark."[107]

Mark was Peter's companion in bringing the Word to the Jewish believers in Jerusalem. As recorded in the book of Acts, Peter went to Mark's home in Jerusalem after Peter was rescued from Herod having arrested him:[108] "And when Peter came to himself, he said, 'Now I know for sure that the Lord has sent forth His angel and rescued me from the hand of Herod and from all that the Jewish people were expecting.' And when he realized this, he went to the house of Mary, the mother of John, who was also called Mark, where many were gathered together and were praying."

Mark also traveled along with Paul in some of Paul's journeys. However, in reporting that John Mark accompanied Paul and Barnabas on Paul's first missionary journey, Luke also alluded to John Mark initially being a disappointment to Paul. "And Barnabas and Saul returned from Jerusalem when they had fulfilled their mission, taking along with them John, who was also called Mark."[109] The trio left Seleucia, a seaport in Antioch, and sailed to Cyprus.[110] As recorded in Acts, they landed at Salamis, which was

---

102. Acts 12:12. John Mark's mother is mentioned only once in the Bible; thus, nothing is known about his mother, Mary. The name Mary was a common Hebrew name. Because the reference in Acts 12:12 is to Mary, John Mark's mother, rather than to his father, she probably was a widow. She may also have been wealthy and had a large home as several believers had gathered at her home for prayer, indicating that she also was a believer. Luke records in Acts 12:13 that she had a servant-girl named Rhoda, who answered the door when Peter knocked "at the door of the gate." She may have been a sister of Barnabas's mother or father as Paul referred to Mark as being Barnabas' cousin in Col 4:10.

103. See Col 4:10.

104. Acts 12:12.

105. Discussion in Bauckham, *The Christian World Around the New Testament*, 109.

106. Eusebius, *The History of the Church*, 201. Eusebuis, in *Ecclesiastical History*, Chapters 14 and 25, refers to the gospels as having been written first by Matthew, then Mark, followed by Luke, and lastly, John. Others contend the Gospel of Mark was the first Gospel and that Matthew and Luke used much of it to write their Gospels.

107. 1 Pet 5:13.

108. Acts 12:11–12, NASB. Discussion of Herod arresting Peter in Chapter 3.

109. Acts 12:25, NASB.

110. Acts 13:4.

a city on the east coast of Cyprus, and "... began to proclaim the word of God in the synagogues of the Jews ...."[111] "From Paphos, Paul and his companions sailed to Perga in Pamphylia where John left them to return to Jerusalem."[112]

Although it is unclear why John Mark deserted Paul and Barnabas at Perga on Paul's first missionary journey,[113] his desertion did cause a major disagreement between Paul and Barnabas that led to Barnabas's failure to accompany Paul on any more of his missionary journeys. Luke recorded the remaining travels of Paul and Barnabas after Mark left them:[114] "But Paul and Barnabas stayed in Antioch, teaching and preaching, with many others also, the word of the Lord. And after some days Paul said to Barnabas, 'Let us return and visit the brethren in every city in which we proclaimed the word of the Lord, and see how they are.' And Barnabas was desirous of taking John, called, Mark, along with them also. But Paul kept insisting that they should not take him along who had deserted them in Pamphylia and had not gone with them to the work. And there arose such a sharp disagreement that they separated from one another, and Barnabas took Mark with him and sailed away to Cyprus. But Paul chose Silas and departed, being committed by the brethren to the grace of the Lord. And he was traveling through Syria and Cilicia, strengthening the churches."

Paul later reconciled with Mark. Mark grew in strength and gained the courage, devotion, and faith to become a valuable fellow worker with Paul.[115] As written to the Colossians as Paul was imprisoned, Paul referred to Mark as being his fellow worker:[116] "Aristarchus, my fellow prisoner, sends you his greetings; and also Barnabas' cousin Mark (about whom you received

---

111. Acts 13:5, NASB.

112. Acts 13:13, NIV. Paphos was a coastal city in Cyprus; Perga was the capital of Pamphylia, which was a province in Asia Minor.

113. As noted previously, some have suggested that Mark did not, at that time, fully accept Paul's doctrine of salvation by grace through faith alone. Discussion in McBirnie, *The Search for the Twelve Apostles*, 194. McBirnie stated that at that time Mark was still a devout Jew and perhaps unable to accept the doctrine of faith for salvation. Additionally, Mark was young then and may not have been strong enough for another strenuous journey.

114. Acts 15:34–41, NASB.

115. Discussion in McBirnie, *The Search for the Twelve Apostles*, 194. McBirnie stated that the breach between Paul and Mark was healed eleven years later in Rome, noting that Mark was one of the few faithful Jewish Christians in Rome who stood by Paul.

116. Col 4:10, NASB. Paul undoubtedly wrote to the Colossians when he was imprisoned in Rome in his last days.

instructions; if he comes to you, welcome him)." While imprisoned, Paul also stated to Philemon, a "beloved brother" that he greeted him "... as do Mark, Aristarchus, Demas, Luke, my fellow workers."[117] In his last days, in writing to Timothy, Paul stated that he wanted Mark to be with him:[118] "Pick up Mark and bring him with you, for he is useful to me for service."

After Peter and Paul's death in Rome, Mark is reported to have gone to Alexandria, a Greco-Roman city in Egypt that had a large Jewish population,[119] and, according to Eusebius, established the first church in the city of Alexandria.[120]

Mark was martyred in Egypt in AD 68.[121] He was buried in Alexandria, but his remains were later taken to Venice, "... where the church of St. Mark was built to receive them."[122]

V. Barnabas, the Son of Encouragement

Barnabas,[123] who was also called Joseph, was a Levite and a native of Cyprus.[124] He apparently was a devout believer and person of some wealth, as he sold a tract of land "... and brought the money and laid it at the apostles' feet."[125] Eusebius reported that, while no list had ever been found of the seventy disciples Jesus had appointed, it was "... stated that one of them was Barnabas."[126]

As noted previously, the Jewish Christians in Jerusalem did not at first accept Paul; they were afraid of him because he had been influential in earlier attempting to destroy the believers. Later, Barnabas convinced the Jewish believers that Paul had been converted and had become a zealous

117. Phlm 1:24, NASB.
118. 2 Tim 4:11, NASB.
119. McBirnie, *The Search for the Twelve Apostles*, 195.
120. Eusebius, *Ecclesiastical History*, 50. These now Egyptian Christians are called Coptic Christians. Coptic means Egyptians.
121. Discussion in McBirnie, *The Search for the Twelve Apostles*, 197–98.
122. McBirnie, *The Search for the Twelve Apostles*, 199.
St. Mark's Square, the Piazza di San Marco, and St. Mark's Basilica are the most favored tourist sites in Venice, Italy.
123. The name, Barnabas, means "Son of Encouragement." See Acts 4:36.
124. Acts 4:36.
125. Acts 4:37, NASB.
126. Eusebius, *The History of the Church*, 29.

and loyal apostle for the Lord: "And when he [Paul] had come to Jerusalem, he was trying to associate with the disciples; and they were all afraid of him, not believing that he was a disciple. But Barnabas took hold of him and brought him to the apostles and described to them how he had seen the Lord on the road, and that He had talked to him, and how at Damascus he had spoken out boldly in the name of Jesus."[127]

Barnabas was the first teacher to the Gentiles at Antioch.[128] When believers in the church in Jerusalem heard of a great revival in Antioch, they sent Barnabas to check it out. Believers in Jerusalem sent him to Antioch[129] ". . . for he was a good man, and full of the Holy Spirit and of Faith. And considerable numbers were brought to the Lord."[130] As recorded in the book of Acts,[131] the believers at Antioch were the first to be called Christians.

Barnabas labored alone in Antioch for a time, but there was great work to be done there, and the church had grown to the extent that Barnabas needed a helper. He thought of his friend, Saul of Tarsus, whom he had befriended in Jerusalem. The "newly named Christians" in Antioch then sent for Saul of Tarsus, who was then called Paul, to help Barnabas in Antioch.[132] Luke recorded in Acts,[133] that Barnabas left Antioch to find Paul, and that he brought Paul with him back to Antioch.[134] Paul and Barnabas worked with the believers in Antioch for about two years.

While in Antioch, Barnabas, Paul, and the Gentile believers there were made aware of ". . . a great famine throughout all the world . . ."[135] The believers then put Paul and Barnabas in charge of carrying to the elders at Jerusalem ". . . a contribution for the relief of the brethren living in Judea."[136] Luke recorded in the book of Acts,[137] that after Barnabas and Paul delivered the offering to the Jewish believers in Jerusalem, they then left Jerusalem, and taking John Mark with them, returned to Antioch.

---

127. Acts 9:26–27, NASB.
128. Antioch is in Syria, about 300 miles north of Jerusalem.
129. Acts 11:22.
130. Acts 11:24.
131. Acts 11:25.
132. Discussion in McBirnie, *The Search for the Twelve Apostles*, 8.
133. Acts 11.
134. Barnabas was an "encourager" for Paul as he later was for John Mark.
135. Acts 11:28b, NKJV.
136. Acts 11:29, NASB.
137. Acts 13.

Other God-Fearing Followers of Jesus

Luke further recorded that after Barnabas and Paul left Jerusalem and returned to Antioch: ". . . while they were ministering to the Lord and fasting, the Holy Spirit said, 'Set apart for Me Barnabas and Saul for the work to which I have called them.' Then, when they had fasted and prayed and laid their hands on them, they sent them away."[138] Luke reported that after Barnabas and Paul were ordained for their ministry to the Gentiles, they left Antioch to bring the message of salvation to Cyprus. As Luke recorded in Acts: "The two of them, sent on their way by the Holy Spirit went down to Seleucia and sailed from there to Cyprus. When they arrived at Salamis, they proclaimed the word of God in the Jewish synagogues. John was with them as their helper. They traveled through the whole island until they came to Paphos."[139] Luke records that Paul and Barnabas informed the Gentiles to whom they preached that the Lord had commanded them: "'I have set you as a light to the Gentiles, That you should be for salvation to the ends of the earth.'"[140]

One historian related that the destination of the first missionary journey was Barnabas's nearby island home of Cyprus and that Barnabas and Paul founded the Church of Cyprus while on that journey, in 45 AD.[141] This historian maintained that at this time a process had begun to remove Christianity from its Jewish exclusiveness and make it a universal faith for all persons.[142]

From Cyprus, Barnabas and Paul traveled to Perga in Pamphylia, but as recorded in Acts,[143] while they were in Perga, John Mark left Barnabas and Paul and returned to Jerusalem. Following their first missionary journey and after Barnabas and Paul ". . . had spoken the word in Perga, they went down to Attalia; and from there they sailed to Antioch, from which

---

138. Acts 13:2b, NASB.

139. Acts 13:1–6a. Luke notes in Acts 13:5 that "John" was with Barnabas and Paul as their helper. This "John" was John Mark, Barnabas' cousin. However, as recorded in Acts 13:13b, NKJV: ". . . John, departing from then, returned to Jerusalem."
Seleucia was a seaport from where Paul, Barnabas, and Mark left for Paul's first missionary journey. Salamis is an ancient Greek city on the coast of Cyprus. Paphos was the capital of the island of Cyprus.

140. Acts 13:47a, NKJV. Luke further reported, Acts 13:48, NKJV: "Now when the Gentiles heard this they were glad and glorified the word of the Lord. And as many as had been appointed to eternal life believed."

141. McBirnie, "*The Search for the Twelve Apostles,* 202, 8. Barnabas is the patron of Cyprus.

142. McBirnie, "*The Search for the Twelve Apostles,* 8.

143. Acts 13:13.

they had been commended to the grace of God for the work that they had accomplished. And when they had arrived and gathered the church together, they began to report all things that God had done with them and how He had opened a door of faith to the Gentiles."[144]

After Barnabas and Paul had returned again to Antioch, and while they were there, some Jewish believers ". . . came down from Judea and began teaching the brethren, 'Unless you are circumcised according to the custom of Moses, you cannot be saved. And when Paul and Barnabas had great dissension and debate with them, the brethren determined that Paul and Barnabas and certain others of them should go up to Jerusalem to the apostles and elders concerning this issue.'"[145] Paul and Barnabas then left Antioch to travel to Jerusalem to meet with the Council at Jerusalem.[146] There Peter and James convinced the Jewish believers that the Gentiles should not be required to be circumcised.[147] Later, when Paul and Barnabas returned to Antioch and delivered the message from the Jewish believers, there was much rejoicing and encouragement among the Gentile believers at Antioch.[148]

After Paul and Barnabas delivered the letter to the Gentile believers at Antioch, Paul told Barnabas that they should go on a second missionary journey to return to cities they had visited on their first missionary journey. Barnabas agreed but wanted to take John Mark with them. When Paul refused to take John Mark along with them, Paul and Barnabas parted ways. Barnabas took Mark with him to Cyprus, and Paul appointed Silas to travel with him on his second missionary journey.[149] As recorded in the book of Acts: "And there arose such a sharp disagreement that they separated from

---

144. Acts 14: 25–27, NASB.

145. Acts 15: 1–2, NASB.

146. Concerning his meeting with the Council at Jerusalem, Paul wrote to the Galatians, Gal 2:1–3, NASB, that ". . . after an interval of fourteen years I went up again to Jerusalem with Barnabas, taking Titus along also. And it was because of a revelation that I went up; and I submitted to them the gospel which I preach among the Gentiles, but I did so in private to those who were of reputation, for fear that I might be running, or had run, in vain. But not even Titus who was with me, though he was a Greek, was compelled to be circumcised."

147. Acts 15:4–29.

148. Acts 15:30–32. Paul reported to the Galatians, Gal 2:9, NASB, that ". . . recognizing the grace that had been given to me, James and Cephas and John, who were reputed to be pillars, gave to me and Barnabas the right hand of fellowship, that we might go to the Gentiles, and they to the circumcised."

149. See Acts 15.

one another, and Barnabas took Mark with him and sailed away to Cyprus. But Paul chose Silas and departed, being committed by the brethren to the grace of the Lord, and he was traveling through Syria and Cilicia, strengthening the churches."[150]

There is no reference in the Bible to Barnabas after his disagreement with Paul except for Paul's reference to him in his letter to the Corinthians.[151] Paul spoke to the Corinthians of his having traveled with Barnabas and mentioned that both of them supported themselves on their missionary journeys. He asked the believers at Corinth:[152] "Or do only Barnabas and I not have a right to refrain from working?" Paul did not indicate though that Barnabas was with him in Corinth. Still, with Paul's reference to Barnabas, the believers in Corinth must have heard of Barnabas and apparently Paul remembered him favorably.

Although there is no evidence that Paul reconciled with Barnabas, it is evident that Paul did reconcile with John Mark. While Paul was imprisoned in Rome, shortly before the end of his life, Paul wrote to the "... saints and faithful brethren in Christ who are at Colossae"[153] that they greet Mark, whom he stated was Barnabas's cousin.[154] During his last years, Paul also requested Timothy to bring Mark to him and stated that only Luke was with him.[155] Paul did not mention Barnabas; thus, it appears that Barnabas was not with Paul when he was imprisoned and possibly had not been with him following their disagreement over John Mark. Still, considering that Barnabas and John Mark were very close, it is probable that because Paul and John Mark later became constant companions, Paul and Barnabas would have reconciled as well.[156]

---

150. Acts 15:39–41, NASB. In the book of Acts, Luke referred first to Barnabas when he described the journeys of "Barnabas and Paul" in spreading the Gospel to the Gentiles. Beginning in Acts 14:42, Luke referred to "Paul and Barnabas" going out to spread the Word. Some have speculated that John Mark may have left Paul because, as Barnabas' cousin, he might have been concerned originally that, as Luke recognized, the mission to the Gentiles had passed from Barnabas' leadership, to Paul.

151. 1 Cor 9:6.

152. 1 Cor 9:6, NASB.

153. Col 1:2, NASB.

154. Col 4:10.

155. 2 Tim 4:11.

156. Because Paul had reconciled with John Mark, he undoubtedly had also reconciled with Barnabas. One advantage of their disagreement is that Barnabas and John Mark began another mission to carry the Word to Cyprus and other areas while Paul continued to spread the Word in Asia Minor and in Greece.

Barnabas is reported to have died in his native city of Salamis, Cyprus, one historian stating it occurred in 58 AD,[157] another as late as 73 AD,[158] and to have suffered a martyr's death by a mob of some Jews who were enraged after Barnabas continued to preach fearfully and aggressively in Cyprus. According to reports, a mob of Jews incited pagans to stone Barnabas. One historian wrote that John Mark witnessed Barnabas's death and secretly buried him in Cyprus after placing Matthew's gospel on his chest.[159]

VI. Timothy, Beloved Companion of Paul

Timothy was from Lystra,[160] and was ". . . the son of a Jewish woman who was a believer, but his father was a Greek."[161] Timothy was a devout believer and a great man of faith, having been taught by his grandmother Lois, and his mother Eunice, both of whom were faithful believers.[162]

Paul taught Timothy the role of a deacon.[163] He referred to Timothy as "my fellow worker"[164] and "my beloved and faithful child in the Lord."[165] Although Paul refused to permit the Jewish believers to circumcise Titus, who was a Gentile, Paul did have Timothy circumcised ". . . because of the Jews who lived in that area, for they all knew that his father was a Greek."[166]

After his second missionary journey and while he was in Athens, Greece, Paul ". . . left instructions for Silas and Timothy to join him as soon

---

157. McBirnie, *The Search for the Twelve Apostles*, 202.

158. Foxe, *Fox's Book of Martyrs*, 14.

159. McBirnie, *The Search for the Twelve Apostles*, 202. Mc Birnie also wrote that Barnabas' relics, with a copy of Matthew's Gospel in Barnabas' handwriting, were discovered by the Archbishop of Cyprus. This archbishop, named Anthemios, is reported to have found Barnabas' grave and relics in 478 AD. In opening the grave, he is reported to have found Matthew's gospel on Barnabas' chest.

160. Lystra was one of the principal cities in Lycaonia, in the Roman province of Galatia, and located on the route from Ephesus to Sardis to Antioch in Syria. Its present-day name is Klistra, and it is in present-day Turkey.

161. Acts 16:1b, NASB.

162. See 2 Tim 1:5.

163. 2 Tim 1:6.

164. Rom 16:21.

165. 1 Cor 4:17.

166. Acts 16:3, NIV. Timothy possibly was not circumcised when he was eight days old, as were other Jewish boys, because his father, a Greek, and may not have approved of Timothy being circumcised.

Other God-Fearing Followers of Jesus

as possible;"[167] Silas and Timothy then departed for Athens, but when Paul chose to remain in Athens for a time, he sent Timothy, along with Erastus,[168] to Macedonia.[169] In then later sending Timothy to Corinth, Paul stated to the Corinthians:[170] "Now if Timothy comes, see that he is with you without cause to be afraid; for he is doing the Lord's work, as I also am."

Timothy was a scribe for Paul and possibly a co-author of some of Paul's letters. Paul wrote four of his epistles while he was in prison. These letters, called the Prison Epistles, are Ephesians, Philippians, Colossians, and Philemon. Timothy may have joined with Paul in writing three of these letters—Philippians, Colossians, and Philemon. He may also have joined in writing the two letters to the Thessalonians and the second letter to the Corinthians.[171] In writing the second epistle to the believers in Corinth, Paul and Timothy addressed the Corinthians, as follows[172] "Paul, an apostle of Jesus Christ by the will of God, and Timothy our brother; To the church of God which is at Corinth, with all the saints who are in Achaia." Paul then stated to the Corinthians:[173] "For the Son of God, Jesus Christ, who was preached among you by us–by me, Silvanus, and Timothy–was not Yes and No, but in Him was Yes."[174]

Timothy and Paul called themselves "bond-servants of Christ Jesus" in addressing the ". . . saints in Christ Jesus who are in Philippi, including the overseers and deacons."[175] Timothy and Paul similarly addressed the believers at Colossae:[176] "Paul, an apostle of Jesus Christ by the will of God, and

---

167. Act 17:15b, NIV.

168. Erastus, an early believer who was a treasurer in Corinth, became a coworker with Paul. See Rom 16:23.

169. Acts 19:22. Luke mentions in Acts 20:4 that Timothy was later with Paul in Macedonia.

170. 1 Cor 16:10, NASB.

171. The name Timothy is included with Paul's in the salutation to Philippians, Colossians, the two letters to the Thessalonians, the second letter to the Corinthians, and in Philemon. Silas, called Silvanus in the two letters to the Thessalonians, is also listed in the greeting in these two epistles; thus, he may have joined with Paul, and also with Timothy, in writing 1 and 2 Thessalonians.

172. 2 Cor 1:1, NKJV.

173. 2 Cor 1:19, NKJV.

174. The name "Silvanus" is a variation of the name "Silas;" thus, Silvanus presumably was Silas. Peter refers to Silvanus as "our faithful brother" in 1 Pet 5:12.

175. Phil 1:1, NASB.

176. Colossae was an ancient city in Phrygia, in Anatolia, located in what is now Asian Turkey.

Timothy, our brother, to the saints and faithful brethren in Christ who are at Colossae: Grace to you and peace from God our Father."[177] Paul stated to the believers at Philippi that he hoped "... in the Lord Jesus to send Timothy to you shortly, so that I also may be encouraged when I learn of your condition."[178] Paul reminded the Philippians of Timothy's worth, stating that he had "... no one else of kindred spirit who will genuinely be concerned for your welfare"[179] and reminded them that "... you know his proven character, that as a son with his father he served with me in the gospel."[180]

Paul, Silvanus, and Timothy also addressed the believers at Thessalonica[181] in like form:[182] "Paul, Silvanus, and Timothy, To the church of the Thessalonians in God the Father and the Lord Jesus Christ: Grace to you and peace from God our Father and the Lord Jesus Christ." Paul reminded the Thessalonians that he had "... sent Timothy, our brother and minister of God, and our fellow laborer in the gospel of Christ, to establish you and encourage you concerning your faith"[183] and affirmed that Timothy "... has come to us from you, and brought us good news of your faith and love, and that you always have good remembrance of us, greatly desiring to see us, as we also to see you ..."[184] Paul, Silvanus, and Timothy wrote a second letter to the Thessalonians shortly after their first letter, addressing the Thessalonians:[185] "Paul and Silvanus and Timothy to the church of the Thessalonians in God our Father and the Lord Jesus Christ: Grace to you and peace from God the Father and the Lord Jesus Christ."

Apparently, Paul, and possibly Timothy, wrote Philemon while Paul was imprisoned in Rome.[186] They called Philemon "... our beloved brother and fellow worker." Paul referred to himself as "a prisoner of Christ Jesus,"

---

177. Col 1:1–2, NASB.

178. Phil 2:19, NASB.

179. Phil 2:20, NASB.

180. Phil 2:22, NKJV.

181. Thesalonica was an ancient city in Macedon in Greece; it is now the city of Thessaloniki in Greece, sometimes called Salonika.

182. 1 Thess 1:1, NKJV.

183. 1 Thess 3:2, NKJV.

184. 1 Thess 3:6a, NKJV.

185. 2 Thess 1:1–2, NASB.

186. Phlm 1:1.

Other God-Fearing Followers of Jesus

and to Timothy as "our brother."[187] Mark and Luke, as well as Timothy, apparently were with Paul when he wrote the epistle to Philemon.[188]

Paul wrote two letters to Timothy while he was imprisoned in Rome, addressing Timothy in the first letter as "my true child in the faith,"[189] and "my beloved son" in the second.[190] Timothy at this time had been left in charge of the church in Ephesus. In his first letter to Timothy, Paul stated to him:[191] "O Timothy, guard what has been entrusted to you, avoiding worldly and empty chatter and the opposing arguments of what is falsely called 'knowledge'–which some have professed and thus gone astray from the faith." In his second letter to Timothy, written just prior to his death, Paul reminded Timothy ". . . to kindle afresh the gift of God which is in you through the laying on of my hands,"[192] stating that "God has not given us a spirit of fear, but of power and of love and of a sound mind."[193] Paul admonished Timothy that he should never ". . . be ashamed of the testimony of our Lord, or of me His prisoner" but rather to ". . . join with me in suffering for the gospel according to the power of God, who has saved us, and called us with a holy calling, not according to our works, but according to His own purpose and grace which was granted us in Christ Jesus from all eternity."[194]

Paul reminded Timothy that he had been appointed a preacher, an apostle, and a teacher when ". . . our Savior Christ Jesus, who abolished death, and brought life and immortality to light through the gospel . . . ," appeared to him.[195] Paul avowed to Timothy: ". . . I am not ashamed, for I know whom I have believed and am persuaded that He is able to keep what I have committed to Him until that Day."[196] Paul then admonished Timothy to ". . . retain the standard of sound words which you have heard from me, in the faith and love which are in Christ Jesus . . ." and to ". . . guard, through the Holy Spirit who dwells in us, the treasure which has been entrusted to you."[197]

---

187. Phlm 1:1.
188. See Phlm 1:23.
189. 1 Tim 1:1.
190. 2 Tim 1:2.
191. 1 Tim 6:20–21, NASB.
192. 2 Tim 1:6, NASB.
193. 2 Tim 1:7, NKJV.
194. 2 Tim 1:8–9, NASB.
195. 2 Tim 1:10–12, NASB.
196. 2 Tim 12b, NKJV.
197. 2 Tim 1:13–14, NASB.

In his last days, Paul asked Timothy to "... make every effort to come to me soon," stating that "Demas, having loved this present world, has deserted me and gone to Thessalonica; Crescens has gone to Galatia, Titus to Dalmatia..."[198] and that only Luke was with him.

Paul's last words and admonition to Timothy and to all believers was: "I solemnly charge you in the presence of God and of Christ Jesus, who is to judge the living and the dead, and by His appearing and His kingdom; preach the word; be ready in season and out of season; reprove, rebuke, exhort, with great patience and instruction. For the time will come when they will not endure sound doctrine; but wanting to have their ears tickled, they will accumulate for themselves teachers in accordance to their own desires; and will turn away their ears from the truth, and will turn aside to myths. But you, be sober in all things, endure hardship, do the work of an evangelist, fulfill your ministry. For I am already being poured out as a drink offering, and the time of my departure has come. I have fought the good fight, I have finished the course, I have kept the faith; in the future there is laid up for me the crown of righteousness, which the Lord, the righteous Judge, will award to me on that day, and not only to me, but also to all who have loved His appearing."[199]

Timothy kept the faith. He must also have been imprisoned at one time because of preaching the Gospel. The writer of Hebrews stated to its readers:[200] "Take notice that our brother Timothy has been released, with whom, if he comes soon, I shall see you."

According to tradition, Timothy served as a bishop at the church in Ephesus[201] and faithfully preached the gospel for many years after Paul's death.[202] He probably would have been in Ephesus with John. Pagans allegedly beat Timothy with clubs after he reproved them for their idolatry; he is reported to have died two days after that beating, in 97 AD.[203]

---

198. 2 Tim 4:9–10, NASB.

199. 2 Tim 4:1–8, NASB.

200. Heb 13:23, NASB.

201. See Eusebius, *The History of the Church*, 424, and Eusebius, *Ecclesiastical History*, 69.

202. See also Foxe, *Fox's Book of Martyrs*, 15.

203. Foxe, *Fox's Book of Martyrs*, 15–16.

VII. Silas, Follower with Paul

Silas, who was also called Silvanus,[204] was chief among the first apostles in Jerusalem. He was called a prophet[205] and may have been one of the seventy that Jesus appointed.

Following the Council at Jerusalem in 50 AD, wherein Paul and Barnabas convinced the Jewish believers that the Gentiles should not be required to be circumcised, Silas was chosen by leaders in the Jerusalem church to accompany Paul and Barnabas to Antioch.[206] Luke reported in Acts[207] that Silas ". . . encouraged and strengthened the brethren . . ." at Antioch, ". . . with a lengthy message."

Paul and Barnabas stayed in Antioch for a time after delivering to the believers there the message from the Jerusalem church.[208] However, ". . . after some days Paul said to Barnabas, 'Let us return and visit the brethren in every city in which we proclaimed the word of the Lord, and see how they are.'"[209] This marked the beginning of Paul's second missionary journey, but because Barnabas wanted John Mark to accompany them, and Paul refused to take Mark along because Mark had deserted them on their first missionary journey,[210] Paul chose Silas to accompany him, they both ". . . being commended by the brethren to the grace of the Lord."[211]

---

204. The name "Silvanus" is a variation of "Silas." See, 2 Cor 1:19, 1 Thess1:1, and 2 Thess 1:1, wherein Paul referred to Silas as Silvanus.
Peter also called Silas "Silvanus." In 1 Pet 5:12, Peter referred to Silas as "Silvanus, our faithful brother" and stated that ". . . for so I regard him."

205. Acts 15:32.

206. Acts 15:22. As discussed previously, Paul and Barnabas had a lengthy discussion with leaders in the Jerusalem church, at the Council at Jerusalem, regarding the question of whether the Gentile believers should be circumcised. After Peter and James, the half-brother of Jesus and bishop of the Jerusalem church, convinced the Jewish believers in Jerusalem that circumcision should not be required of the Gentiles, the church leaders in Jerusalem prepared a letter for Paul to deliver to the Gentiles at Antioch expressing that decision.

207. Acts 15:32.

208. Acts 15:35.

209. Acts 15:36, NASB.

210. Acts 15:37–39. See discussion in Chapter 4 and above, in the discussion of Barnabas, about how the disagreement between Paul and Barnabas concerning John Mark accompanying them caused a final break between Paul and Barnabas.

211. Acts 15:40, NKJV.

On Paul's second missionary journey, Paul and Silas traveled through Derbe and Lystra, to Troas, to Neapolis,[212] and from there to Philippi, which was a leading city in the Roman colony of Macedonia.[213] Paul and Silas were both arrested and beaten in Philippi after they healed a slave-girl ". . . who brought her masters much profit by fortune-telling."[214] As recorded in Acts:[215] "But when her masters saw that their hope of profit was gone, they seized Paul and Silas and dragged them into the market place of the authorities, and when they had brought them to the chief magistrates, they said, 'These men are throwing our city into confusion, being Jews, and are proclaiming customs which it is not lawful for us to accept or to observe, being Romans.'"

After their arrest, Silas and Paul witnessed to other prisoners and to the jailor, who later became a believer. As recorded in Acts:[216] "But about midnight Paul and Silas were praying and singing hymns of praise to God, and the prisoners were listening to them; and suddenly there came a great earthquake, so that the foundations of the prison house were shaken; and immediately all the doors were opened, and everyone's chains were unfastened. And when the jailer had been roused out of sleep and had seen the prison doors opened, he drew his sword and was about to kill himself, supposing that the prisoners had escaped. But Paul cried out with a loud voice, saying, 'Do yourself no harm, for we are all here!' And he called for lights and rushed in and, trembling with fear, he fell down before Paul and Silas, and after he brought them out, he said, 'Sirs, what must I do to be saved?' And they said, 'Believe in the Lord Jesus and you shall be saved, you and your household.'" The jailer then ". . . brought them into his house and set food before them, and rejoiced greatly, having believed in God with his whole household."[217] Later, when the chief magistrates learned that Silas and Paul were Romans, they were afraid and begged them to leave the city. Silas and Paul then left for Thessalonica.[218]

After a mob stirred up the city of Thessalonica, stating that Silas and Paul were acting ". . . contrary to the decrees of Caesar, saying that there

---

212. Acts 16:1–11. Neapolis was an ancient city in Edonis, a region of Macedon.
213. Acts 16:12.
214. Acts 16:16, NKJV.
215. Acts 16: 19–21, NASB.
216. Acts 16:25–31, NASB.
217. Acts 16:34, NASB.
218. Acts 16:38–40; 17:1.

Other God-Fearing Followers of Jesus

is another king, Jesus . . . ,"[219] Silas and Paul left for Berea[220] and there ". . . went into the synagogue of the Jews."[221] Many persons in Berea believed, but when some of the Jews of Thessalonica ". . . found out that the word of God had been proclaimed by Paul in Berea also, they came there likewise, agitating and stirring up the crowds."[222] Paul then left Berea for Athens, Greece, but ". . . Silas and Timothy remained there . . ." until Paul later commanded them to come to him in Athens.[223] After Paul left Athens, he went to Corinth where Silas and Timothy joined him.[224]

There is little additional information about Silas though he may have been a secretary to Peter. Peter referred to Silas, whom he called Silvanus, as having helped him write one of his epistles. As Peter recorded:[225] "Through Silvanus, our faithful brother (for so I regard him), I have written to you briefly, exhorting and testifying that this is the grace of God. Stand firm in it!" Silas may also have been the first bishop of Corinth. There is no record of the time or place of his death.

VIII. Titus, Child of the Faith

Titus was a Greek[226] who became a partner and fellow worker with Paul after Paul led him to faith in Christ.[227] Paul referred to him as "my true child in a common faith."[228] In a letter to the Corinthians,[229] he called Titus a messenger of the churches and "a glory to Christ."

Titus was born in Greece; one historian reported that he was born in Crete, which is the largest of the Greek islands. Some historians contend that Titus went to Antioch to study philosophy and there heard Paul preach about Jesus when Paul was in Antioch on his first missionary journey. Titus reportedly responded to Paul's message and believed in Jesus. He also is

---

219. Acts 17:7, NASB.
220. Berea is a city in Macedonia, in northern Greece.
221. Acts 17:10b, NKJV.
222. Acts 17:12–13, NASB.
223. Acts 17:14–15.
224. Acts 8:1, 5.
225. 1 Pet 5:12, NASB.
226. Gal 2:3.
227. 2 Cor 8:6.
228. Titus 1:4.
229. 2 Cor 8:23.

reported to have been one of the seventy and, if so, would have been a witness to Jesus's preaching. In whatever context, Titus heard Jesus' message of salvation and became one of the first Gentile believers.

Titus is not mentioned in the book of Acts. However, Paul did report to the Galatians[230] that he brought Titus with him and Barnabas when they went to Jerusalem in 50 AD to meet with the Council of Jerusalem regarding the issue of whether Gentiles had to be circumcised to be saved. Paul pointed to Titus as the example of a devout Gentile believer who was saved without circumcision. Paul informed the Galatians that he refused to have Titus circumcised and, because of Titus' great faith, that he convinced the Jewish believers circumcision was not necessary for the Gentiles to be saved. Paul stated to the Galatians: ". . . not even Titus who was with me, though he was a Greek, was compelled to be circumcised."[231]

Paul had written a harsh letter to the believers in Corinth telling them they were not to associate with immoral persons.[232] Titus had gone to Corinth to deliver the letter from Paul. Paul later became concerned that he may have been too harsh in his letter and wanted to acquire Titus' report of the Corinthian's reaction to the letter. Thus, on Paul's second missionary journey, he left Ephesus to go to Macedonia by way of Troas to find Titus. On his third missionary journey, probably while he was in Ephesus for about three years, in a second letter to the Corinthians, Paul expressed his disappointment that he did not find Titus in Troas earlier[233] but stated that he nonetheless went on to Macedonia and did find Titus there.[234]

When Paul met Titus in Macedonia, he was elated because the letter to the Corinthians apparently was a success. Paul wrote to the Corinthians that he had been comforted by Titus' coming to him in Macedonia ". . . not only by his coming, but also by the comfort with which he was comforted to you, as he reported to us your longing, your mourning, your zeal for me; so that I rejoiced even more."[235] Paul had informed the Corinthians that even though the letter caused them sorrow ". . . though only for a while . . . ," he, Paul,

---

230. Gal 2.

231. Gal 2:3, NASB. Recall that Paul did have Timothy circumcised. Although Timothy's father was a Greek, his mother was Jewish. Paul had Timothy circumcised because he wanted Timothy to be accepted among his fellow Jewish believers. This was not required for Titus as he was a Gentile.

232. Recorded in 1 Cor 5:9.

233. 2 Cor 2:12–13.

234. 2 Cor 2:12–13.

235. 2 Cor 7:7, NASB.

Other God-Fearing Followers of Jesus

rejoiced, not because they "... were made sorrowful according to the will of God..." but rather, as Paul stated to them, that they "... might not suffer loss in anything through us."[236] He told them that godly sorrow brings repentance that leads to salvation and leaves no regret, but worldly sorrow brings death. Paul also informed the Corinthians that he "... rejoiced even more for the joy of Titus, because his spirit had been refreshed by you all. For if in anything I have boasted to him about you, I was not put to shame; but as we spoke all things to you in truth, so also our boasting before Titus proved to be the truth. And his affection abounds all the more toward you, as he remembers the obedience of you all, how you received him with fear and trembling."[237] Paul further stated to the Corinthian believers: "I rejoice that in everything I have confidence in you."[238] Paul was refreshed by the news from Titus that there was great progress in his ministry to the Corinthians.

During his third missionary journey, Paul had collected money for the poor believers in Jerusalem—from churches in Macedonia-Philippi, Thessalonica, and Berea. Believers there had given more than Paul expected considering that they also were poor. Apparently, the Corinthian church, which had more money than the churches in Macedonia, had also elected to send money to the Jewish believers in Jerusalem.[239] Paul informed the Corinthians that he was sending Titus and another believer to go with him to deliver the collection to Jerusalem.[240] Paul reported to the Corinthians that Titus and "... a brother whose fame in the things of the gospel has spread through all the churches"[241] would carry the offering back to the church in Jerusalem to take, as Paul stated "... precaution that no one should discredit us in our administration of this generous gift."[242]

236. 2 Cor 7:8–10, NASB.
237. 2 Cor 7:13b-15, NASB.
238. 2 Cor 7:16, NASB.
239. See 2 Cor 8:10.
240. 1 Cor 8:16-23.
241. Acts 8:18, NASB.

242. Acts 8:20, NASB. Recall, as recorded in Acts 11:28-30, that before his first missionary journey, Paul and Barnabas carried an offering to Jerusalem believers from the Gentile believers at Antioch. Paul felt hostility in Jerusalem, yet he wanted to carry offerings from Gentile Christians to the poor Jewish believers to show that his outreach to the Gentiles was a ministry to Israel—the Gentiles were a ministry to Israel. Paul reported to the Roman believers his vision that Jewish and Gentile believers would be united in their love of God and in obedience to Christ. Some contend that Paul's concern about the poor believers in Jerusalem and the offerings of the Gentile believers showed that the Gentiles were a ministry to Israel.

Paul appointed Titus over the churches in Crete,[243] noting that he had left Titus in Crete for Titus to ". . . set in order what remains and appoint elders in every city."[244] Titus was to visit Crete and restore order to the churches there. The gospel did take root in Crete, and Crete remains strongly Christian.

Paul later requested Titus to travel from Crete to join him in Nicopolis, which was in Epirus, Greece.[245] In Paul's last years in Rome, he stated that he had only Luke with him and remarked that Titus was in Dalmatia,[246] which was in modern day Croatia. There is no additional record of Titus's missionary work, but records indicate that Titus returned to Crete after Paul's death. Some contend he was the first bishop of Crete.

Titus has been reported to have died in Crete at age 97 and that, at the time of his death, his face shone like the sun.[247] Titus' body was later moved to Venice and is located in St. Mark's Basilica.

IX. Erastus, Treasurer in Corinth and Minister to Paul

Little is known about Erastus; Paul referred to him as the city treasurer in Corinth.[248] Luke described him as a believer who ministered to Paul along with Timothy.[249] In his last years while imprisoned in Rome, Paul reported to Timothy that "Erastus remained at Corinth" during Paul's imprisonment. Nothing else is recorded about this city official, who, according to Luke was a faithful believer and minister with Paul.

Paul's vision has not yet been realized. Many Jewish people rejected Jesus, and when the Gentiles became dominant in the Christian churches, they, the Gentiles, rejected the Jewish people.

243. Eusebius, *Ecclesiastical History*, p, 69.

244. Titus 1:5.

245. Titus 3:12.

246. 2 Timothy 4:10–11.

247. Https://www.oca.org/saints/lives/2010/08/25/102393-apostle-titus-of-the-seventy-and-bishop-of-crete.

248. Rom 16:23.

249. Acts 19:22.

X. Linus, Second Bishop of the Roman Church

Linus is referred to only once in the Bible,[250] Still, it is evident that Linus was very close to Paul from Paul's referral to Linus in his letter to Timothy,[251] wherein he reported to Timothy that Linus sent greetings. Linus was one of the few faithful companions who remained loyal to Paul to the end of Paul's ministry when many others had deserted Paul during his imprisonment in Rome.

Eusebius reported that Linus was the first after Peter to obtain the episcopate at Rome.[252] Eusebius stated that after "... the martyrdom of Paul and Peter the first man to be appointed Bishop of Rome was Linus."[253]

XI. Aquila and Priscilla, Tent Makers and Companions to Paul

Aquila, who was from Pontus in Asia Minor,[254] and his wife, Priscilla, whose formal name was Prisca, were Jewish believers who probably were Roman citizens. They likely lived in Rome until they had to leave Italy because of Jewish persecution in about 50 AD during the reign of Claudius. Paul met them later in Corinth during his second missionary journey.

Luke refers to the Jewish persecution in Italy and to Aquila and Priscilla's companionship with Paul in the book of Acts,[255] reporting that after Paul had left Athens and had gone to Corinth, "... he found a certain Jew named Aquila, a native of Pontus, having recently come from Italy with his wife Priscilla, because Claudius had commanded all the Jews to leave Rome."[256] Because Paul was of the same trade as Aquila and Priscilla, Paul "... stayed with them and worked," for, as Luke recorded: "... by occupation they were tent-makers."[257]

---

250. See 2 Tim 4:21. Paul referred to Linus as sending greetings to Timothy; thus, Linus apparently was with Paul in Rome.

251. 2 Tim 4:21.

252. Eusebius, *Ecclesiastical History*, 69.

253. Eusebius, *A History of the Church*, 65.

254. Pontus was located along the south shore of the Black Sea.

255. Acts 18:1–3.

256. Acts 18:2, NASB.

257. Acts 18:3, NKJV.

Luke reports in Acts that Paul stayed a year and a half in Corinth,[258] but then, because the Jews "rose up against Paul," Paul left Corinth to go to Syria, taking Aquila and Priscilla with him.[259] Luke notes that, while Aquila and Priscilla accompanied Paul on his travels from Corinth to Ephesus, Paul left them in Ephesus.[260] After Paul had left Aquila and Priscilla, they worked in the early church there and often had believers meet in their home. Paul apparently remained in contact with them and thought highly of them and their ministry. In a letter to the Corinthians, Paul sent his greetings from "the churches of Asia" and also wrote them that ". . . Aquila and Prisca greet you heartily in the Lord with the church that is in their house."[261]

While in Ephesus, Aquila and Priscilla "took aside" a Jewish believer named Apollos who Luke recorded was ". . . an Alexandrian by birth, an eloquent man . . . ," who ". . . came to Ephesus . . ." and who ". . . was mighty in the Scriptures . . . ,"[262] but who was ". . . acquainted only with the baptism of John."[263] Luke wrote that ". . . when Priscilla and Aquila heard him, they took him aside and explained to him the way of God more accurately."[264] In helping Apollos understand salvation by grace through faith in Christ, they made Apollos' preaching much more effective.

Aquila and Priscilla later left Ephesus and returned to Rome where they also opened their home for worship with the believers there. During his third missionary journey, in a letter written from Corinth to Jesus' followers in Rome, Paul called for the believers there to "greet Prisca and Aquila," whom he called "my fellow workers in Christ Jesus," and requested the Roman believers to ". . . also greet the church that is in their house."[265] Paul expressed his great affection and respect for Aquila and Priscilla, affirming to the Roman believers: "They risked their lives for me."[266]

Aquila and Priscilla evidently returned to Ephesus where they then helped Timothy, who was the church leader in Ephesus at that time. In his

---

258. Acts 18:11.
259. Acts 18:18.
260. Acts 18:19.
261. 1 Cor 16:19, NASB.
262. Acts 18:24, NASB.
263. Acts 18:25b.
264. Acts 18:26b, NASB.
265. Rom 16:1, 3a, NASB.
266. Rom 16:4a, NIV.

last days in Rome, and in a last letter to Timothy,[267] Paul also told Timothy to "greet Prisca and Aquila." Aquila and Priscilla apparently continued to open their house where their fellow followers of Jesus could meet for worship.

It is interesting that Paul mentioned Prisca before Aquila when he addressed the believers in Rome and also when he addressed Timothy while he was imprisoned in Rome. Luke also referred to her first when he reported that she and Aquila explained to Apollos ". . . the way of God more accurately."[268] Priscilla then may have been more active than Aquila in their missionary work. She also may have been more instrumental in helping Apollos understand the message of salvation. It is conceivable that Aquila maintained his work as a tent maker while Priscilla was more active in Christian missionary work. Priscilla clearly was a missionary pastor and teacher and co-worker with Paul and, thus, one of the women who were devout and fearless followers of the Lord.

XII. Apollos, Jewish Christian from Alexandria

Apollos, like Paul, was a devout Jew who became a devout Christian. As Luke[269] described him, he was ". . . an Alexandrian by birth, an eloquent man, came to Ephesus . . . mighty in the Scriptures." Luke reported in the book of Acts:[270] "This man had been instructed in the way of the Lord; and being fervent in spirit, he was speaking and teaching accurately the things concerning Jesus, being acquainted only with the baptism of John; and he began to speak out boldly in the synagogue. But when Priscilla and Aquila heard him, they took him aside and explained to him the way of God more accurately."

Apollos had been baptized by John the Baptist. The Jews had a ritual of purification that involved being cleansed by water. They baptized Gentile converts to "cleanse" them. However, John the Baptist thought everyone needed repentance and baptized everyone, not just the Gentiles. His baptism looked ahead to the coming of Christ of which he was the precursor. It differed from the later baptism with the Holy Spirit that looked back to the proven fact of Jesus' death and resurrection. As recorded by Mark:[271]

267. 2 Tim 4:19a.
268. Luke 19:26.
269. Acts 18:24, NASB.
270. Acts 18:25–26, NASB.
271. Mark 1:4, NIV.

"And so John the Baptist appeared in the wilderness, preaching a baptism of repentance for the forgiveness of sins." Mark reported John the Baptist as stating: "I baptized you with water; but He will baptize you with the Holy Spirit."[272] Jesus Himself stated: "For John baptized with water, but in a few days you will be baptized with the Holy Spirit."[273] Jesus instructed the disciples to "Go therefore and make disciples of all the nations, baptizing them in the name of the Father and the Son and the Holy Spirit."[274]

There were other early believers who were baptized only by John the Baptist. It concerned Paul that these believers probably had not received the Holy Spirit. He thought they may not have even known of the Holy Spirit. As recorded in Acts:[275] "While Apollos was at Corinth, Paul took the road through the interior and arrived at Ephesus. There he found some disciples and asked them, 'Did you receive the Holy Spirit when you believed?' They answered, 'No, we have not even heard that there is a Holy Spirit.' So Paul asked, 'Then what baptism did you receive?' 'John's baptism,' they replied. Paul said, 'John's baptism was a baptism of repentance. He told the people to believe in the One coming after him, that is, in Jesus.' On hearing this, they were baptized in the name of the Lord Jesus."

After Aquila and Priscilla explained to Apollos "the way of God more adequately"[276] and Apollos became knowledgeable of the Holy Spirit and of baptism with the Holy Spirit, Apollos grew, as Peter had admonished the early believers, in ". . . the grace and knowledge of our Lord and Savior

---

272. Mark 1:8, NASB.

273. Acts 1:5, NIV. In being baptized with the Holy Spirit, a believer receives the gifts of the Holy Spirit, which are listed in Isa 11:2 and 1 Cor 12:8–10. As stated in Isa 11:2, NKJV, "The Spirit of the Lord shall rest on Him, The spirit of wisdom and understanding, The Spirit of counsel and strength, The Spirit of knowledge and of the fear of the Lord." Paul recorded in his letter to the Corinthian believers, 1 Cor 12:8–9, NASB: "For to one is given the word of wisdom through the Spirit and to another the word of knowledge according to the same Spirit; to another faith by the same Spirit and to another gifts of healing by the one Spirit."

The Holy Spirit lives in believers and thus brings to them the gifts of wisdom, understanding, direction (counsel), strength, knowledge, and service in the Lord. Nonbelievers do not accept that the Holy Spirit can live in every believer, but those who believe can know this truth; they have the gifts of the Spirit.

274. Matt 28:19, NASB.

275. Acts 19:1–5, NIV.

276. Acts 18:26b, NIV.

Other God-Fearing Followers of Jesus

Jesus Christ."[277] As Luke recorded in Acts:[278] "When Apollos wanted to go Achaia, the brothers and sisters encouraged him and wrote to the disciples there to welcome him. When he arrived, he was a great help to those who by grace had believed. For he vigorously refuted his Jewish opponents in public debate, proving from the Scriptures that Jesus was the Messiah."

Unfortunately, Apollos' eloquent preaching in Corinth became the focus of a division in the church. Some Christians later identified with Apollos, while others with Paul. This was of great concern to Paul. Matthew recorded Jesus' words:[279] "I will build my church and the gates of hell will not prevail against it," but there were early divisions in the first church that Jesus built. There unfortunately are many divisions in modern churches.

Paul stated to the Corinthians:[280] "For when one says, 'I follow Paul,' and another, 'I follow Apollos,' are you not mere human beings? What, after all, is Apollos? And what is Paul? Only servants, through whom you came to believe—as the Lord has assigned to each his task. I planted the seed, Apollos watered it, but God has been making it grow. So neither the one who plants nor the one who waters is anything, but only God, who makes things grow. The one who plants and the one who waters have one purpose, and they will each be rewarded according to their own labor. For we are co-workers in God's service; you are God's field, God's building. By the grace God has given me, I laid a foundation as a wise builder, and someone else is building on it. But each should build with care. For no one can lay any foundation other than the one already laid, which is Jesus Christ."

Paul admonished the Corinthian believers:[281] "Therefore let no one boast in men. For all things are yours: whether Paul or Apollos or Cephas, or the world or life or death or things present or things to come—all are yours. And you are Christ's, and Christ is God's." He further affirmed:[282] "Now these things, brethren, I have figuratively transferred to myself and Apollos for your sakes, that you may learn in us not to think beyond what is written, that none of you may be puffed up on behalf of one against the other."

Paul's rebuke to the Corinthians was not aimed at Apollos but at them. Apollos became a friend and helper of Paul. He left Corinth to return with

---

277. 2 Pet 3:18, NIV.
278. Acts 18:27–28, NIV.
279. Matt 16:18, NIV.
280. I Cor 3:4–11, NIV.
281. 1 Cor 3:21–22, NKJV.
282. 1 Cor 4:6, NKJV.

Paul to Ephesus and, because of the dissension that his presence there had caused, would not return to Corinth when believers there requested his return. Paul though evidently encouraged Apollos to return. Paul later informed the Corinthians that "... concerning Apollos our brother, I encouraged him greatly to come to you with the brethren, and it was not at all his desire to come now, but he will come when he has opportunity."[283] There is no record of whether Apollos returned to Corinth, but some historians contend he did return when the religious differences in Corinth were settled.

Apollos apparently helped in the growth and development of churches in Ephesus and Corinth. Apollos did not plant churches as did Paul; rather he strengthened those already established. Paul stated:[284] "I planted the seed, Apollos watered it, but God has been making it grow."

There is no record of what happened to Apollos after he began his fervent preaching of the Gospel to strengthen the churches in Corinth and Ephesus. He was last mentioned by Paul when Paul wrote to Titus from Rome prior to ending his ministry. Paul wrote to Titus,[285] to "... diligently help Zenas the lawyer and Apollos on their way so that nothing is lacking for them."[286]

Some contend, but without evidence, Martin Luther among them, that Apollos was the writer of Hebrews.

XIII. Women Who Followed Jesus

Priscilla, who was so instrumental in making Apollos' preaching more effective, was not the only early woman pastor and teacher. There were many other women who were loyal and fearless followers of Jesus even though little is recorded about them. Some of these were supporters of Jesus during his three-year ministry. Others were teachers, apostles, and evangelists in the early churches; several were Paul's partners in his efforts to spread the Gospel. Women clearly played important roles in spreading the message of salvation.

---

283. 1 Cor 16:12, NASB
284. 1 Cor 3:6, NIV.
285. Titus 3:13, NASB
286. Paul wrote his last epistles to Titus and Timothy.

Other God-Fearing Followers of Jesus

A. Women Who Assisted Jesus during His Ministry

The most important woman in the life of Jesus would have been his mother, Mary. Paul recorded[287] that Jesus was a descendant of King David. Both Mary and Joseph, her husband, were of the tribe of Judah and lineage of David. The genealogy of Joseph is set out in Matthew.[288] Joseph was a descendant of David from David's son Solomon. Joseph's father was Jacob. However, Joseph's genealogy obviously is not as important as that of Mary's. Her genealogy[289] shows her to be a descendant of King David from David's son Nathan. Mary's father was Heli. Luke attributes Heli to Joseph, but Heli was Joseph's father-in-law.

Paul recorded:[290] "But when the fulness of the time had come, God sent forth His Son, born of a woman, born under the Law, in order that He might redeem those who were under the Law, that we might receive the adoption as sons." Being human, born of a Jewish woman, Jesus fulfilled completely God's law to which, in His Jewish humanity, He was born and was subject.

There is very little known about Mary because the gospels do not concentrate on her role in the life of Christ. Still, while there is never a focus on Mary, her amazingly wondrous position as the mother of Jesus is set out in the first chapters of the Gospels of Matthew and Luke. Although Mary had the indescribable, but wondrous, blessing of being the mother of Jesus in His humanity, and thus was the first person to be present at Jesus' birth, she also was confronted with the indescribably terrible event of being present at His earthly death.

While Elizabeth and Zacharias did not believe an angel who told them they would conceive the child who was John the Baptist.[291] Mary immediately submitted to God's will for her life. She believed the angel's words and agreed to bear the child Jesus, even under humanly impossible circumstances. Mary knew the prophecies about a coming Messiah, and as recorded in the Gospel of Luke, she said to the angel who informed her of her coming

---

287. Rom 1:3.
288. Matt 1:7–15.
289. Set out in Luke at Luke 3:23–31.
290. Gal 4:4–5, NASB.
291. See Luke 1:18–25. As a result, Zacharias could not speak until the birth of his son, John the Baptist. As recorded in Luke 1:22, NASB: "But when he came out, he was unable to speak to them; and they realized that he had seen a vision in the temple; and he kept making signs to them; and remained mute."

birth:[292] "I am the Lord's servant, ... May your word to me be fulfilled." Luke recorded Mary's song of praise:[293] "My soul glorifies the Lord, and my spirit rejoices in God my Savior, For He has mindful of the humble state of His servant; From now on all generations will call me blessed, for the Mighty One has done great things for me—holy is His name."

The gospels record Mary being at the cross when Jesus was crucified. John recorded:[294] "But there were standing by the cross of Jesus His mother and His mother's sister, Mary the wife of Clopas and Mary Magdalene." Although there was great joy for Mary in being the mother of the Messiah, she also bore indescribably horrendous pain in being present for His crucifixion. Mary participated in bringing forward a life that made salvation possible, but she had to witness the horrific death of Jesus on the cross.

Mary evidently had four other sons although some would disagree. As recorded in Mark, many persons in Nazareth scoffed about Jesus having divinity, stating: "Is not this the carpenter, the son of Mary, brother of James, and Joses, and Judas, and Simon?"[295] Mary was never listed as a follower of Jesus in Jesus' ministry, but Luke[296] does record that she and Jesus' apparent half-brothers joined the disciples in the upper room for prayer on the Day of Pentecost. There is nothing in the Scriptures about Mary after that date. Although James, the half-brother of Jesus, is mentioned in the book of Acts as being a pillar in the early church in Jerusalem, there are no further references to Jesus' other half-brothers. Still, the fact that they joined the disciples on the Day of Pentecost indicates they also became devout followers of Jesus after the resurrection.[297]

---

292. Luke 1:38, NIV.

293. Luke 1:46b-49, NIV. See also Luke 1:50–55.

294. John 19:25, NASB.

295. Mark 6:3a, NASB. Some contend the four sons listed in Mark were either Jesus' cousins or His step-brothers. The supposition is they may have been children of Joseph from a previous marriage if not His cousins. There is no evidence to support either of these theories. Paul referred to James as being the "Lord's brother" in Galatians 1:19. Luke referred to Jesus' "brothers" in Acts 1:14.

296. Acts 1:14.

297. Some contend Jesus' half-brother Simon was the Simon who became bishop of the church in Jerusalem after James, Jesus's beloved half-brother, was put to death. Some also contend another half-brother of Jesus, Jude, wrote the Epistle of Jude. More likely though the book of Jude was written by Jude Thaddaeus, one of Jesus' twelve disciples. Additionally, Eusebius recorded that Simon the Zealot became the bishop in Jerusalem after James. See Eusebius, *The History of the Church*, 95, and *Ecclesiastical History*, 134.

Other God-Fearing Followers of Jesus

Some churches contend that Mary was without sin.[298] Additionally, some churches and many countries celebrate the assumption of Mary, called the Virgin, which is referred to as the Feast of the Assumption. There is no burial place for Mary nor for John, the disciple and apostle who cared for her after Jesus's death and resurrection; thus, some have assumed that both Mary and John ascended into heaven. Other churches have reacted in opposition to this belief.[299]

Clearly, as an angel had told Mary, she found favor with God.[300] Mary indeed has a special, most unparalleled, relationship with God that no one else can ever have. Nonetheless, Jesus confirmed that all who "hear the word of God and obey it" also have a special affinity with the Lord. As recorded in Luke,[301] a woman in a crowd following Jesus called out, 'Blessed is the mother who gave your birth and nursed you.' Jesus replied, 'Blessed rather are those who hear the word of God and obey it.'" Matthew recorded:[302] "While He was still speaking to the multitudes, behold, His mother and brothers were standing outside, seeking to speak to Him. And someone said to Him, 'Behold, Your mother and Your brothers are standing outside seeking to speak to you.' But He answered the one was telling him and said, 'Who is My mother and who are My brothers? And stretching out His hand toward His disciples, He said, 'Behold, My mother and My brothers. For whoever does the will of My Father in heaven, he is My brother and sister and mother.'"

There were other faithful and devout women, some also named Mary, who played significant roles in Jesus' life and ministry. Luke mentioned "Mary (called Magdalene)," "Joanna the wife of Chuza, the manager of Herod's household," "Susanna," and affirmed that there were ". . . many others."[303] Indeed, it was women followers of Jesus who did not desert the Lord after he was arrested and crucified. Mark recorded that at Jesus crucifixion: "There were also women looking on from afar, among whom

---

298. Still, Paul affirmed at Romans 3:23, NIV, that ". . . all have sinned and fall short of the glory of God."

299. John wrote at John 3:13, NKJV: "No one has ascended to heaven but He who came down from heaven, that is the Son of Man who is in heaven." Still, John wrote this in his Gospel obviously prior to his death and possibly prior to Mary's death as well. He and Mary could have ascended into heaven sometime after he made this statement.

300. See Luke 1:28.

301. Luke 11:27–28, NIV.

302. Matt 12: 46–50, NASB.

303. Luke 8:2, NIV.

were Mary Magdalene, Mary the mother of James the Less and of Joses, and Salome, who also followed Him and ministered to Him when He was in Galilee, and many other women who came up with Him to Jerusalem."[304] Luke reported that after Joseph of Arimathea, "... a member of the Council, a good and upright man who had not consented to their decision and action ... Going to Pilate, he asked for Jesus' body. Then he took it down, wrapped it in linen cloth, and placed it in a tomb cut in the rock, one in which no one had yet been laid. It was the Preparation Day, and the Sabbath was about to begin."[305] Luke further stated:[306] "The women who had come with Jesus from Galilee followed Joseph and saw the tomb and how His body was laid in it. Then they went home and prepared spices and perfumes. But they rested on the Sabbath in obedience to the commandment." Mark reported that, after Jesus's crucifixion "... when the Sabbath was over Mary Magdalene, and Mary the mother of James, and Salome brought spices, that they might come and anoint Him.[307]

Luke recorded the event as follows:[308] "On the first day of the week, very early in the morning, the women took the spices they had prepared and went to the tomb. They found the stone rolled away from the tomb, but when they entered, they did not find the body of the Lord Jesus. While they were wondering about this, suddenly two men in clothes that gleamed like lightning stood beside them. In their fright the women bowed down with their faces to the found, but the men said to them, 'Why do you look for the living among the dead? He is not here, He has risen! Remember how He told you, while He was still with you in Galilee: 'The Son of Man must be delivered over to the hands of sinners, be crucified and the third day be raised again.' Then they remembered His words. When they came back from the tomb, they told these things to the Eleven and to all the others. It was Mary Magdalene, Joanna, Mary the mother of James, and the others with them who told this to the apostles. But they did not believe the women, because their words seemed to them like nonsense. Peter, however, got up and ran to the tomb. Bending over, he saw the strips of linen lying by themselves, and he went away, wondering to himself what had happened."

304. Mark 15:40, NKJV.
305. Luke 23:50–54, NIV.
306. Luke 24:55–56, NIV.
307. Mark 16:1, NASB.
308. Luke 24:1–12, NIV.

Other God-Fearing Followers of Jesus

Luke reported that later, after Jesus appeared to the women and then also to the disciples, the disciples were "... all continually with one accord in prayer and supplication, with the women and Mary the mother of Jesus, and with His brothers."[309] Luke recorded in Acts that both women and men became courageous apostles and that many were imprisoned for their zeal in spreading the Gospel.[310]

Perhaps because of the great devotion of the women who had ministered to Him, Jesus first appeared to women after His resurrection rather than to His disciples or to any other men. Mark wrote that after Jesus had risen, "... He appeared first to Mary Magdalene" and that she then "... went and told those who had been with Him, as they mourned and wept."[311]

There are references in the Bible to many women named Mary, in addition to Mary, the mother of Jesus, who helped spread the gospel. Most of the references are to Mary Magdalene, but there also are references to other Marys—Mary, the wife of Cleophas and probably the sister of Mary, the mother of Jesus; Mary Salome, the wife of Zebedee whom some also contend was the sister of Mary, the mother of Jesus; Mary of Bethany, although some assert strongly that she was Mary Magdalene; and to the Mary who washed Jesus' feet, who some also contend was Mary Magdalene.

Mary Magdalene was a Jewish believer from the town of Magdala, which was a fishing town on the shore of the Sea of Galilee. Many consider her to have been a penitent sinner who became a devout believer. Luke referred to her as "... Mary who was called Magdalene, from whom seven demons had gone out," and, in reporting that Jesus first appeared to her after his resurrection, Mark called her "Mary Magdalene, out of whom He had cast seven demons."[312]

There was another woman named Mary,[313] whom Jesus commended for listening and learning from Him and who some claim was Mary Magdalene. As recorded in Luke:[314] "Now as they were traveling along, He entered a certain village; and a woman named Martha welcomed Him into her home. And she had a sister called Mary who moreover was listening to

---

309. Acts 1:14, NKJV.

310. See Acts 1–8:1–4.

311. Mark 16:9b-10, NKJV. See also John 20:9-21.

312. Luke 8:2b, NASB and Mark 16:9, NKJV.

313. This was Mary of Bethany the sister of Lazarus and Martha. See John 11:1-2. Some postulate that this Mary was also Mary Magdalene.

314. Luke 10:38-42, NASB.

the Lord's word, seated at His feet. But Martha was distracted with all her preparations; and she came up to Him, and said, 'Lord, do You not care that my sister has left me to do all the serving alone? Then tell her to help me.' But the Lord answered and said to her, 'Martha, Martha, you are worried and bothered about so many things; but only a few things are necessary, really only one, for Mary has chosen the good part, which shall not be taken away from her.'"

Some also have contended that Mary Magdalene is the sinful woman Luke reports anointed Jesus with expensive perfume. As recorded in John, this person was Mary of Bethany, the sister of Lazarus and Martha.[315] Luke wrote in the Epistle of Luke:[316] "When one of the Pharisees invited Jesus to have dinner with him, He went to the Pharisee's house and reclined at the table. A woman in that town who lived a sinful life learned that Jesus was eating at the Pharisee's house, so she came there with an alabaster jar of perfume. As she stood behind Him at His feet weeping, she began to wet His feet with her tears. Then she wiped them with her hair, kissed them and poured perfume on them. When the Pharisee who had invited Him saw this, he said to himself, 'If this man were a prophet, He would know who is touching Him and what kind of woman she is—that she is a sinner.' Jesus answered him, 'Simon, I have something to tell you.' 'Tell me, teacher,' he said. 'Two people owed money to a certain moneylender. One owed five hundred denarii, and the other fifty. Neither of them had the money to pay him back, so he forgave the debts of both. Now which of them will love him more?' Simon replied, 'I suppose the one who had the bigger debt forgiven.' 'You have judged correctly,' Jesus said. Then he turned toward the woman and said to Simon, 'Do you see this woman? I came into your house. You did not give me any water for my feet, but she wet my feet with her tears and wiped them with her hair. You did not give me a kiss, but this woman, from the time I entered, has not stopped kissing my feet. You did not put oil on my head, but she anointed perfume on my feet. Therefore, I tell you, her many sins have been forgiven—as her great love has shown. But whoever has been forgiven little loves little. For this reason, I say to you, her sins, which are many, have been forgiven, for she loved much; but he who is forgiven little, loves little.' Then Jesus said to her 'Your sins are forgiven.' The

---

315. John 11:1–2. John reported that Mary of Bethany was the "... Mary who anointed the Lord with ointment and wiped His feet with her hair..." and that her brother was Lazarus.

316. Luke 7:36–50, NIV.

Other God-Fearing Followers of Jesus

other guests began to say among themselves, 'Who is this who even forgives sins?' Jesus said to the woman, 'Your faith has saved you; go in peace.'"

There is no evidence that Mary Magdalene is the sinful woman Luke described in his Epistle. Additionally, there is no evidence she was any more a sinful person than the other followers of Jesus even though Luke and Mark reported that she had been demon possessed. There also is no evidence that she was Lazarus' sister, Mary of Bethany, although John reported that the woman who anointed Jesus with ointment and wiped His feet with her hair was Mary of Bethany.[317] Actually little is known about Mary Magdalene despite her being referred to in several scriptural verses. It is clear though that while she may have suffered originally under demon control, she became a devout apostle for Christ.

Some contend that sometime after Jesus instructed His followers to spread the message of salvation to the world and after the Holy Spirit had appeared to the believers at Pentecost, Mary Magdalene journeyed to southern France with Lazarus, alleged to be her brother, and others, to spread the Gospel there. Others who reportedly brought the message of salvation to France were Mary, the wife of Cleophas, and Mary Salome, both of whom allegedly were sisters of Mary, the mother of Jesus. Although Joseph of Arimathea and Philip the Apostle were also reported to be with the group, they supposedly left the others when they arrived in France and traveled to England to proclaim the good news of salvation there.

Whether or not it is a myth that the Marys carried the message of salvation to France, Mary Magdalene is a saint to Christians in southern France. In addition, Lazarus is reported to have been the first bishop of Marseilles. Some historians report that Lazarus converted the whole of Provence before he was beheaded in France.[318]

Another Mary and Salome, named Mary Salome, who was the mother of James and John, were with Mary Magdalene at Jesus' crucifixion. There are no historical facts about these women except that it is reported that Mary was the wife of Cleophas and a sister to Mary, the mother of Jesus.[319]

---

317. See John 11:2.

318. There are two versions of where Lazarus proclaimed the Gospel. Another version is that he left Bethany because of Jewish opposition to him and journeyed to Cyprus where Paul and Barnabas later appointed him the first bishop of Larnaca. In this version Lazarus reportedly lived in Cyprus for over thirty days and died a natural death there.

319. See John 19:25.

Additionally, Mary Salome, the mother of James and John, was the wife of Zebedee and reportedly was also a sister to Mary, the mother of Jesus.[320]

Another of the women who were a part of Jesus's ministry was Joanna, the wife of Chuza, who was a steward to Herod Agrippa I. Joanna was a faithful follower of Jesus despite her husband's vocation. She is only mentioned twice in the Bible. Luke notes that she contributed to the support of Jesus and his disciples from her "*private means*."[321] Joanna was obviously a loyal and close follower of Jesus because she was at the crucifixion. Luke mentions that she was with Mary Magdalene and Mary, the mother of James, after Jesus' resurrection and that she also told Peter and the other apostles of Jesus' empty tomb.[322] Joanna would have been a most fearless believer because she had to be risking her safety by following Jesus. Herod Agrippa I, for whom her husband worked, was the son of Herod the Great, who had attempted to kill Jesus when he learned of Jesus' birth. Additionally, Herod Agrippa I was the Herod who had the disciple James put to death and who also tried to kill Peter. Joanna then would have been in constant peril by supporting Jesus.

A woman named Susanna also supported Jesus in His ministry. Susanna was a wealthy woman, who like Joanna, provided financial support for Jesus and His disciples during Jesus' three-year ministry.[323] She is only mentioned once in the Bible. Luke alone referred to her as one of the women who ministered to Jesus and who provided Him and His disciples with financial support.[324]

B. Women Leaders in the Early Churches

One of the first women to be involved in the spread of Jesus' message of salvation after Jesus ascension and the coming of the Holy Spirit at Pentecost, was a woman named Dorcas. She made clothing for the poor. Dorcas not only was called a disciple; she also had importance in the early spreading of the gospel because Peter had brought her back to life after she had died. This event was testimony of the divinity of Jesus.

---

320. See Matt 27:56 and Mark 15:40.
321. Luke 8:3.
322. See Luke 24:8–10.
323. See Luke 8:3.
324. Luke 8:3.

Other God-Fearing Followers of Jesus

As recorded in Acts:[325] "In Joppa, there was a disciple named Tabitha (in Greek her name is Dorcas); she was always doing good and helping the poor. About that time she became sick and died, and her body was washed and placed in an upstairs room. Lydda was near Joppa, so when the disciples heard that Peter was in Lydda, they sent two men to him and urged him, 'Please come at once!' Peter went with them, and when he arrived he was taken upstairs to the room. All the widows stood around him, crying and showing him the robes and other clothing that Dorcas made while she was still with them. Peter sent them all out of the room; then he got down on his knees and prayed. Turning toward the dead women, he said, 'Tabitha, get up.' She opened her eyes, and seeing Peter, she sat up. He took her by the hand and helped her to her feet. Then he called for the believers, especially the widows, and presented her to them alive. This became known all over Joppa, and many believed in the Lord."

One of the leaders in the early church in Ephesus was Priscilla, an important woman follower of Jesus, who was discussed earlier. Another woman, Lydia, was a church leader in Philippi in Macedonia.

Paul's original intent for his travels in his second missionary journey was to stay in Asia, in what is now Turkey, to visit the cities he had visited in his first missionary journey; however, God changed his plans. Paul had a vision[326] to go westward across the Aegean Sea to Macedonia; thus, on his second missionary journey, Paul traveled to Philippi, a leading city in Macedonia, and there met Lydia and some other women believers.

Lydia was originally from the city of Thyatira, which was a city in a place called Lydia, a province in western Turkey. Because her name was the same as a city in the country of her origin, some speculate that Lydia may have been a slave girl originally. However, at the time Paul encountered her, she was a wealthy dye merchant. Although Lydia was a resident of Asia, she was saved in Europe. She is recorded as being the first Christian convert in Europe.

As Luke wrote in Acts, he and Paul stayed in Philippi for several days.[327] There not being a synagogue in Philippi, they went to a riverbank hopefully to locate a place of prayer and found there worshipers, all of whom were women. Luke recorded that ". . . on the Sabbath day we went outside the gate to a riverside, where we were supposing that there would

---

325. Acts 9:36–42, NIV.
326. See Acts 16:6–10.
327. Luke 16:12.

be a place of prayer, and we sat down and began speaking to the women who had assembled. And a certain woman named Lydia, from the city of Thyatira, a seller of purple fabrics, a worshiper of God, was listening; and the Lord opened her heart to respond to the things spoken by Paul. And when she and her household had been baptized, she urged us, saying, 'If you have judged me faithful to the Lord, come into my house and stay.' And she prevailed upon us."[328]

While they were staying with Lydia, Paul and Silas were imprisoned for healing a slave girl who had brought ". . . her masters much profit by fortune telling;"[329] however, they were released from the jail when an earthquake shook the prison and opened all the doors. They then delivered the message of salvation to the jailor who was saved. Later, the city magistrates were concerned when they were made aware that Paul and Silas were Romans and begged them to leave the city. Luke recorded:[330] "And they went out of the prison and entered the house of Lydia and when they saw the brethren, they encouraged them and departed."

Lydia remained in Philippi, and the church there grew significantly because of her ministry. Unfortunately. there is no further record of her or her ministry.

Phoebe was another early believer who helped Paul in his ministry. She was an evangelist and a leader in the church at Cenchrea, which was a port village just east of Corinth. In his letter to the Romans, Paul told the believers in Rome: "I commend to you our sister Phoebe, who is a servant of the church[331] which is at Cenchrea; that you receive her in the Lord in a manner worthy of the saints, and that you help her in whatever matter she may have need of you; for she herself has also been a helper of many, and of myself as well."[332] There is no further information about Phoebe, but she apparently greatly contributed her support to Paul to help him in his ministry.

Euodia and Syntyche of Philippi were women evangelists who were leaders in the church in Philippi, along with Lydia. They, however, apparently had some disagreement. In his letter to the Philippians,[333] Paul urged

---

328. Luke 16:13–15, NASB.

329. Acts 16:16.

330. Acts 16:40, NASB.

331. The Revised Standard Version of the Bible refers to Phoebe as a "deacon of the church."

332. Rom 16:1–2, NASB.

333. Phil 4:2, NASB.

Other God-Fearing Followers of Jesus

Euodia and Syntyche "... to live in harmony in the Lord.." and requested an unnamed church leader at Philippi "... to help these women ..." who had shared his "... struggle in the cause of the gospel."[334]

The brief mention of Euodia and Syntyche demonstrates that there may have been some dissension in the early church that Paul helped to heal. Their disagreement is reminiscent of the disagreement between Paul and Barnabas, but Paul's request to church leaders at Philippi to help them "live in harmony in the Lord" is a recognition that Paul encouraged believers to be in agreement and that Paul undoubtedly mended his relationship with Barnabas. Paul's message to the Philippians to help believers heal their discord is an admonition to current Christians as well.

In his letter to the Romans, Paul also refers to another woman, named Junias, who was an early believer and called an apostle. She was one of the first women to have been called an apostle. Paul referred to her as such when he told the believers in Rome to greet "... Andronicus and Junias, my countrymen, and my fellow prisoners, who are of note among the apostles, who also were in Christ before me."[335] Apparently Andronicus was Junias' husband. Little else is recorded about Junias and Andronicus, but some contend they were founders of the church in Rome.

Luke mentions four women who were called prophetesses.[336] They were daughters of Philip, the Evangelist, and they lived in Caesarea with their father.[337] Unfortunately there is no other reference in the Bible to these obviously faithful believers. Still, Eusebius reported that these prophetesses "remained unmarried;"[338] thus, they must have taken care of their father and undoubtedly taught in the early church in Hierapolis. Eusebius affirmed that they were "endowed with the prophetic gift"[339] and called them "luminaries," which means guiding lights.[340] Eusebius was impressed with Philip's daughters; he stated that the daughters "lived in the Holy Spirit."[341]

---

334. Phil 4:3, NASB.
335. Rom 16:7, NKJV.
336. Luke stated in Acts, 21:9, that Philip had "four virgin daughters who were prophetesses."
337. See Acts 21:8–9.
338. Eusebius, *The History of the Church*, 94.
339. Eusebius, *The History of the Church*, 94.
340. Eusebius, *Ecclesiastical History*, 96.
341. Eusebius, *Ecclesiastical History*, 96.

These daughters obviously had spiritual gifts and used them to minister to others and to spread the word of God.

Eusebius reported that two of the daughters were buried with Philip, their father, in Hierapolis and that one was buried in Ephesus, but he also stated that all the daughters were buried with their father in Hierapolis.[342] Little else is known about these early women prophetesses. However, some historians have called one of the sisters, Hermione, and have stated she was somewhat of a physician in Ephesus where she ministered to homeless and travelers.[343]

In summary, several women are mentioned in the Bible as being faithful early followers of Jesus. There were five possible women apostles—Mary Magdalene, Joanna, Susanna, Dorcas, and Junias.[344] Priscilla and Lydia were teachers in the early church. Phoebe was called a deacon. Euodia and Syntyce were referred to as evangelists. The four daughters of Philip the Evangelist were called prophetesses. While there is little record of the lives and activities of these early women believers, it is clear that Jesus called and trained women to proclaim the good news of salvation and that Paul had as partners in his mission several, very prominent, devout, and courageous women. The major roles that many women played during Jesus' ministry and in the early churches in spreading the message of salvation should not be overlooked.

---

342. Eusebius, *The History of the Church*, 94.

343. Https://www.markcarlson-ghost.com/index.php/2016/09/17/philips-daughters-prophets-names/. As recorded here, the other three sisters were possibly named Eutychis, Mariamne, and Eukhidia.

344. Luke referred to Dorcas as a disciple in Acts 9:36.

6

The Establishment of a Kingdom of Justice and Righteousness

I. Introduction
II. Importance of the Prophecies
III. Jerusalem, the Pivotal City
IV. Return of the Jewish People to their Homeland
V. The Message of Peace Jesus and His Followers Gave to the World
VI. A Remembrance to Serve the Lord Always

I. Introduction

THIS FINAL CHAPTER REFERS to some prophecies that are significant in a study of the lives and ministries of Jesus' early followers–some from the Old Testament scriptures that pointed to Jesus' first coming and some from writings of the early believers that pointed to Jesus' second coming. The chapter also includes a brief history of the city of Jerusalem and a summarization of biblical portrayals of its role in God's plan of redemption as well as many believers' affirmations regarding the importance of the return of the Jewish people to their homeland. It closes with an acknowledgment and confirmation that a solid and unswerving faith in the Lord Jesus, patterned on that of the first and early followers of Jesus, brings believers help and peace during the continuing difficulties and tribulations of the current society.

The review in the prior chapters of the lives and ministries of the early followers of Jesus proves the first believers knew without doubt that Jesus was the fulfillment of the scriptural promise that God would send a Messiah who would bring salvation to the world. As set out in the previous chapters, these early believers sacrificed their lives to bring Jesus' message of salvation to the "ends of the earth." Their almost unbelievable courage was based on the proven fact, as established by their lives and ministries, that they met with the resurrected Jesus and witnessed His ascension into Heaven. After these most devout and confident believers were filled with the Holy Spirit on Pentecost, they were given a divine power that permitted them to pay ". . . no heed to torture in all its terrifying forms."[1] As Eusebius, the Greek Christian historian, confirmed, the heroic and "splendid martyrs of Christ" suffered their martyrs' deaths for the Lord while, all the time, sending up ". . . hymns of thanksgiving to the God of the universe till their very last breath."[2] The first believers brought an assurance to the first century world, as well as to current society, that Jesus will return again one day to establish a kingdom of justice and righteousness. Present society then must be reminded, and never forget, the lives and sacrifices of the early followers of Jesus; their lives and sacrifices must serve as a remembrance and assurance to the world that Jesus is one with God and Savior of the world. That remembrance and assurance should bring a complete trust in the Lord and, with it, an absolute and lasting peace and a commitment to serve the Lord always.

II. Importance of the Prophecies

Prophecies of Isaiah, Jeremiah, Ezekiel, and Zachariah, as well as an amazing prediction of the prophet, Daniel, all discussed below, should lead the reader to a recognition of the importance of examining scriptural prophecies as did the early followers of Jesus. An in-depth study of the prophecies, both from the Old Testament and those of Jesus and some of His followers, can bring the reader further validation that Jesus' coming signified the fulfillment of God's plan of redemption, that Jesus is the Christ, that He will return again, and that the Bible is the inspired Word of God.

---

1. Eusebius, *The History of the Church*, 267.
2. Eusebius, *The History of the Church*, 271, 265.

The Establishment of a Kingdom of Justice and Righteousness

Luke recorded in the last chapter of his Gospel that Jesus ". . . opened their minds so they could understand the Scriptures."[3] Additionally, Peter tells believers[4] "Dear friends, this is my second letter to you. I have written both of them as reminders to stimulate you to wholesome thinking. I want you to recall the words spoken in the past by the holy prophets and the command given by our Lord and Savior through your apostles. Above all, you must understand that in the last days scoffers will come, scoffing and following their own evil desires. They will say, 'Where is this coming He promised? For ever since our ancestors died, everything goes on as it has since the beginning of creation.' But they deliberately forget that long ago by God's word the heavens came into being and the earth was formed out of water and by water. By these waters also the world of that time was deluged and destroyed, By the same word the present heavens and earth are reserved for fire, being kept for the day of judgment and destruction of the ungodly. But do not forget this one thing, dear friends: With the Lord a day is like a thousand years, and a thousand years are like a day. The Lord is not slow in keeping His promise, as some understand slowness. Instead He is patient with you, not wanting anyone to perish but everyone to come to repentance. But the day of the Lord will come like a thief. The heavens will disappear with a roar; the elements will be destroyed by fire, and the earth and everything done in it will be laid bare." Peter also stated that "But in keeping with His promise we are now looking forward to a new heaven and a new earth, where righteousness dwells."[5]

Matthew recorded[6] that the disciples came to Jesus as He was sitting on the Mount of Olives and asked him ". . . when will these things be? And what will be the sign of Your coming, and of the end of the age?" Jesus answered them that nations will rise against nations and kingdoms against kingdoms,[7] and informed them:[8] "Therefore when you see the abomination of desolation, spoken of by Daniel the prophet, standing in the holy place (whoever reads let him understand), then let those who are in Judea flee to the mountains."

---

3. Luke 24:45, NIV.
4. 2 Pet 3:1–10, NIV.
5. 2 Pet 3:13, NIV.
6. Matt 24:3, NKJV.
7. Recorded at Matt 24:7.
8. Matt 24:15, NKJV.

The disciple Matthew cited to Jesus' referring to the words of Daniel recorded in 538 BC, which was more than 500 years before the birth of Jesus. Daniel predicted the beginning of Jesus' ministry and the time of his crucifixion to the very year these events occurred at a time over 500 years before they occurred. As recorded in Daniel:[9] "Seventy weeks have been decreed for your people and your holy city, to finish the transgression, to make an end to sin, to make atonement for iniquity, to bring in everlasting righteousness, to seal up vision and prophecy, and to anoint the most holy place. So you are to know and discern that from the issuing of a decree to restore and rebuild Jerusalem until the Messiah the Prince there will be seven weeks and sixty-two weeks; it will be built again, with plaza and moat, even in times of distress. Then after the sixty-two weeks the Messiah will be cut off and have nothing, and the people of the prince who is to come will destroy the city and the sanctuary. And its end will come with a flood; even to the end there will be war; desolations are determined. And he will make a firm covenant with the many for one week, but in the middle of the week he will put a stop to sacrifice and grain offering; and on the wing of abominations will come one who makes desolate, even until a complete destruction, one that is decreed, is poured out on the one who makes desolate."

It is difficult to interpret Daniel's prophecy; but a consideration of his prediction becomes relevant because not only did Jesus refer to it as noted above, it also leads to a prophecy from John in Revelation, noted below, and, additionally, proves the validity of the Scriptures to which Jesus and His early followers often referred. A summary of the prophecy from the interpretations by biblical scholars[10] follows.

Daniel's prophecy records a time period of seventy weeks. As set out in Numbers[11] and Ezekiel[12] a day can represent a year. With a day representing a year, a week becomes seven years and seventy weeks becomes 490 years. In the seventy weeks that Daniel set out, with each day in each week representing a year, there would be 490 years (each week of seven years times seventy, for the seventy weeks, equals 490 years). According to

---

9. Dan 9:24–27, NASB.

10. See discussion in Andrew Van Niekerk, "From Daniel to Revelation," https://revelationbyjesuschrist.com/daniel-9-24-27/ and Richard H. Perry, "Of the Last Days: Listen, I tell you a mystery," https:// www.lastdaysmystery.info/the_prophet_daniel.htm.

11. Num 14:34.

12. Ezek 4:6.

The Establishment of a Kingdom of Justice and Righteousness

Daniel, sixty-nine of the seventy weeks, would be the time from the issuance of a decree to rebuild Jerusalem to the coming of the Messiah, who would bring an end of sin and would bring in everlasting righteousness. According to some biblical scholars, the beginning time to which Daniel was referring would be 457 BC, the year Artaxerxes issued the decree to Ezra to restore and rebuild Jerusalem after the Jews had stopped work in the temple for nearly sixty years. By subtracting 483 years (based on the sixty-nine weeks, or 483 years (seven years in each week times the sixty-nine referenced weeks equates to 483 years) from 457 BC (the year of the decree to restore and rebuild Jerusalem), the year becomes 26 AD. By prophesying that the Messiah would come sixty-nine weeks (or years) after the issuing of the decree to restore and rebuild Jerusalem, Daniel, in effect, predicted that the the Messiah, would come in 26 AD, which was the year Jesus was baptized and then began His ministry. Daniel referred to the middle of the remaining week (seven years), or the last week (or seven years) in the seventy weeks (or 490 years), as the time that the covenant with the many would be stopped. According to Daniel, the middle of the last week, or seven years, was the time when there would be a "stop to sacrifice and grain offering." Adding 3 1/2 years (the middle of the remaining week, or seven years) to 26 AD, and the adding of a year,[13] provides the date of Jesus' crucifixion, or 30 AD. This was the date Daniel recorded as the end of sacrifice and grain offerings. The end of sacrifice and grain offerings to which Daniel predicted occurred with the ultimate sacrifice of Jesus on the cross in approximately 30 AD.

What is the significance of the rest of the remaining "week" or the last 3 ½ years? Some contend this time, which would end at 34 AD (when an additional year must be added because there is no zero year,) referred to

---

13. Because there is no zero year, an additional year must be added. This then makes the year of Jesus' crucifixion to be 30 AD, which is stated by most to be the year He was crucified.

Daniel divided the sixty-nine weeks into seven weeks and sixty-two weeks. The seven weeks of the sixty-nine weeks is forty-nine years (7 x 7). (Again, when each day is a year, each week would equal seven years so that seven weeks would be forty-nine years–7 X 7.) It took this time period, from 457 BC to 408 BC (457 minus 49), to restore Jerusalem. The sixty-two weeks represents 434 years (7 x 62); 434 years after 408 BC also marks the year the Messiah began His ministry (434—408 = 26 AD). Additionally, by subtracting 457 BC from the seventy weeks or 490 years (7 x 70) that Daniel predicted would be the time there would "... an atonement for iniquity ... ," and eliminating the last 3 ½ of the last week or seven years, the year again becomes 30 AD, the year Jesus was crucified and died for the sins of the world. Daniel prophesied that this year would "... bring in everlasting righteousness ..."

the time Stephen would be stoned to mark the date Jewish leaders rejected Christ. Stephen was stoned in 34 or 35 AD; the stoning marked the date Jewish leaders rejected the Gospel. Still, other biblical scholars have interpreted Daniel's prophecy as a prediction of the tribulation. They contend Daniel was prophesying that Jesus' sacrificial offering would end at that time and that the "abomination" that causes "desolation," which he predicted would be set up until the end is decreed, would be the tribulation. As Daniel stated ". . . on the wing of abominations will come one who makes desolate, even until a complete destruction, one that is decreed, is poured out on the one who makes desolate." In other words, at the end times, "one" will come who will cause an "abomination" until there is a complete "destruction."

As noted above, Daniel recorded:[14] "The end will come like a flood. War will continue until the end, and desolations have been decreed. He will confirm a covenant with many for one 'seven.' In the middle of the 'seven' he will put an end to sacrifice and offering. And at the temple he will set up an abomination that causes desolation, until the end that is decreed is poured out on him." Based on these last words of Daniel in his prophecy, some biblical scholars contend the clock was paused after Jesus' crucifixion and the last 3 ½ years, or the "middle of the week" (that being 3 ½ years when a day is a year) to which Daniel referred, has not come. These scholars contend the last 3 ½ years remains—that at a later date an abomination will come that will cause desolation. According to these biblical scholars, this will be the great tribulation that will last 3 1/2 years, and after the 3 ½ years, the Messiah will rule the world from Jerusalem for 1,000 years. Some predict a great blessing on the nation of Israel at that time with the blindness removed from Israel.[15]

John also referred to a 3 ½ year period in Revelation; John recorded:[16] "The beast was given a mouth to utter proud words and blasphemies and to exercise its authority for 42 months." The 42 months equals 1260 days (42 months x 30 days in each month equals 1260 days–42 x 30). The 3½ years also equals 1260 days (360 x 3.5 = 1260). Thus, the 42 months to which John refers can be the same as the 3 1/2 years to which Daniel possibly was referring when he mentioned the "middle of the week," it being 3 ½ years, when the abomination would begin. John states that the "beast"

---

14. Dan 9:26b-27, NIV.

15. See discussion of end time at Richard H. Perry, "Of the Last Days: Listen, I tell you a mystery," www.lastdaysmystery.info/the_prophet_daniel.htm.

16. Rev 13:5, NIV.

The Establishment of a Kingdom of Justice and Righteousness

will exercise authority for these 3 ½ years. John further referred in Revelation to a measuring of the temple and the altar with its worshipers, but he excluded the outer court and did not measure it because, according to John, it was given to the Gentiles.[17] John wrote: "Go and measure the temple of God and the altar, with its worshipers. But exclude the outer court; do not measure it, because it has been given to the Gentiles. They will trample on the holy city for 42 months. And I will appoint my two witnesses, and they will prophesy for 1,260 days, clothed in sackcloth."[18] Some contend these two witnesses are Moses and Elijah, both of whom appeared with Jesus at the transfiguration.

In his gospel, Luke recorded Jesus' words that:[19] "Jerusalem will be trampled under foot by the Gentiles until the times of the Gentiles be fulfilled." The Gentile rule began when the Temple was destroyed in 586 BC; at that time, the Gentiles began to "trample Jerusalem." Although the temple was rebuilt after Cyrus had conquered the Babylonians and had permitted the Jews to return to Jerusalem to rebuild the temple, the Jewish people were still under control of a Gentile nation, at that time, the Persians. Additionally, even though the temple was rebuilt, it was destroyed again in 70 AD, and, to this date, has not been rebuilt. Further, there was not a new Israelite nation until 1948, and even then, Jerusalem continued to be ruled by other nations.

Some contend that the "time of the Gentiles" will end when Jerusalem is fully restored to the Jewish people. After this, some believe Jesus will return and then defeat all nations. Referring again to Daniel's prophecy, it can be assumed that after 3 ½ years, the misery on earth will end and that the predicted 1,000 years of peace will begin. The Israelis did take back Jerusalem, in 1967, in a six-day war. However, despite the Israelis taking back Jerusalem, the Temple Mount was returned to the Muslims in 1994 when President Clinton, Israel Prime Minister Yitzhak Rabin, and the Jordanian King Hussein recognized Jordanian custody of the Temple Mount. Currently, the Jewish people may only visit the site. This undoubtedly means the Gentiles still are trampling Jerusalem, and clearly, the misery on earth had not ended.

---

17. Rev 11:2. With reference to Paul's discussion of the Jewish people's rejection of Jesus, Chapter 4 directs the reader to Luke's recording, in Luke 21:24b, of Jesus' words that Jerusalem would be "trampled under foot" by the Gentiles until "the times of the Gentiles" is fulfilled.

18. Rev 11:1a-3, NIV. John equates the 42 months to 1260 days in this verse.

19. Luke 21:24, NIV.

III. Jerusalem, the Pivotal City

The history of Jerusalem goes back 4,000 years to the time when Abraham met Melchizedek at Salem.[20] Abraham later returned to Salem, afterwards called Jerusalem, to Mount Moriah or Mount Zion, now called the Temple Mount, to offer to sacrifice Isaac, his son. Later, in about 1000 BC, King David conquered Jerusalem from the Jebusites and moved the capital of Israel to Jerusalem. Jerusalem has been named the City of God, God's "holy mountain."[21]

The Hebrew Temple was built on Mount Moriah, about 1,000 years after Abraham had offered to sacrifice his son. Animals were sacrificed in the Temple as a prelude to the ultimate sacrifice of Jesus, which occurred about 2,000 years after Abraham went to Mount Moriah to offer his sacrifice. The early church was born in Jerusalem and it was God's plan that the church would expand from Jerusalem. However, the Temple was destroyed in 70 AD. At that time the early church in Jerusalem almost disappeared. Additionally, the city of Jerusalem was completely destroyed by 73 AD after the final siege of Masada, a fortress outside Jerusalem to which the Jewish people had fled. Yet Jerusalem has been restored and remains as the most significant focal point in the world.

The law of Moses came from Mount Sinai; Isaiah prophesied that the new Testament law, the law of Christ, will come from Zion and the word of the Lord from Jerusalem. Additionally, over 2,000 years after Isaiah prophesied that the new law would go forth from Zion, John recorded in Revelation:[22] "Then I looked, and there before me was the Lamb, standing on Mount Zion . . ." All believers, Jews and Gentiles, can come to Zion and, quoting Isaiah, discussed below, will go up to the "mountain of the Lord." When Jesus returns, it is predicted He will come to Jerusalem and, as John prophesied in Revelation,[23] He will stand on Mount Zion.

---

20. Melcizedek was the king of Salem, the ancient city now called Jerusalem. Melchizedek was called a priest king of righteousness and peace. Eusebius referred to Melchizedek as being ". . . produced in the sacred record as priest of God Most High." See Eusebius, *The History of the Church*, 13.

Some contend Mechizedek was the pre-incarnate Jesus. Jesus is also called a priest king of righteousness and peace and, as noted in Heb 6:20, a High Priest "in the order of Melchizedek."

21. Ps 48:1. God stated Jerusalem is the city where He chose to put His name. See 1 Kgs 11:36.

22. Rev 14:1, NIV.

23. Rev 14:1a.

The Establishment of a Kingdom of Justice and Righteousness

In pointing the way to a new promised city of Jerusalem,[24] Ezekiel foretold that "... the name of the city from that day shall be, 'The Lord is there.'"[25] Further, as recorded in Hebrews,[26] there will be a new covenant with Jesus as the mediator: "But you have come to Mount Zion, to the city of the living God, the heavenly Jerusalem, You have come to thousands upon thousands of angels in joyful assembly, to the church of the first-born, whose names are written in heaven. You have come to God, the Judge of all, to the spirits of righteous made perfect, to Jesus, the mediator of a new covenant..."

Ezekiel predicted[27] a new city of Jerusalem that would have twelve gates named after the twelve tribes of Israel. However, Ezekiel included in the twelve tribes the tribe of Levi but listed only one gate for the tribes of Manasseh and Ephraim, which he called the gate of Joseph, to make up the twelve tribes.[28] In Revelation,[29] John also described a new Jerusalem with the wall of the city having twelve gates and the name of one of the twelve tribes listed on each of the gates. Interestingly, John[30] lists the tribe of Manasseh, refers to what was the tribe of Ephraim as the tribe of Joseph, does list the tribe of Levi, but does not list the tribe of Dan, to make up the twelve tribes.[31]

John expanded upon Ezekiel's prophecy, writing in Revelation that on the *foundations* of the new city would be listed the names of the twelve apostles.[32] The foundation of the new Jerusalem represents the life of Christ

---

24. Ezek 40:1—48:35.

25. Ezek 48:35b, NASB.

26. Heb 12:22–24a, NIV.

27. Ezek 48:30–35.

28. Recall in Chapter 1 in the discussion of the twelve tribes that the twelve tribes that were given land in the then nation of Israel did not include a portion for the tribe of Levi but portions were allotted to the two sons of Joseph, Manasseh and Ephraim.

29. Rev 21:12.

30. Rev 7:5–8.

31. The tribe of Ephraim lost its preferential status among the ten tribes because it was Jeroboam from the tribe of Ephraim who conducted the resistance that led to a division of Israel into the two Israelite nations, the Northern Kingdom called the Kingdom of Israel, and the Southern Kingdom, called the Kingdom of Judah. Jeroboam became the first king of the Northern Kingdom. The tribe of Dan, which was part of the Northern Kingdom, undoubtedly lost its status because of the great sins of members of this tribe. The tribe of Dan set up two golden calves that its members then worshiped.

32. Rev 21:14. The humble apostles who never sought recognition for themselves are made great in the new Jerusalem. As referred to previously, Matthew recorded at Matt 19:28, NASB, the words of Christ Jesus telling His disciples: "Truly I say to you, that you

Jesus who is the foundation of His church and His people. Paul informed the believers at Ephesus that the gospel church is ". . . built on the foundation of the apostles and prophets, with Christ Jesus Himself as the chief cornerstone . . ."[33] and is ". . . joined together and rises to become a holy temple in the Lord."[34] Paul stated to the Corinthians: "For no one can lay a foundation other than the one which is laid, which is Jesus Christ.[35] Luke recorded Peter as stating to the Jewish leaders:[36] "He is the stone which was rejected by you the builders, but which became the very cornerstone. And there is salvation in no one else; for there is no other name under heaven that has been given among men, by which we must be saved." The Hebrew or Israelite religion, which is the religion of the Jewish people, was founded on twelve patriarchs. The gospel church is founded on the twelve apostles with Jesus the cornerstone. The foundation of a new Jerusalem is symbolic of the believers who knew without doubt that Jesus is the Christ.

Jerusalem means City of Peace,[37] but Jerusalem has not been a city of peace. Luke recorded Jesus' words about Jerusalem in about 30 AD as Jesus was approaching Jerusalem shortly before His crucifixion:[38] "As He approached Jerusalem and saw the city, He wept over it and said, 'If you, even you, had only known on this day what would bring you peace—but now it is hidden from your eyes. The days will come upon you when your enemies will build an embankment against you and encircle you and hem you in on every side. They will dash you to the ground, you and the children within your walls. They will not leave one stone on another, because you did not recognize the time of God's coming to you."

Jesus foretold the destruction of Jerusalem;[39] it had rejected His love, and Jesus knew some of its people would be taking His life. The Jewish people were visited by their Savior, and while many received Him, many of the Jewish leaders wanted Him crucified. Shortly after Jesus' crucifixion,

---

who have followed Me, in the regeneration when the Son of Man will sit on His glorious throne, you also shall sit upon twelve thrones, judging the twelve tribes of Israel."

33. Eph 2:20b, NIV.
34. Eph 2:21b, NIV.
35. 1 Cor 3:11, NASB.
36. Acts 4:11, NASB.
37. "Jeru" means city and "salem" means peace.
38. Luke 19:41-44, NIV.
39. Jesus' words about the destruction of Jerusalem became true beginning in 70 AD—about forty years after Jesus wept over the city.

The Establishment of a Kingdom of Justice and Righteousness

Jerusalem was completely destroyed. When Jesus returns as the recognized Christ, believers point to a new Jerusalem; Jerusalem then will be the City of Peace.[40]

IV. Return of the Jewish People to their Homeland

As noted above, Peter informed believers that they should study the Scriptures and the words of the prophets to remember God's promises and to know that His promises are certain. The reader should consider some of the prophecies that set out His promises and some that appear to relate to the end times. Prophecies of Isaiah, Jeremiah, Ezekiel, Daniel, and Zechariah that are especially intriguing and very relevant in this context, are summarized below.

The Jewish people have not had a homeland for centuries. They lost their sovereignty as a nation in 605 BC when God finally departed from them because of their then rejection of His law and His presence among them. As discussed in Chapter 1, and as predicted by the prophets Jeremiah and Isaiah, the Babylonians carried members of the Southern Kingdom into captivity in 605 BC, and although Cyrus the Persian permitted their return to their homeland in 537 BC, they remained under control of other nations until 1948. Amazingly, in 1948, over 2,500 years later, many of the Jewish people have returned to their original homeland in Israel, and it again has become a nation as foretold by the prophets Jeremiah, Isaiah, and Ezekiel. Ezekiel also predicted that Israel would be restored as *one* nation.[41]

---

40. Jerusalem became the capital of the Southern Kingdom, the Kingdom of Judah, over 3,000 years ago when King David moved the capital there. However, the Jewish people lost Jerusalem in 70 AD and did not regain control of it until 1967. Although the new Jewish state recognized Jerusalem as its capital early in the reestablishment of Israel as a nation, the United States formally recognized it as the capital of Israel in December of 2017. Jerusalem now is the national capital of Israel and has been designated the spiritual capital for Gentile believers.

41. As discussed in Chapter 1, the Israelite nation was divided into two kingdoms, the Northern Kingdom of Israel and the Southern Kingdom of Judah. The Northern Kingdom was destroyed in 722 BC when the Assyrians captured its people; the ten tribes from the Northern Kingdom were then lost in history. The Southern Kingdom of Judah lost its status as a nation in 605 BC when the Babylonians took its people into captivity.

It is amazing that even though the Jewish people did not have a nation for over 2,500 years and even with almost unspeakable suffering through the generations, the Jewish people have, through the grace of God, been preserved as a people and now have regathered to their homeland, which again, after more than 2,500 years, is the *nation* of Israel. As discussed below and in Chapter 1, the prophet Ezekiel prophesied over 2,500 years

About 2,700 years ago, the Evangelical prophet Isaiah predicted:[42] "And it shall come to pass in the last days, that the mountain of the Lord's house shall be established in the top of the mountains, and shall be exalted above the hills, and all the nations shall flow unto it. And many people shall go up and say, 'Come ye, and let us go up to the mountain of the Lord, to the house of the God of Jacob; and He will teach us of His ways, and we will walk in His paths, for out of Zion shall go forth the law, and the word of the Lord from Jerusalem.'" Isaiah prophesied that all nations will stream to Jerusalem, to the house of the Lord established on the Temple Mount–Mount Zion. While the uncircumcised Gentiles could not enter the Temple located on the Temple Mount, Isaiah prophesied that all will enter the new house of the Lord to be located on that mount, then to be referred to as Zion.

Isaiah spoke of the remnant from the tribes of Judah, Benjamin, and Levi being returned from Babylon when he recorded the Lord's pronouncement:[43] "Do not be afraid, for I am with you; I will bring your children from the east and gather you from the west. I will say to the north, 'Give them up!' and to the south, 'Do not hold them back. Bring My sons from afar, and My daughters from the ends of the earth—everyone who is called by My name, whom I created for My glory, whom I formed and made.'" However, Isaiah's words have a broader meaning—all God's people will be regathered when Christ comes to rule in peace over the world. Isaiah further recorded the word of the Lord:[44] "'these I will bring to My holy mountain and give them joy in My house of prayer. Their burnt offerings and sacrifices will be accepted on My altar; for My house will be

---

ago, in Ezek 37:22, that God would restore Israel as *one* nation rather than two kingdoms into which Israel had been divided. Although many of the children of Israel from the Kingdom of Judah returned to their homeland after the Persians conquered the Babylonians, and Cyrus, the Persian king, permitted their return, they were not in control. Beginning in 605 BC, the Israelites were controlled or ruled first by the Babylonians, then by Persians, later by Greeks, then the Romans, Arabs, Turks, Egyptians, the Ottoman Empire, Islamists, and even by Britain. The Jewish people were driven almost completely from Israel shortly after the temple in Jerusalem was destroyed in 70 AD. Additionally, the first church of the believers that was first established in Jerusalem almost completely disappeared shortly thereafter. The church of the first followers of Jesus then became principally a Gentile church. Presently though, many Jewish people also are returning to the faith in Jesus that their ancestors, the early followers of Jesus, brought to the world and, as a result, changed the world forever.

42. Isa 2:2–3, KJV.
43. Isa 43:5–7, NIV.
44. Isa 56:7–8, NIV.

The Establishment of a Kingdom of Justice and Righteousness

called a house of prayer for all nations.' The Sovereign Lord declares—He who gathers the exiles of Israel: I will gather still others to them besides those already gathered.'" God's house then will be a house of prayer for all people–Jews and Gentiles.

About 2,550 years ago, Ezekiel, a prophet who went into exile in Babylon with the Israelites, foretold the redemption of the Israelites and their return to the land God had promised them:[45] "Therefore say, 'This is what the sovereign Lord says: Although I sent them far away among the nations and scattered them among the countries, yet for a little while I have been a sanctuary for them in the countries where they have gone.' Therefore say, 'This is what the Sovereign Lord says: I will gather you from the nations and bring you back from the countries where you have been scattered, and I will give you back the land of Israel again. They will return to it and remove all its vile images and detestable idols. It will give them an undivided heart and put a new spirit in them; I will remove from them their heart of stone and give them a heart of flesh. Then they will follow my decrees and be careful to keep my laws. They will be My people, and I will be their God.'"

Additionally, Ezekiel foretold that the Israelite tribes would become *one* nation:[46] ". . . say to them, 'This is what the Sovereign Lord says: I will take the Israelites out of the nations where they have gone. I will gather them from all around and bring them back into their own land. I will make them one nation in the land, on the mountains of Israel. There will be one king over all of them and they will never again be two nations or be divided into two kingdoms . . . They will be My people, and I will be their God.'" As noted previously, Israel was restored as one nation in 1948. Ezekiel further recorded God's foretelling:[47] "Then they shall know that I am the Lord their God, which caused them to be led into captivity among the heathen; but I have gathered them unto their own land, and have left none of them any more there."

About 2,000 years ago, the Prophet Jeremiah quoted the word from God that after the Israelites had returned to their homeland, the Messiah would establish a new nation of justice and righteousness:[48] "'I Myself will gather the remnant of My flock out of all the countries where I have driven them and will bring them back to their pasture, where they will be fruitful

---

45. Ezek 11:16–20, NIV.
46. Ezek 37:21–23, NIV.
47. Ezek 39:28, KJV.
48. Jer 23:3–8, NIV.

and increase in number. I will place shepherds over them who will tend them, and they will no longer be afraid or terrified, nor will any be missing,' declares the Lord. 'The days are coming,' declares the Lord, 'when I will raise up for David a righteous Branch, a King who will reign wisely and will do what is just and right in the land. In His days Judah will be saved and Israel will live in safely. This is the name by which He will be called, the Lord our righteous Savior. So then, the days are coming,' declares the Lord, 'when people will no longer say, 'As surely as the Lord lives, who brought the Israelites up out of Egypt,' but they will say, 'As surely as the Lord lives, who brought up the descendants of Israel up out of the land of the north and out of all the countries where He had banished them.' Then they will live in their own land.'"

When the Jewish leaders rejected Jesus, they and the majority of the Jewish people were temporarily cut off from the blessings of a special relationship with God. The Gospel was given to the Gentiles who gladly received it. Still, as Paul recorded,[49] "I say then, has God cast away His people? Certainly not! For I also am an Israelite, of the seed of Abraham, of the tribe of Benjamin. God has not cast away His people whom He foreknew."[50] It is recorded in Psalms[51] Paul's assertion that: "God has not rejected His people whom He foreknew."[52] Paul stated to the believers at Rome:[53] "I am talking to you Gentiles. Inasmuch as I am the apostle to the Gentiles, I take pride in my ministry in the hope that I might somehow arouse my people to envy and save some of them;" he affirmed that he did not want them[54] ". . . to be ignorant of this mystery," because, as he stated, "Israel has experienced a hardening part until the full number of the Gentiles has come in." Paul referred the prophecy of Isaiah: "The Deliverer will come from Zion; He will turn ungodliness from Jacob. And this is My covenant with them when I take away their sins.'" Isaiah recorded about 2,700 years prior, that the

---

49. Rom 11:1–2a, NKJV.

50. Additionally, not all Jews rejected Jesus. As pointed out, nearly all of the early followers of Jesus were Jewish, as was Jesus. These first Jewish believers were vital to the Christian movement. Their great value to the spread of the Gospel has continued through the years as Jewish persons also have served as missionaries and preachers in the continuous growth of the Church.

51. Ps 94:14.

52. See Rom 11:2a. Psalms 94:14, NKJV, records "For the Lord will not cast off His people, Nor will He forsake His inheritance."

53. Rom 11:13–15, NIV.

54. Rom 11:25–27, NIV. See Isaiah 59:20–21.

Lord had declared:[55] "'The Redeemer will come to Zion, to those in Jacob who repent of their sins.'"

Daniel also prophesied that[56] "... in the days of those kings, the God of heaven will set up a kingdom which will never be destroyed, and that kingdom will not be left for another people; it will crush and put an end to all kingdoms, but it will itself endure forever." Isaiah earlier foretold that[57] "He will judge between the nations, and will settle disputes for many peoples... Nation will not take up sword against nation, nor will they train for war anymore."

Zechariah seemed to point prophetically to Jesus' second coming and the ultimate end of all things, when God will dwell among believers who will live with Him forever. Zechariah recorded:[58] "'Sing and rejoice, O daughter of Zion; for lo, I come, and I will dwell in the midst of thee,' saith the Lord.' And many nations shall be joined to the Lord in that day and shall be my people; and I will dwell in the midst of thee, and thou shalt know that the Lord of hosts has sent me unto thee. And the Lord shall inherit Judah his portion in the holy land, and shall choose Jerusalem again. Be silent, O all flesh, before the Lord: for he is raised up out of his holy habitation.'" Zechariah also recorded:[59] "And it shall come to pass, that every one that is left of all the nations which came against Jerusalem shall even go up from year to year to worship the King, the Lord of hosts, and to keep the feast of tabernacles."[60]

V. The Message of Peace Jesus and His Followers Gave the World

Isaiah prophesied to the Hebrew people:[61] "And the work of righteousness shall be peace; and the effect of righteousness, quietness and assurance forever." The "work of righteous" that is "peace" and that has the "effect of

---

55. Isa 59:20, NIV.
56. Dan 2:44, NASB.
57. Isa 2:4, NIV.
58. Zech 2:10–13, KJV.
59. Zech 14:16, KJV.
60. Recall from the discussion in Chapter 1 that the Feast of Tabernacles, also called the Feast of Booths, is the seventh and last of the seven feasts the Jewish people were commanded to celebrate. Jesus' first coming did not fulfill this feast.
61. Isa 32:17, KJV.

righteousness, quietness and assurance" was exemplified in Melchizedek, called a "priest forever," and in Jesus, the Messiah, who is referred to in the book of Hebrews as a "high priest forever."

David referred to the Messiah[62] as "... a priest forever after the order of Melchizedek." The writer of Hebrews[63] informed believers that "Jesus has entered as a forerunner for us, having become a high priest forever according to the order of Melchizedek." Melchizedek, a contemporary of Abraham who is referred to in Genesis as ... the priest of the Most High God"[64] and called a king of righteousness and peace, was above the priests of Levi. This was evidenced when Abraham gave Melchizedek a tithe.[65] Melchizedek then was greater than Abraham, the founder of the Israelite nation; it should mean that he was a priest for *all* people. The reader should consider that for Jesus to be an eternal priesthood after the order of Melchizedek, the salvation Jesus gives to *all* people is forever; it cannot be destroyed. The writer of Hebrews confirms that Jesus forever and continually mediates with God for sinners. This awareness found in the pages of Hebrews should bring peace to all believers.

John, the beloved disciple, quoted Jesus as saying to all believers:[66] "The thief comes only to steal and kill, and destroy; I came that they might have life, and might have it abundantly." Jesus' early followers knew from personal experience that Jesus brought to them the "abundant" life and were willing to devote their lives, even suffering a violent death, to bring to the world knowledge of that abundant life and the miracle of salvation. The assurance, confidence, boldness, and fearlessness with which Jesus' first believers spread the message of salvation to the world remain as testimony today, and conclusive proof, that Jesus is the Son of God and Savior of the world. With the message of salvation, the early followers of Jesus brought to believers who followed them "... the peace of God, which surpasses all understanding."[67]

Paul assured believers that:[68] "... having been justified by faith, we have peace with God through our Lord Jesus Christ." John, the beloved

---

62. Ps 110:4b, KJV.
63. Heb 6:20, NASB.
64. Gen 14:18b, KJV.
65. See Gen 14:20.
66. John 10:10, NASB.
67. Phil 4:7a, NKJV.
68. Rom 5:1, NKJV.

The Establishment of a Kingdom of Justice and Righteousness

disciple recorded Jesus' words to all believers: "Peace I leave with you; My peace I give to you; not as the world gives do I give to you. Let not your heart be troubled, neither let it be afraid."[69] Jesus gave believers His trust that: "... in Me you may have peace," and promised that although "... in the world you will have tribulation ... [to] be of good cheer" because Jesus affirmed: "I have overcome the world."[70]

The lives, sacrifices, and deaths of Jesus' early followers should serve as a remembrance to the reader and to all believers of the indisputable fact that Jesus is one with God; that knowledge and remembrance should bring to all peoples a peace that "... surpasses all understanding."[71] Only Christ can bring peace, not governments nor a society that is fundamentally corrupt. To have real peace, the Spirit must come and indwell in believers.

At the second coming, most biblical scholars believe that the three remaining unfulfilled fall feasts that God commanded His people to observe[72] will then also be fulfilled. The first of the three remaining feasts, and the fourth feast of the seven important festivals ordained by God, is the Feast of Trumpets. This feast occurs on the first day of the Jewish seventh month. As many believers contend, it will be fulfilled when the trumpet will sound to announce the arrival of the King of Kings. Some believers contend the Church at that time will be taken out of the world, that the trumpet represents the rapture of the Church. Paul recorded:[73] "For this we say to you by the word of the Lord, that we who are alive and remain until the coming of the Lord will by no means precede those who are asleep. For the Lord himself will descend from heaven with a shout, with the voice of an archangel, and with the trumpet of God. And the dead in Christ shall rise first. Then we who are alive and remain shall be caught up together with them in the clouds to meet the Lord in the air. And thus we shall always be with the Lord."

The fifth feast, the Day of Atonement, or Yom Kippur,[74] which occurs on the tenth of the Jewish seventh month, is the highest of Jewish

---

69. John 14:27, NKJV.
70. John 16:33, NKJV.
71. Phil 4:7, NKJV.
72. Lev 23. See discussion in Chapter 1. These are the Feast of Trumpets, the Day of Atonement (or Yom Kippur), and the Feast of Tabernacles (also called the Feast of Booths).
73. 1Thess 4:15–17, NKJV.
74. Kippur means ransom.

holy days. It is the most important feast for the Jewish people and precedes the Feast of Tabernacles.[75] Some believers contend that the ultimate fulfillment of this feast will occur at Jesus' second coming when Jesus will restore Israel completely after, as Luke recorded of Jesus' words,[76] the fullness of the Gentiles has come. Luke recorded Jesus' words as follows:[77] "Israel has experienced a hardening in part until the full number of the Gentiles has come in, and in this way all Israel will be saved. As it is written: 'The deliverer will come from Zion; He will turn godlessness away from Jacob. And this is My covenant with them when I take away their sins.'" The writer of Hebrews[78] affirmed that "Christ was sacrificed once to take away the sins of many; and He will appear a second time not to bear sin, but to bring to salvation to those who are waiting for Him."

The Feast of Tabernacles follows the Day of Atonement and occurs on the fifteenth day of the Jewish seventh month. This feast points to God's desire to dwell with His people. John recorded:[79] "And the Word became flesh, and dwelt among us, and we beheld His glory, the glory as of the only begotten of the Father, full of grace and truth." Jesus' first coming did not fulfill the Festival of Tabernacles. The Feast of Tabernacles is still celebrated; many believers contend its culmination will be the establishment of a central point of nation worship at Jerusalem on Mount Zion.

John described the culmination of the Feast of Tabernacles as follows:[80] "Then I saw a new heaven and a new earth, for the first heaven and the first earth had passed away, and there was no longer any sea. I saw

---

75. As noted in Chapter 1, before the temple was destroyed, the atonement ritual began with a high priest coming into the holy of holies. A bull was sacrificed for a sin offering. Then two goats were brought, one to be sacrificed because of the Israelites' sinfulness and rebellion. The blood of the first goat was to appease the God's wrath for the sins of the people for another year. The other goat was used as a scapegoat. The high priest would place his hand on the goat's head, confess over it the rebellion and immorality of the Israelites, and would set the goat out with an appointed man who would release it into the wilderness. The goat carried on itself all the sins of the people, which were forgiven for another year. It removed the sins of the people into the wilderness where they were forgotten. The two goats represent Jesus; He is the fulfillment of both goats. Jesus had to be sacrificed for the sins of the world, which He, as the sacrificial goat, transferred to Himself as the second goat, the scapegoat.

76. Luke 21:24b.
77. Rom 11:25b-27, NIV.
78. Heb 9:28, NIV.
79. John 1:14, NKJV.
80. Rev 21:1-7, NIV.

The Establishment of a Kingdom of Justice and Righteousness

the holy city, the new Jerusalem, coming down out of heaven from God . . .And I heard a loud voice from the throne, saying 'Look! God's dwelling place is now among the people, and He will dwell with them. They will be His people, and God Himself will be with them and be their God. He will wipe away every tear from their eyes. There will be no death or mourning or crying or pain, for the old order of things has passed away.' He was seated on the throne and said, 'I am making all things new!' Then He said, 'Write this down, for these words are trustworthy and true.' He said to me, 'It is done. I am the Alpha and the Omega, the Beginning and the End. To the thirsty I will give water without cost from the spring of the water of life. Those who are victorious will inherit all this, and I will be their God and they will be My children.'" The writer of Hebrews recorded:[81] "So Christ was offered once to bear the sins of many. To those who eagerly wait for Him He will appear a second time, apart from sin, for salvation." Jesus' second coming will bring a fulfillment of the Feast of Tabernacles.

Zechariah prophesied:[82] "And it shall come to pass, that in the whole land, saith the Lord, two parts therein shall be cut off and die; but the third shall be left therein. And I will bring the third part through the fire, and will refine them as silver is refined, and will try them as gold is tried; they shall call on my name and I will hear them: I will say 'It is my people: and they shall say, The Lord is my God.'" One third of the world population is now Christian. Perhaps the one third to whom Zechariah referred is symbolic of believers. This third will be refined through fire like silver and gold.

VI. A Remembrance to Serve the Lord Always

About 2,700 years ago Isaiah referred to the Messiah and recorded: "That unto me every knee shall bow, every tongue shall swear. Surely, shall one say, in the Lord have I righteousness and strength . . ."[83] Paul reported to the Philippians,[84] "And being found in appearance as a man, He humbled Himself by becoming obedient to the point of death, even death on a cross. Therefore also God highly exalted Him, and bestowed on Him the name which is above every name, that at the name of Jesus every knee should bow, of those who are in heaven, and on earth, and under the earth, and

---

81. Heb 9:28, NKJV.
82. Zech 13:8–9, KJV.
83. Isa 46:23b, 24a, KJV. The "me" to whom Isaiah was referring is the Messiah.
84. Phil 2:9–11, NASB.

that every tongue should confess that Jesus Christ is Lord, to the glory of God the Father."

Jesus' ultimate sacrifice and His message of salvation, which His followers brought to the world through their tremendous and phenomenal sacrifices, brings to all a need to bow before Jesus and, like as Joshua instructed the twelve tribes,[85] an obligation to serve the Lord forever.

---

85. Josh 4:24.

Bibliography

Bauckham, Richard. *The Christian World Around the New Testament*. Grand Rapids: Baker Academic, 2017.

Eusebius. *The Ecclesiastical History*. Translated by C.F. Cruse. Reprint, Hendrickson Publishers, 1998.

———. *The History of the Church from Christ to Constantine*. Translated by G. A. Williamson. Revised and edited by Andrew Louth. Penguin Books, 1965.

Foxe, John. *Fox's Book of Martyrs*. Wilder Publications, 2009.

King James Bible. Living Word Reference Edition. Riverside Book and Bible House: Iowa Falls, Iowa.

Levitt, Mark. Edited by Parson, John. "The Jewish Holidays –A Simplified Overview of the Feast of the Lord," https://www.hebrews4christians.com/holidays/Introduction/introduction.html

Master Study Bible, New American Standard. Holman Bible Publishers: Nashville, 1981. Copyright, Lockman Foundation: La Habra, California, 1960–1977 (used by permission).

McBirnie, William Steuart. *The Search for the Twelve Apostles*, Revised Edition. Tyndale House Publishers, 2008.

New American Standard Bible. Edited by Frank Charles Thompson. Indianapolis: B.B. Kirkbride Bible Co., Inc., 1993.

New International Bible. Grand Rapids: Tyndale House Publishers, Inc., 2007.

New King James Bible. Nashville: Thomas Nelson, 2018.

Perry, Richard H. "Of the Last Days: Listen, I tell you a mystery," www.lastdaysmystery.info/the_prophet_daniel.htm.

Vander Laan, Ray. "That the World May Know, "https://www.thattheworldmayknow.com/jewish-feasts.

Van Niekerk, Andrew. "From Daniel to Revelation," https://www. revelationbyjesuschrist.com/daniel-9-24-27/

www.ingramcontent.com/pod-product-compliance
Lightning Source LLC
Chambersburg PA
CBHW051925160426
43198CB00012B/2037